WEST CHICAGO PUBLIC LIBRARY DISTRICT

3 6653 00019 4070

P9-CQA-982

92
SAR

Thompson, Kenneth

SARTRE

West Chicago Public Library
231-1552

1. Books may be kept two weeks and may be renewed once for the same period, except 7 day books and magazines.

2. A fine is charged for each day a book is not returned according to the above rule. No book will be issued to any person incurring such a fine until it has been paid.

3. All injuries to books beyond reasonable wear and all losses shall be made good to the satisfaction of the Librarian.

4. Each borrower is held responsible for all books drawn on his card and for all fines accruing on the same.

ABG-7342

DEMCO

SARTRE:
LIFE AND WORKS

Facts On File Chronology Series

SARTRE: LIFE AND WORKS

Kenneth and Margaret Thompson

Facts On File Publications
New York, New York • Bicester, England

92
SAR

Sartre:
Life and Works

Copyright © 1984 by Facts on File, Inc.

All rights reserved. No part of this book may be
reproduced or utilized in any form or by any means,
electronic or mechanical, including photocopying,
recording or by any information storage and retrieval
systems, without permission in writing from the
Publisher.

Library of Congress Cataloging in Publication Data

Thompson, Kenneth A.
   Sartre, his life and works.

   Includes index.
   1. Sartre, Jean Paul, 1905–   . 2. Philosophers—
France—Biography. 3. Authors, French—20th century—
Biography.   I. Title.
B2430.S34T52   1983   848'.91409 [B]   82-15585
ISBN 0-87196-719-7

Printed in United States of America

10 9 8 7 6 5 4 3 2 1

Composition by Seham Associates

Printed By Maple Press

Contents

Preface and Acknowledgements

The titles listed at the start of each year or period of years indicate Sartre's principal writings during that time.

The main sources used are: Sartre's own works, especially the many published interviews in which he discussed his life and works; Simone de Beauvoir's autobiographical writings and interviews; the various bibliographical works of Michel Contat and Michel Rybalka, especially their *Les Ecrits de Sartre* (Paris: Gallimard, 1970); *The Writings of Jean-Paul Sartre,* two volumes, translated by Richard C. McCleary (Evanston, Illinois: Northwestern University Press, 1974), updated in *Obliques,* Nos. 18–19 (1979), pages 331–47; and François H. Lapointe, *Jean-Paul Sartre and His Critics: An International Bibliography (1938–1980),* revised edition (Bowling Green, Ohio: Bowling Green State University Philosophy Documentation Center, 1981).

In addition to the above, we wish to acknowledge our indebtedness to M. Anicet Sénéchal, who supplied much information, guidance and inspiration, and to whom we dedicate this book.

To Séné

Introduction

Few intellectuals in the 20th century have produced so many weighty works and attracted so much attention as Jean-Paul Sartre. His death in 1980 did not halt the flow of publications. Since that time, three large volumes of new material have been published, stimulating more discussion and calling for further reassessment of his life and thought.[1] Perhaps more than the life and works of any other major figure who has aroused intellectual controversy in the last 50 years, Sartre's life and works require a chronological treatment in order to comprehend their scope and complexity. They constitute an intricate web that can only be unraveled and their connections disclosed by following their development on a month-by-month, year-by-year basis. Only in this way can the full picture emerge, taking in the personal, political and scholarly features: the intellectual polymath—novelist, playwright, existentialist and Marxist philosopher; political protester—founder of a resistance group for socialist intellectuals during the German occupation, rejecting the Nobel prize for literature, attracting bomb attacks and arrest for protesting against the Algerian War, chairing the Russell Tribunal on American war crimes during the Vietnam War, peddling Maoist newspapers at street corners in his old age; the lover of many women, who yet remained true, in his own fashion, to his lifelong companion, Simone de Beauvoir. Even the scrapbook images can find their place, such as the description by one admirer of "the glasses, the octopus eye, the thick cigarette, the short, plastered-down hair, all that urbane French knowledge about communism and brothels."

The chronological approach yields a chronicle of the events, personal and political, that made Sartre a focus of public attention for nearly half a century. It traces the course of his

1. The three volumes, published by Gallimard (Paris, 1983), are: *Carnets de la drôle de guerre, Cahiers pour une morale* and *Lettres au Castor et à quelques autres.*

friendships, disputes and campaigns, including the celebrated quarrel with Camus and the disputes with the French Communist Party. Despite their disagreements, Camus and Sartre were alike in their refusal to abdicate their critical independence of judgment to a doctrine or dogma fashioned elsewhere. Sartre is revealed taking up a succession of unpopular stances, from opposition to the wave of anticommunism in the early years of the Cold War to the dangerous minority opposition to the Algerian War and the much-derided support for the young Maoists in the 1970s. During the Cold War he was criticized by the Communists, whose defense he had undertaken, and the Maoists often attacked his bourgeois scruples and preoccupations; he in return criticized the dogmas of Communists and Maoists, while being prepared to stand shoulder to shoulder with them when he thought their cause was just. The accounts of his visits to Russia and America show that he had great admiration for the ideals of both countries, but he denounced the betrayal of those ideals—branding both the USSR for its "war crime" in invading Czechoslovakia and the United States for its actions in Vietnam. Freedom was his guiding principle, and he fiercely denounced threats to it from whichever source they emanated. In his pursuit of freedom, and in its defense, he was not afraid to get his hands dirty; he recognized that, in order "to influence men who are struggling, one must first participate in the struggle." The Algerian War taught him the lesson that violence may be the only way the oppressed can attain their freedom. It was here that he disagreed with Camus's ethic of moderation, which, in practice, he believed, would serve to perpetuate the status quo rather than change it. Carmus's scruples were like those of the vacillating liberal priest in Sartre's play *Le Diable et le bon Dieu,* of whom the peasant leader says: "You are for us when we are killed, against us when we dare to defend ourselves." And yet, as the chronology reveals, although Sartre moved from his early detached position as a café intellectual and engaged himself in constant struggles on behalf of the oppressed, he could never bring himself to submit to the compromising disciplines of a political party.

Much has been made of a supposed break or rupture in Sartre's philosophy, separating the earlier phenomenological and existentialist works, such as *Being and Nothingness,* from the later neo-Marxist and more sociological approach, to be found in the *Critique of Dialectical Reason*. However, as the chronology shows, although there were important changes, there is a striking continuity in the development of his thought and in his method of analysis, which finds its summation and application in the multi-volume study of Flaubert—*The Idiot of the Family*. Despite its overtly literary topic, the main question the book addresses is social philosophical, embracing sociology and psychology: "What can we know about a man in the present state of our knowledge?" In his efforts to answer that question, taking Flaubert as a case study, Sartre calls upon concepts and methods that he had first begun to develop in his earliest works, such as *L'Imaginaire* (1940), as well as those of his later works, as in the *Critique* (1960) and *Search for a Method* (1957). The fully developed method of analysis that he employed was the progressive-regressive approach that he had first begun to explore in the context of the existential psychoanalysis outlined in *Being and Nothingness* (1943) and that he had developed in a sociological direction in *Search for a Method*. The regressive analysis involved examining the childhood and family relations that led Flaubert to accept a definition of himself as the idiot of his family—a nothing in terms of what his family regarded as of real value. The progressive analysis entailed tracing the process by which Flaubert was led to personalize himself through his project of subordinating the "real" world to his novelist's imaginary, or "unreal" world. The existential psychoanalytic dimension was concerned with the link between Flaubert's concept of art and his personal neurosis. The Marxist sociological methods and concepts are used to answer the question of how that concept of art and the artist reflected the general condition of French society in the second quarter of the 19th century. The ambitiousness of Sartre's own project lay in his attempt to chart a way between determinism and free will. Thus, in his existential psychoanalysis, he refused to resort to an explanation of Flaubert in terms of unconscious motives. Flaubert's neurosis was consciously chosen, in the sense that one chooses one's meanings or directions by the practical projects one sets for oneself. Flaubert's personalizing project was to be a literary artist, and he chose the life of a neurotic, *l'homme imaginaire,* in order to be able to write.

However, the concept of art and the artist that he chose was socially given; it corresponded to the "objective neurosis" of French society in the 1830s and 1840s.

In English-speaking countries there has always been a time lag in the appreciation of Sartre's ideas, due to the delay in bringing out translations of his works, and so judgments of his thought or actions have often been outdated or irrelevant. During the 1950s Anglo-American philosophers were mounting an attack on the deficiencies of his existentialist writings of the 1940s, which had been inspired by the wartime situation, in which there was scope for individual heroism. But Sartre had already moved on to confront the misadventures of dialectical reason, a topic relevant to the ideological confrontation of the Cold War, and then to the opportunity opened up by the death of Stalin. When the English translation of *Being and Nothingness* finally appeared in 1956, Sartre was already writing his preface to the *Critique of Dialectical Reason,* now known as *Search for a Method.* The English translation of the *Critique* appeared in 1976, 16 years after its French publication. In the meantime, the ideas of that work had already been tested in practice during the student rebellion of May 1968, and the debates had moved considerably further on, so that even outside France there was a sense that this was a book whose time had come and gone. Sartre had long since returned to working on his three-volume study of Flaubert, which came out in France in the period 1971–72, and the long wait before an English translation appeared meant that the development of his thought went unappreciated outside France. Because of its overtly literary topic, many English-speaking philosophers and sociologists are still not familiar with it, even though they may have come to appreciate the *Critique.*

And yet there was more to follow after the Flaubert study, as Sartre went on thinking aloud, publishing his conversations with the young *gauchistes* Philippe Gavi and Pierre Victor, in *On a raison de se révolter* (1974), and later conversations with Benny Lévy (Pierre Victor). The chronology follows his pilgrim's progress down the various roads to freedom that he explored until he reached the end of his life. In his trio of novels with the general title *The Roads to Freedom,* Sartre had explored a series of ways, mostly inauthentic, of using or fleeing from one's freedom. In his youth he believed that art, writing, was the most authentic use of freedom, through its ability to transcend the given and to create a harmonious, well-ordered world. It is illustrated at the end of *Nausea* (1938) by the character Roquentin, Sartre's alter ego, who listens to a melody on a jukebox and wants to attain that same purity, solidity and harmony in his own disordered life. After the experience of wars and other examples of social oppression, Sartre's purpose in the *Critique* was to examine the social restraints on individual freedom. And in *On a raison de se révolter,* he attempted to develop a theory of "freedom in the organization" and to show how freedom is the foundation of revolutionary praxis and the goal to which socialism is directed.

It is fitting that, after his death, we should be reminded of Sartre's lifelong struggle to reconcile individual freedom and social constraint and determinism. The publication of *Cahiers pour une morale* in 1983 enables us to see why it was that, as Simone de Beauvoir reported, throughout the 1950s Sartre filled notebook after notebook with ideas on morality. He was attempting to resolve the contradiction between his growing political awareness of the need for radical social change, as he involved himself more and more in protest movements, and the concept of individual freedom, which his existentialist fictional and philosophical works had made famous. In retrospect it is clear that the early works lacked a dynamic, or dialectical, concept of the reciprocal interaction between the individual and his or her social environment. In *Being and Nothingness* he had maintained a belief in an absolute and unadulterated freedom of the individual, and yet society, the Other, was an alienating and repressive power that constrained freedom. This anguish at the heart of freedom was escaped either by assuming the identity of a Being-for-others, adopting the safest and most convenient form demanded by society, or through pretending that one was a Being-in-itself, complete, self-contained and immune from the claims made upon one. Either way, "Hell is other people," as the famous line in his play *Huis clos* put it.

The truly free man was one who truly met the challenge of his Being-for-others, who lived with the moral tension and did not succumb to bad faith. But this was a purely individualistic morality and a generalization from the privileged position of the bourgeois intellectual, who generalized his relative freedom into an ontological notion supposedly valid for all men. It was suitable for the artist, who could transcend the given without evading it and in so doing help to free others by subverting oppressive reality by way of the imagination. This was the message of his essay *What Is Literature?* (1948). But by the time he came to write his autobiography, *Words* (1964), his experiences had brought him to the conclusion that there was no salvation through literature, and he regarded his youthful espousal of the vocation of writer as a neurosis. He renounced his vocation, but as he put it: "I have not unfrocked myself. I still write. What else can I do?" Culture could save nothing and nobody, but it could still act as a critical mirror in which we might recognize ourselves, neuroses and all.

His immersion in social protest movements and activities on behalf of what his friend Frantz Fanon called "the wretched of the earth" broadened his focus from the individual to the group, so that progressively from the 1950s onward, he is to be found arguing that freedom makes sense and is of importance only if it is freedom for everyone. Whereas earlier he had spoken of individual freedom, his later statements on morality are concerned with groups in revolt creating common values and, in so doing, perhaps creating or discovering universal values. In the *Critique,* in order to make sense of his radical politics, he set out to show the process by which individuals could fuse into a group and so overcome their ontological solitude and hostility to each other. For this purpose, he drew on Marxist and sociological sources to develop his version of the dialectical method and the concepts of series, collectives, groups and groups in fusion. However, using the case study of Communist parties, his application of this historical sociology of social movements led to a somewhat pessimistic conclusion: revolutionary movements tended to pass from being groups, fused in a common purpose and ideal, into institutions, which serialized and rendered passive the class in whose name they claimed to rule. But he did not despair nor sink into pessimism. He learned from the student movement of 1968 and his subsequent involvement in the activities of the young Maoists, and *On a raison de se révolter* elaborates a model of a revolutionary organization that, in its practice of direct democracy, would also serve as a model of the new society.

However, the decline of a sense of common purpose and fraternity on the Left and the swing to the Right in many countries (including the Soviet Union) led Sartre to say in 1980 that, for the first time since the Second World War, he felt the temptation of despair. He found the invasion of Afghanistan particularly troubling and thought a third world was not impossible, as the Cold War seemed to be coming back to life. The planet appeared divided between the extremely poor, who were dying of hunger, and the small number of wealthy, who were beginning to become less wealthy. Expressing these fears in a conversation with Benny Lévy shortly before his death, he described the world as "ugly, bad and without hope." And yet, being Sartre, he could not let things rest there and he added that he nevertheless would die in hope, but that it was necessary to create a foundation for this hope. He sought to explain why this present world, which appeared so horrible, was but a moment in a long historical development. Hope had always been one of the dominant forces of revolutions and uprisings, which was why he again felt hopeful in his conception of the future.[2]

This chronology of the events and works of Sartre's life will chart the progress of his incessant struggle to liberate himself from false ideas and to pursue the cause of freedom and justice for others. It is a chronicle that substantiates the tribute paid to Sartre after his death by the leading French Communist intellectual, Louis Althusser, who described him as a generous and courageous man, defender of the exploited and oppressed, who always struggled for freedom, "most often with the communists and, if necessary against them." Comparing Sartre to Jean-Jacques Rousseau, Althusser quoted Marx's tribute to Rousseau as "This man, who, no matter what his follies, was of a profound intransigence, and who never accepted the least compromise with established power." Sartre would have agreed with Althusser when he added, "There is no greater compliment for an intellectual, in my opinion."[3]

Kenneth Thompson

2. Sartre in *Le Nouvel Observateur* (26 March 1980).
3. *Le Monde,* 17 April, 1980.

1905

21 June: Jean-Paul Charles Aymard Sartre was born at the home of his parents, Jean-Baptiste and Anne-Marie (née Schweitzer), rue Mignard, in Paris. The maternal grandparents, Charles and Louise Schweitzer, lived in the same apartment building. The young couple had met the year before in Cherbourg, where Anne-Marie's brother was a naval engineer; Jean-Baptiste Sartre was a naval officer who suffered from ill health as a result of fevers contracted in Cochin, China. He had also suffered an unhappy home life, as his father, a country doctor, seemed to bear a grudge against Jean-Baptiste's mother, and the two never spoke to each other. The maternal grandparents were to play a much greater part in Jean-Paul Sartre's life. Charles Schweitzer, although he never attained the same fame as his nephew Albert Schweitzer, gained something of a following by developing the direct method of teaching languages. His father had wanted him to be a Protestant pastor, but he had rebelled and run off in pursuit of a bareback rider, subsequently taking up the profession of teacher. Nevertheless, despite this refusal of the clerical vocation, Charles Schweitzer still "looked so much like God the Father that he was often taken for him," according to Jean-Paul Sartre.[1]

20 July: Sartre was baptized at Notre-Dame de Grâce in Passy.

---

1. Jean-Paul Sartre, *Words,* trans. Irene Clephane (London: Penguin Books, 1967), p. 16.

1906

Jean-Baptiste Sartre's illness got steadily worse, and he was taken to rest at a small farm a few miles outside Thiviers, his home town. The days and nights of vigil exhausted Anne-Marie, and her milk dried up; Jean-Paul had to be sent to a wet nurse who lived nearby, where he became very ill with enteritis. Looking back, Sartre thought this was fortunate for his own psychological development.

Since he was forcibly weaned at nine months, he was prevented by fever and exhaustion from feeling "the last snip of the scissors" which severed the bond between mother and child. . . .[1]

17 September: Jean-Baptiste Sartre died. Once again, Sartre's autobiographical account of the loss emphasized the benefits for his own psychological development:

"Jean-Baptiste's death was the great event of my life: it returned my mother to her chains and it gave me my freedom." Having no paternal bond to inhibit him, Sartre felt that this allowed him to develop a psyche that was entirely without a Superego.[2]

Knowing so little of him, there was not much more Sartre could say about his father, except that he was amazed how little he knew about him. . . . No one in the family had been able to rouse his curiosity about his father. For some years, Sartre saw, over his bed the portrait of a junior officer with frank eyes, a round, balding head and a heavy moustache: But when his mother remarried, the portrait disappeared.[3]

---

1. Jean-Paul Sartre, *Words,* trans. Irene Clephane (London: Penguin Books, 1967), p. 13.
2. Ibid., pp. 14–15.
3. Ibid., p. 15.

1906–15

Penniless and jobless, Anne-Marie decided to go back to live with her parents. The ensuing years of his childhood in that household are the subject of Sartre's autobiography *Les Mots (Words),* in which he describes the situation and its effects on him of the fact that, "Until the age of ten, I was alone between one old man and two women."[1] It was an upbringing of great indulgence and without any attempt to impose discipline on him. He was the "golden boy" and child prodigy. His young mother, living in her parents' home, was more like a sister, and his grandfather, once a strong disciplinarian with his own children, indulged his grandson. Not only was Jean-Paul intellectually precocious, he was also very pretty in his early years. The pretty looks gradually disappeared as the result of an eye infection, which began after he caught a chill at the age of 3 or 4 during a stay in Arcachon, eventually producing a strabism in his right eye. The effect on his looks became apparent when his grandfather took him, at the age of 7, to have his long hair cut, because he thought the boy looked effeminate. The response from his mother was dramatic and left a deep imprint on the young Sartre. She went and shut herself up in her bedroom to weep, unable to deny to herself that not only had her little girl been transformed into a little boy, but that that little boy was also very ugly.[2]

Sartre's intellectual precocity and obsession with words were evident from an early age. He was fortunate in being surrounded with books in his grandparents' home: "I began my life as I shall no doubt end it: among books." Even before he could read them, he revered them and realized the family prosperity depended on them. By the age of about 4, he was going through the motions of reading, seizing upon a work called *Tribulations d'un Chinois en Chine* and pretending to read it, thereby attracting cries of admiration. He virtually taught himself to read by deciphering in private Hector Malot's *Sans famille (Nobody's Boy).* He was soon devouring encyclopedias and by the age of

1. Jean-Paul Sartre, *Words,* trans. Irene Clephane (London: Penguin Books, 1967), p. 53.
2. Ibid., p. 66.

7 had read *Madame Bovary,* Corneille, Rabelais, Voltaire, Vigny, Mérimée, Hugo and many other writers. He also began to write, corresponding in verse with his grandfather, rewriting the fables of La Fontaine in alexandrine form and attempting to write novels with titles like *Pour un papillon (For a Butterfly)* and *Le Marchand de bananes (The Banana Man).* He even wrote a letter of appreciation to Georges Courteline (the pseudonym of Georges Moinaux, 1858–1929), the author of light comedies, with some help from his grandfather. Much to Sartre's annoyance, the letter, which contained many spelling mistakes, was published in 1950 by some newspapers, under the title "Jean-Paul Sartre's Début in the Literary Life."

After living in Meudon for a number of years, the family had moved to Paris in 1911, taking up residence at 1 rue le Goff, in the 5th arrondissement, where Charles Schweitzer founded a language institute. In 1913 he decided that his grandson should be subjected to ordinary educational disciplines and so took him along to the lycée Montaigne, where he extolled the boy's merits to the headmaster and told him Jean-Paul's only fault was being too advanced for his age. The headmaster cooperated and put him in an advanced class. But after the first dictation, the grandfather was hastily summoned to the school by the irate headmaster and given Sartre's paper, which was full of scrawls and atrocious misspellings. The doting grandfather decided the school did not understand or appreciate Sartre and so took him away from the lycée. Jean-Paul was unmoved: "I had not understood what was going on and my setback did not bother me: I was an infant prodigy who could not spell, that was all."[3]

Sartre went back to his lonely ways, which he liked, despite the cost to him of being separated from the real world. A private tutor was hired. However, the family spent some time in Arcachon the following year, and Sartre was sent to the local school there because his grandfather had decided his democratic principles required it. But Sartre was treated to a great deal of favoritism which he took to be absolutely right and proper, and affected great superiority towards the "working class boys."[4]

3. Ibid., p. 50.
4. Ibid., pp. 50–51.

After Arcachon there was one term at the Poupon School, which was not very satisfactory, and then Sartre was withdrawn and given private lessons at home by one of the teachers at the school, Mademoiselle Marie-Louise, who insisted on telling her young charge about all her personal problems. When she was dismissed, Sartre had a succession of tutors, all of whom were eminently forgettable.

From time to time he would go to Thiviers to spend time with his paternal grandparents, but on 22 October 1913, his grandfather, Dr. Aymard Sartre, died.

1915

In October Sartre's real formal education began when he entered the excellent lycée Henri-IV in Paris. His teachers found him an unusual mixture of talent and impetuosity. At the end of his first term, one teacher found him to be: "An excellent little boy. Never gets the answer right the first time. Must get used to thinking more."[1] However, he soon became accustomed to the new disciplines, and by the end of the year his teachers reported that he was "excellent in every respect."

1916–17

On entering the fifth year at the lycée Henri-IV, Sartre met Paul Nizan, who was to be his closest friend. Once, during the year, he and Nizan wrote a bawdy story, which was confiscated by the teacher, at which point Nizan denied his authorship and said the work was Sartre's. Nevertheless, Sartre made a good impression, especially on the French teacher, who described

1. Archives of the lycée Henri-IV, 1915–16; Michel Contat and Michel Rybalka, "Chronologie," in Jean-Paul Sartre, *Oeuvres romanesques* (Paris: Gallimard, 1981), p. xxxviii.

him as having an open mind, a little kit of literary tools and a good memory.[1]

1917

26 April: Sartre's mother remarried, an event that greatly upset Sartre's schoolwork. The new stepfather was Joseph Mancy, a naval engineer, aged about 40. Anne-Marie had first met him at her brother's house in Cherbourg, at around the same time she met her first husband. He came from a modest background, the son of a railroad worker, and although he would have liked to propose marriage to her even then, he had considered himself unworthy. Now he was more successful and had contacted her again. Sartre's mother felt herself a burden on her family, and marriage seemed the only solution in view of the fact that she had not been able to secure work. In later life Sartre expressed the opinion that she certainly did not marry out of love for Mancy, who, in his opinion, was not a very nice person. For the first few months, the couple had an apartment in the rue Condorcet, while Sartre continued to live with his grandparents and attended the lycée Henri-IV as a day student.

Sartre's education was then disrupted when his mother and stepfather moved to La Rochelle. In November he was entered in the fourth year at the boys' lycée in La Rochelle (the school is now known as the lycée Eugène-Fromentin). His class teacher, M. Loosdreck, was a victim of constant class rowdiness and died two years later.

1. Archives of the lycée Henri-IV, 1916–17; Michel Contat and Michel Rybalka, "Chronologie," in Jean-Paul Sartre, *Oeuvres romanesques* (Paris: Gallimard 1981). P. xxxviii.

1918–19

Despite problems in adjusting to the new school, Sartre's achievements in class 3A were fairly good: he gained first-class honors, taking first prize in French composition and Latin translation and a first-class certificate in German. Less impressive was his performance in gymnastics, where he received a fourth-class certificate.

1919–20

In class 2A (equivalent to American 10th grade), Sartre was the only student of Greek and was awarded a prize. Among the first prizes given to him at the award ceremonies on 12 July 1920 were those for Latin translation and composition. However, despite these results, it was clear to Sartre's family that he was unhappy and unsettled at the school. According to his own later accounts, he was often the victim of raggings and beatings. In order to gain acceptance, he joined in the class baiting of M. Loosdreck (the model for the protagonist in "Jesus the Owl, Small-town Schoolteacher," his first attempt at novel writing) and even stole money from his mother in order to buy popularity among his classmates (the discovery of which, in the spring of 1919, provided material for a later short story). This latter incident lost him the support of his grandfather, who was staying with them, and Sartre became even more isolated and experienced deep emotional loneliness. His relations with his stepfather were very strained and distant. Joseph Mancy made no attempt to play the role of father but confined himself to supervising his stepson's studies and urging him in the direction of preparing for a career as a teacher of mathematics or physics. Sartre resisted this urging to the point of insolence, and his stepfather gave up. A final emotional setback was when Sartre discovered his ugliness as the result of a rebuff from a girl of his own age whom he tried to go out with. He later described the time in La Rochelle as the worst years of his life. Certainly they were the only years when he experienced a complete drying up of his urge to write. In the fourth and third years (8th and 9th grades), he had tried to write cloak-and-dagger–type novels and dreamed of writing librettos for operettas; he even taught himself the piano. By second year (10th grade), he had stopped writing completely.

Despite Sartre's negative appraisal of his years at La Rochelle, at least one of his contemporaries was to offer a different impression, noting: "He was exciting to listen to, he could get discussions going and he could keep it going for hours. He was ambitious and he had an original mind, with a sort of imaginative exuberance. We all felt that we would hear more of him."[1]

His parents were not so impressed with his progress and decided to send him back to Paris for the following year, so as to take him away from the "bad influences."

1920

Back at the lycée Henri-IV in class 1A, Sartre was reunited with Nizan. The two were inseparable and eventually became known as "Nitre and Sarzan." Together they launched into literary studies. Nizan was the more up to date in his reading and introduced Sartre to Giraudoux, Gide, Valéry and others. Together they discovered Proust, for whom they developed a great passion. And their French literature teacher, M. Georgin, introduced them to the great works of literature, although Sartre's response to Flaubert was to say that he hated him and that *Madame Bovary* was disgusting (in contrast to his later obsession with both).

Unlike his isolated position at La Rochelle, at the lycée Henri-IV Sartre was in the center of things and occupied the position of official class organizer of amusements and japes. M. Georgin's report commented: "Definitely has what it takes."[1]

1. Michel Guillet, "Jean-Paul Sartre au lycée de La Rochelle," *Sud-Ouest Dimanche* (25 October 1964).

1. Archives of the lycée Henri-IV, 1920–21.

1921

In *June* Sartre was awarded the prize for excellence and first prize for French composition. He also entered for the general concours and took the first part of his baccalauréat.

1922

Sartre's twin talents for literature and philosophy were already becoming evident. In addition to his literary studies, he was winning plaudits from his philosophy teacher, M. Chabrier, who said of him, "Excellent student: mind already lively, good at discussing questions, but needs to depend a little less on himself."[1] However, the young Jean-Paul was less happy with philosophy as it was presented to him, and he confessed to finding it boring and not something he would wish to continue with. He had begun writing again and was working on fictional pieces, two of which were to be published the following year— "The Angel of Morbidity" and "Jesus the Owl." He systematically noted down his ideas on all kinds of subjects, inscribing them in an alphabetically ordered notebook that he had found on the Métro.

In *June* Sartre took the second part of his baccalauréat.

Later in the *summer* he went on a trip to Alsace with his grandfather. The holidays were spent with his family in La Rochelle.

At the beginning of the academic year 1922–23, Sartre and Nizan were transferred after the summer to the lycée Louis-le-Grand, which had a better record for teaching the two preparatory years leading up to the competitive examination that gave entrance to the École Normale Supérieure. Sartre was registered as a half-boarder, as his parents had now moved back

---

1. Archives of the lycée Henri-IV, 1921–22.

to Paris, living at 2 Square Clignancourt, in the 18th arrondissement. The shipyard in La Rochelle, where his stepfather
was manager, had gone bankrupt.

1923

"L'Ange du morbide" ("The Angel of Morbidity"), a short story; *La Revue sans titre,* no. 1, 15 January.

"Jésus la Chouette, professeur de province" ("Jesus the Owl, Small-town Schoolteacher"), a fragment of a novel; *La Revue sans titre,* no. 2, 10 February; no. 3, 25 February; no. 4, 10 March; no. 5, 25 March.

Sartre's first publications, when he was still only 17, consisted
of the short story "The Angel of Morbidity" and a fragment of
a novel, "Jesus the Owl, Small-town Schoolteacher," both published in *La Revue sans titre.* The short story showed many of
the concerns and ideas that were to appear in Sartre's mature
works—the contrast between the world as imagined and the
world as experienced; the self-deception that he was to brand
as "bad faith," bourgeois complacency and literary affectation;
and the subjective experience of the world in the form of a sick-
ness. It was a satirical narrative about a schoolteacher with
aspirations to be a poet, to which end he seeks to cultivate a
taste for the morbid and decadent. Attempting to seduce a young
girl suffering from tuberculosis, he recoils in horror when she
succumbs to a coughing fit and spits blood. It ends with the
young man marrying a "pink, blonde, dumb, and healthy Alsatian girl" and concludes: "He never wrote a thing again and
at the age of fifty-five was awarded the Legion of Honor, the
indisputable mark of 'Bourgeoisie.' " The fragment of a novel
was faintly autobiographical, as it involved a youth being sent
to the lycée at La Rochelle, and contains observations on bourgeois mediocrity and a way of life in which "the tedium of virtue
ruled unrestrained."

At the conclusion of the academic year 1922–23, Sartre finished second to Nizan in his strongest subject, French, and in

philosophy he could only make fifth place. He was still having trouble coming to terms with his philosophy teachers. In this case it was a M. Bernes, who commented on him: "Active and alert mind; will succeed; must avoid being over-facile and writing too much about inadequately clarified ideas." Sartre reciprocated by saying that he could not understand anything in M. Bernes' course. He was also at loggerheads with Nizan from March to October, although he had made a new friend in René Maheu.

1924

In the final year at the lycée Louis-le-Grand, Sartre shone in only one subject, and that was philosophy. The breakthrough in the subject came when he wrote an essay for his teacher, M. Colonna d'Istria, on the subject of "The Consciousness of Duration," which involved reading Bergson's *Essai sur les données immédiates de la conscience.* He was also introduced to the works of Schopenhauer and Nietzsche. A fellow student at the time, Georges Canguilhem, later recollected that Sartre made an impression, not only with his hard work and brilliance but also with his liveliness and humor.

In **August** Sartre gained seventh place in the entrance exam for the École Normale Supérieure, and so began one of the happiest periods of his life, spent in the company of stimulating fellow students such as Raymond Aron, Albert Bédé, Georges Canguilhem, Maurice Merleau-Ponty, Jean Hyppolite, René Maheu and, of course, Nizan, with whom he shared lodgings. As Sartre put it: "The École Normale was, from the first day, for me and for most of us, the beginning of independence. Many of us can say, as I do, that they had four years of happiness there."[1] They were years not only of intellectual stimulation but also of fun and passion. Sartre's group was not above indulging in youthful gang warfare against other groups of students, especially those they identified as Nietszchean élitists.

1. Jean-Paul Sartre, *Situations,* vol. IV (Paris: Gallimard, 1964), p. 149.

Water bombs were the favorite weapon. The inner trio of the group was composed of Sartre, Nizan and Réné Maheu. (It was Maheu who introduced Simone de Beauvoir into the group.) Sartre quickly established a work routine that lasted him throughout his time at the École. He hardly ever attended lectures at the Sorbonne, unless they particularly interested him, such as those by Bréhier on the Stoics or a course on psychology. He worked hard during fixed hours: from 9 a.m. to 1 p.m. and from 5 p.m. to 9 p.m.—hours that he kept to for most of his working life.

1925

This year saw the beginning of Sartre's first serious love affair, which lasted on and off for two years. It was with Camille, whose full name was Simone-Camille Sans, later known as Simone Jollivet. They met at the funeral of a mutual cousin at Thiviers in Périgord, when she was 22 and he 19. She was a beautiful woman, with long blonde hair and a reputation for sexual intrigue, having frequented fashionable *maisons de rendez-vous* from the age of 18 and enjoyed great success and profit from it. According to Simone de Beauvoir's description: "Camille possessed an acute sense of the appropriate *mise en scène;* while awaiting a client in the room set apart for him she would stand in front of the fireplace, stark naked, her long hair combed out, reading Michelet or, at a later period, Nietzsche."[1]

At their first meeting Camille's beauty took on a mysterious quality for Sartre, as she was dressed in black mourning crepe. Her initial impression of him was less favorable; he appeared particularly ugly in his dark suit and wearing one of his stepfather's hats, which came down to his eyebrows, and with a look of intense boredom on his face during the funeral ceremonies. Camille was thunderstruck and is said to have muttered: "It's Mirabeau."[2] Nevertheless, they were fascinated with

---

1. Simone de Beauvoir, *The Prime of Life,* trans. Peter Green (New York: Harper Colophon Books, 1976) p. 58.
2. Ibid., p. 59.

each other and stayed together for four days, at the end of which period they had to be separated by their worried families. Camille was being courted by the son of a wealthy furnace manufacturer, but she did not relish the idea of becoming a respectable middle-class housewife any more than that of remaining a tart. Sartre's convincing line was that he could save her from provincial mediocrity; he encouraged her to think for herself and advised her on what to read. While apart they exchanged letters; he signed himself "Vautrin" and she was "Rastignac." She also sent him her attempts at literary essays, and he responded with comments that mingled flattery and truth in a winning combination. The correspondence prompted him to formulate his own philosophy; in two of his letters he developed the idea of the "contingency of consciousness as an emptiness in being," which was to be a central feature of *Being and Nothingness.*

It was six months before he had saved up enough money to visit Camille in Toulouse, where she lived with her parents, who owned a pharmacy. His subsequent visits over the next two years were not as frequent as he would have wished, due to the cost. Sometimes he would sleep on a park bench or in the cinema during the day and not check in at a hotel, so as to save money. At night he would stand outside the pharmacy until Camille had retired to her room, and then she would send her adopted sister Zina to open the door and let him in. At daybreak he had to leave Camille's room and creep out of the house. Not surprisingly, by the third or fourth night of his visit, he would be dropping with fatigue, and then Camille would say, contemptuously: "Oh go to sleep then: I'll read Nietzsche." And then when he awoke, she was quite likely to quote him from Nietzsche's *Also sprach Zarathustra,* emphasizing the passage that deals with the mastery of the body by the will.[3]

3. Ibid.

1926

Sartre continued to pursue an active social life alongside his studies. He was very attracted to jazz and frequented the College Inn in the rue Vavin.

15–25 August: Sartre had been awarded a grant to allow him to participate in a debate on "The Christian Imprint," at a conference in Pontigny. He spoke on Descartes but did not feel very comfortable with the subject. Other participants included Charles Du Bos, Jean Baruzi and L.-M. Chauffier.

In **September** Nizan departed for Aden, where he was to stay until the following spring. Sartre became friendly with Pierre Guille, and he, Sartre and Réné Maheu began to meet regularly with an older woman, Mme. Morel. She was 40 and drew from the young men an "admiring friendship." Sartre was employed to tutor her son for the baccalauréat in philosophy. Sartre had written a novel called *Une défaite (A Defeat)*, which Gallimard had rejected for publication. It was based on the love affairs of Nietzsche and Cosima Wagner and had as its hero a young man, Frédéric, who was notable for his aggressive "voluntarism." Mme. Morel called Sartre "miserable Frédéric" whenever he tried to impose his own tastes and beliefs on her or to dictate her actions, especially concerning her son's education.[1] But despite their arguments, Sartre and Mme. Morel enjoyed each other's company and valued their friendship. He referred to her as "that Lady"—hence the dedication in *Huis clos*.

His relations with his parents were not always easy. When they moved to Paris, he would have Sunday lunch with them and also see his mother alone every 10 days or so. With his stepfather, who regarded him as a spokesman for the Communist Party, there were long political arguments. In fact, although Sartre felt sympathetic to the Communist Party, he was not tempted to join it (unlike Nizan, who joined in 1928); he described himself as too much of an anarchistic individualist. It was opposition to the established order that he enjoyed. It is

---

1. Simone de Beauvoir, *The Prime of Life,* trans. Peter Green (New York: Harper Colophon Books, 1976), p. 35.

symptomatic that Sartre and his friends should have invented a personal mythology for themselves, in which they were a caste called the Eugenes—inspired by Cocteau's *Potomak*. Its principal teaching was that all thoughts of order are unbearably sad.

In a letter to Camille at the time, he described what he believed to be his two basic, and conflicting, character traits: the ambition to *create* something (precisely what was still unclear) and the "sentimentality of an old woman." He was deeply ashamed of the latter and had been ridiculed by his friends and family for it. He had therefore decided that the first thing he would create would be his own character, and this meant repressing this unpleasing aspect of his makeup. As a consequence, he felt he would never be able to act spontaneously.[2]

1927

"La Théorie de l'état dans la pensée française d'aujourd'hui" ("The Theory of the State in Modern French Thought"), an article, *Revue universitaire internationale* no. 1, January, pp. 25–37.

Sartre's first philosophical publication was on "The Theory of the State in Modern French Thought." It appeared in the journal of a university association connected with the League of Nations, published simultaneously in French, English and German. The editor in Paris, who solicited the article, was Sartre's fellow student, Daniel Lagache. In it Sartre compared realist and idealist theories of the state. On the whole, French philosophers had adopted a realist approach, but under pressure of national feelings aroused by the First World War, they had tried to use this method to reach an idealist conclusion—to construct an "ought" out of an "is." French sociologists, under the influence of Durkheim, were particularly prone to put forward evolutionary solutions to explain the emergence of state

2. Jean-Paul Sartre, *Lettres au Castor et à quelques autres* (Paris: Gallimard, 1983), p. 10.

sovereignty as both a fact and a value. But according to Sartre, their notion of "collective consciousness," explaining why the society was greater than the individuals composing it and had an independent life of its own, rested on an unprovable assumption that "the whole is greater than the sum of its parts." This presupposed that the sum and the whole can be compared, but the sum cannot be given without the whole being given. "In the world there are wholes and parts. That is all there is. Consequently, I cannot know whether something completely new may spring from an addition of parts." Sartre's argument showed all the marks of the typical articulate Normalien, but it was stronger on negative critique than on original thought. His dismissal of the distinction between the sum and the whole, as found in Durkheimian sociology, was not something he held to in his own later philosophy, when he contrasted seriality with the group in fusion.

Another completed work was his thesis for the diplôme d'études supérieures, which he had written under the supervision of the professor of psychology, Henri Delacroix. Its title was "The Image in Psychological Life: Its Role and Nature," and it drew on such thinkers as Bergson, Binet, Proust, Jaspers, Freud and the young Piaget, who, although only nine years older than Sartre, had already established his intellectual reputation. In the case of Jaspers, Sartre and Nizan had collaborated in translating his *General Psychopathology* from the German.

This was the second year of Sartre's affair with Camille, and she spent two weeks with him in Paris. She made a great impression on his fellow students when he took her to the École Normale ball. However, in order to entertain her, he had to borrow money, and even then she was disappointed by the poor quality of the hotel he booked her into and the restaurants and dance halls they visited. Sartre wanted her to stay on in Paris and to this end obtained a job for her in a stationer's, but she was not attracted by the prospect of selling postcards for a living, and so, claiming that she did not like Paris, she returned home to Toulouse. By the summer their passionate relationship had come to an end.

Sartre was also in trouble with the authorities at the École Normale Supérieure for having written insulting things in the École journal against the obligation for Normale students to undergo special military training. He was censured by the disciplinary committee.

24 December: Sartre and Aron were the witnesses at Nizan's wedding.

Despite his other activities, he had passed examinations in psychology, ethics, sociology, logic and metaphysics, and failed only in Latin.

1928

Sartre's determination to pursue his own original line in philosophy, which had earlier brought him into dispute with his philosophy teachers, served him badly in his examinations, and he surprised everybody by finishing in 50th place in the written part of the agrégation. His response was to say that it had taught him a lesson as to what was expected: the next time he would reproduce other people's ideas only thinly disguised in an original format. It was after this failure that he sprang a further surprise by asking his parents to find out if he could marry a young girl whom he had met the year before while on holiday in the Massif Central with a friend, Alfred Péron, who was her cousin. This impetuosity had no ill effects, as the girl's parents refused.

In **August** he went to stay with Nizan in La Croix-Valmer, in Provence.

On returning to Paris to prepare for resitting his examination, he took a room at the Cité universitaire. It was there that he met Marc Zuorro, who made a strong impression on him and on whom he modeled the character of Daniel in his novel *Roads to Freedom*.

In **November,** still pursuing his campaign against military training, he was one of 83 Normale students who signed a petition against compulsory military training for students.

1929

Letter on "Enquête auprès des étudiants" ("Investigation of Today's Students"), *Les Nouvelles littéraires* (2 February 1939), p. 10.

Sartre's original philosophy, so different from that of his teachers, received its first published exposition in a letter he wrote in response to an investigation into student opinion being carried out by Roland Alix for *Les Nouvelles littéraires*. In it, Sartre wrote that it was a paradox of the human mind that Man, whose business it was to create the necessary conditions, could not raise himself above a certain level of existence, "like those fortune-tellers who can tell other people's futures, but not their own."

He added, comparing his own generation with the preceding one:

"We are more unhappy, but nicer to know."[1]

In July he met Simone de Beauvoir, who was introduced into their group by Maheu (whom she referred to in her writings as "Herbaud"). She provided a revealing description of the life of the group at that period: they would do most of their work in the mornings, have lunch at the restaurant in the Cité, or near the Parc Montsouris, and then take time off in the afternoons to drive around Paris in Nizan's car, stopping frequently for a glass of beer at a sidewalk café or to play at the pin-table machines at the fun fair at the Porte d'Orléans. They took part in the usual escapades at the École Normale, climbing over roofs and walls, often to the loud accompaniment of Sartre and Maheu singing at the tops of their voices. Sartre had a good voice, could sing all the current jazz songs, and was well known at the École Normale for his comic talents.[2]

Maheu was jealous that he should occupy first place in Simone's affections, but he agreed to let Sartre spend the evening of the 14th of July celebrations with them. After dinner at an

1. Quoted in Simone de Beauvoir, *Memoirs of a Dutiful Daughter,* trans. James Kirkup (London: Penguin Books, 1963), pp. 342–43.

2. Ibid., pp. 335–36.

Alsatian restaurant, they sat on the lawn of the Cité universitaire and watched the fireworks. Sartre, who had a reputation for generosity, then took them in a taxi to the Falstaff in rue Montparnasse, where they drank cocktails until two o'clock in the morning. Simone found Sartre more amusing than Maheu, but she allowed the latter to continue to occupy first place. However, Maheu failed the examinations and left Paris. Sartre told Simone: "From now on, I'm going to take you under my wing."[3] He also gave her their examination results: he had been awarded first place, and she was second. During the fortnight of the oral examinations, they hardly ever left each other except to sleep. They would meet for drinks occasionally with the Nizans; with Aron, who was doing his military service in the Meteorological Corps; or with Politzer, who, like Nizan, had joined the Communist Party. Sartre bought Simone books from the secondhand bookstalls by the Seine, and in the evenings he introduced her to cowboy films. By the time she left him at the beginning of August, it was clear to her that "he would never go out of my life again."[4] Some time later, Sartre suggested that they enter into a two-year trial contract with each other, explaining that: "What we have is an *essential* love; but it is a good idea for us also to experience *contingent* love affairs."[5]

The new relationship had two consequences for Sartre. It meant that Simone became his closest confidante, and other friends, such as Raymond Aron, for this reason felt that their own relationship to him changed at that point. He also widened his circle of friends to include those of Simone, such as Stépha and Fernando Gerassi, the latter supplying the model for Gomez in *Roads to Freedom*.

For a brief period during the year there was the possibility that Sartre might become seriously involved again with Camille, and this produced feelings of jealousy and inadequacy in Simone. Camille had returned to Paris at the beginning of the year with a wealthy lover and had then taken up with the actor Dullin, who set her up in an apartment on the rue Gabrielle. She also began meeting with Sartre because she still found

3. Ibid., p. 339.

4. Ibid., p. 345.

5. Simone de Beauvoir, *The Prime of Life*, trans. Peter Green (New York: Harper Colophon Books, 1976), p. 24.

Paris boring and remembered the lively times they had spent together. She was now more sophisticated and an actress. Sartre enjoyed her scandalous tales of intrigue in the theatrical world, but he decided he did not wish to put their relationship back on its old passionate footing. Camille was resentful and disappointed. Soon the whole thing fizzled out, and they subsequently kept up only an intermittent acquaintance with each other.

Sartre applied for a lecturing post in Japan but did not get it.

In **November** he began an 18-month period of military service in the meteorological office at Saint-Cyr, with Raymond Aron as his sergeant instructor. He had plenty of free time now in which to write, and he produced poems, the first chapter of a novel inspired by the death of Simone's friend Zaza, then "The Legend of Truth" and two plays—"Épiméthée" and "I Shall Have a Fine Funeral."

1930

Although Sartre was filling his free time with reading and some writing, the results of the writing were not very impressive or satisfactory. Indeed, his friend Pierre Guille responded to his poetry and the attempt at a novel by bursting out laughing at some of their incongruous images, and Sartre discarded them.

In **August** Simone de Beauvoir took up residence for a month in a little hotel on the banks of the Loire, near Sartre's meteorological station. They would spend most of the day together, with Sartre returning to the meteorological station every two hours to take a reading. Often Sartre could take a whole day off, and he would use money from the legacy left to him on the recent death of his grandmother Schweitzer in order to hire a taxi for a trip to one of the châteaux of the Loire, and they would treat themselves to an expensive restaurant meal. One September morning they set off for Paris and arrived there extremely hungry. As soon as their favorite café, the Closerie des

Lilas, opened for the day, they sat down on the terrasse and ordered a large pile of croissants and cups of hot chocolate. Finding that they did not have enough money to pay the bill, Sartre left Simone as a kind of hostage and set off in a taxi to find friends to borrow money from. Unfortunately, most of them were away on vacation, and this was the reason he took so long, not returning to the anxious Simone for more than an hour. This style of life gradually eroded Sartre's legacy, and Simone was reduced to selling her books and jewelry.

When Simone returned to her work in Paris, she would visit Sartre in Tours every Sunday, bringing him an armful of books. At first he asked for "entertaining trash," but he was soon disappointed with these and asked for more serious books. Whenever possible they went to the cinema—"the one medium which Sartre ranked almost as high as literature."[1] According to Simone de Beauvoir, "It was while watching images flickering across a screen that he had had his revelation concerning the fundamental necessity of art, and had come to realize how lamentably 'contingent' by contrast our physical background was."[2]

1931

Having finished his national service in February, armed with a document certifying that he had maintained "good conduct all the time that he had remained under the flag, and that he had constantly served with honor and faithfulness," Sartre, disappointed by the rejection of his application for a lectureship in Japan, decided to accept a post teaching philosophy at the lycée in Le Havre, initially as a replacement for a teacher suffering from a nervous breakdown, but with a guarantee of keeping the job for the following year. Since Simone de Beauvoir was offered a teaching post in Marseille, about as far away as it is possible to get from Le Havre, this was the point when

1. Simone de Beauvoir, *The Prime of Life*, trans. Peter Green (New York: Harper Colophon Books, 1976), p. 44.
2. Ibid.

they seriously considered marriage, since married teachers could expect, though not always immediately, to be given posts in the same town. The bourgeois institution of marriage seemed incompatible with freedom, and they both were equally resolved to withstand any encroachment by society on their private affairs. According to Simone de Beauvoir's own testimony,[1] they would have considered the "so-called legitimacy" of marriage had they wanted to have children, but neither of them had any such desires, either for strengthening the bonds that united them or for reflecting and extending their existence in some other being. For Simone de Beauvoir writing was incompatible with maternity: Literature, she thought, was a way of justifying the world by fashioning it anew in the pure context of imagination—and, at the same time, of preserving its own existence from oblivion. Whereas, childbearing seemed no more than a "purposeless and unjustifiable increase of the world's population."[2]

Nevertheless, argued Sartre, in the face of Simone de Beauvoir's extreme anxiety at the thought of their separation, why martyr oneself for a principle? Such a formality as marriage need not seriously affect one's way of life. However, Simone de Beauvoir, according to her account, was not for one moment persuaded by such arguments, but they did at this point enter into a greater commitment to each other. "Our relationship had become closer and more demanding than at first; it could allow brief separations, but not vast solitary escapades. We did not swear oaths of eternal fidelity; but we did agree to postpone any possibility of separation until the distant time when we reached our thirties."[3]

An extract of "The Legend of Truth," written in 1929, was published in the journal *Bifur* in June. Nizan had submitted the manuscript of the complete work to Europe Press, but it was rejected, and he then used his influence to have it published in the journal with which he was associated. In his "Note on Contributors," Nizan wrote: "Young philosopher. Is at work on

---

1. Simone de Beauvoir, *The Prime of Life,* trans. Peter Green (New York: Harper Colophon Books, 1976), pp. 66–67.

2. Ibid., p. 67.

3. Ibid.

a volume of destructive philosophy." For the first time Sartre used a literary mode to convey philosophical arguments because, even at this early stage, he was opposed to the tendency to talk in terms of universal categories and generalizations that obscured the concrete reality of being. In "The Legend of Truth," the story form is used to present a sociology of knowledge in which different ways of thinking are related to different social structures. According to Simone de Beauvoir, he used the medium of a story because he had no faith in universals or generalizations. He could not even formulate his repudiation of these in generalized terms and had to replace proposition by demonstration.[4]

Nizan himself had just published his *Aden-Arabie,* which Sartre found "brilliant rather than profound" and not a little upsetting, since in it Nizan made a furious attack on the École Normale and its ethos and subsequently asserted his strong commitment to the Communist Party. Sartre felt that he had gone a little too far.

12 July: At the award ceremony at the lycée in Le Havre, Sartre gave a lecture entitled "Motion Picture Art," which was published in the local newspaper and later republished under the title "The Movies Are Not a Bad School" in the *Gazette du Cinéma* (1950). From childhood he had been a fan of the movies and loved the egalitarian atmosphere of the neighborhood movie theater. He reassured his students that their parents need not fear the effect of the cinema on them: "It is an art which seems easy but is extremely hard and, if it is approached in the right way, very profitable; because by its nature it reflects civilization in our time."

Summer: Sartre and Simone de Beauvoir traveled to Spain and in Madrid again met Fernando Gerassi, who had been living there since 1929. They made several visits to the Prado, where Sartre admired El Greco and Bosch but decided that he disliked Titian for being too "theatrical." But since they were both convinced that the true quality of a town was to be found only in its poorest quarters, they spent all their evenings in the Barrio Chino, "where big, graceful women sang, danced,

4. Ibid., p. 41.

and offered their favors from little open-air platforms. We were interested in them, but observed their audiences with rather more curiosity: by virtue of the spectacle we were all watching together, we felt ourselves assimilated in the crowd."[5]

October: "The Legend of Truth" was rejected again, and Sartre gave up trying to get it published, having decided on maturer reflection that, although the book contained some lively ideas, they were frozen under a very stiff, artificial, classical style. His pamphlet "On Contingency," which contained the ideas for *Nausea,* seemed to be more promising.

1932

As new, young teachers, Sartre and Simone de Beauvoir found that they now had greater opportunities for travel and time to read. Although they read everything that came out, the book that appealed to them most was Céline's *Journey to the End of Night.* They were enchanted by the style he used to attack war, colonialism, the cult of mediocrity, platitudes, and society generally. It seemed as if Céline had forged a way of writing that was as vivid as the spoken word. Sartre was strongly influenced by it and he abandoned the "starchy verbiage" he had still been using in "The Legend of Truth."[1]

Equally, John Dos Passos's *The 42nd Parallel* taught them a lot. Dos Passos succeeded in presenting his main characters through a bifocal perspective which meant that they appeared both as detailed individuals and as purely social phenomena.[2]

Easter: According to Simone de Beauvoir's testimony, Sartre was "dragged off" by her to Brittany for the holidays. Fired by her reading, she had various romantic notions about Brittany, which—partly because of the weather and partly because of

5. Ibid., p. 71.

1. Simone de Beauvoir, *The Prime of Life,* trans. Peter Green (New York: Harper Colophon Books, 1976), p. 113.

2. Ibid.

uncomfortable transport—were quickly dispelled. Chateau-briand's tomb struck them as "so absurdly pompous in its fake simplicity" that Sartre urinated over it as a token of his contempt!

Summer: Sartre and Simone de Beauvoir made a trip to the Balearics and Spanish Morocco and on the way back met Pierre Guille and Mme. Morel in Seville for a car trip together across Spain. Although all four were good friends, traveling together in the hot Spanish sun brought out certain conflicts, particularly between Sartre and Guille: Sartre was forever railing against the bourgeoisie, while traveling in comfortable bourgeois style; Guille, on the other hand, was more consistent in his bourgeois liberalism. "To Sartre he appeared just the kind of cultivated humanist that Sartre himself did not want to be, yet from which he had not, so far, managed to distinguish himself. Each saw in the other a disquieting image."[3]

On the return journey, Sartre and Simone de Beauvoir met Camille in Toulouse, which she encouraged them to explore. She herself was working on a novel based on her own adolescent experiences, writing every night from midnight until six in the morning. Her determination greatly inspired both Sartre and Simone de Beauvoir, neither of whom felt they were making great progress in their writing, and they resolved, like her, to work six hours a day, every day.

October: Simone de Beauvoir took up a new teaching post at the Jeanne d'Arc lycée in Rouen, which was only an hour's train ride from Le Havre, and there she stayed until 1936. She and Sartre met frequently, either in Le Havre or Rouen or in Paris. Through Camille they met Charles Dullin, actor and director, and, through Nizan, a young Trotskyist called Colette Audry, who was a colleague of Simone de Beauvoir's and was greatly interested in psychoanalysis. At this time there was a popular craze for the yo-yo: people used to walk down the streets with their yo-yos in their hand. Gide was said to be a highly skilled performer; Sartre himself practiced from morning until night with "somber perseverance."

They were as yet not interested in world political events,

3. Ibid., p. 97.

preferring to talk about the various people they knew, about psychoanalysis (Adler interested them more than Freud because "he attached less importance to sexuality")[4] and about all kinds of abnormality, as revealed in sexual and murder trials. Such trials raised the question of individual and collective responsibility. The majority of the verdicts revealed the society's class-ridden, reactionary attitudes.[5]

In order to synthesize their knowledge of people without losing sight of individual qualities Sartre and Simone needed a systematic plan; and this they did not possess. During these years their labors were directed toward isolating and creating such a pattern, and Simone believed this did more for them than any amount of reading or external advice. Sartre worked out the notion of dishonesty *(mauvaise foi)*, which embraced all those phenomena which other people attributed to the unconscious mind.[6]

1933

With the ever-worsening worldwide economic crisis, Sartre often considered the idea of joining those who were working for revolution, but at this point he felt that although the proletarian struggle was of concern to him and that he should always speak out on behalf of the oppressed, it was nonetheless not *his* struggle. His contribution could best be made through his teaching, his writing and his discussions. It was at this time that he discovered Husserl through Emmanuel Lévinas's book *(La théorie de l'intuition dans la phénoménologie de Husserl* [Paris: Alcan, 1930]), and since Husserl's ideas seemed to be so close to his own, Sartre decided to make a serious study of him. He therefore applied for a grant to spend a year at the French Institute in Berlin, where he would succeed Raymond Aron at the latter's instigation. Influential, too, were the writings of Ernest Hemingway, particularly *Fifty Grand* and *The*

4. Ibid., p. 106.
5. Ibid., p. 108.
6. Ibid., pp. 106–7.

Sun Also Rises: "His individualism and his concept of human nature were both very close to ours: there was no split in any of his heroes between head, heart or body. . . ."[1]

Through his love of jazz, Hollywood films and American novels, Sartre found himself attracted to and fascinated by the United States while at the same time condemning its régime. The USSR, on the other hand, whose social policies he admired, nevertheless held no such attraction.

Easter: During a trip to England, Sartre and Simone de Beauvoir had fierce arguments about their different perceptions of "reality," Simone de Beauvoir accusing Sartre of hasty systematizations. She maintained that reality extended beyond anything that could be said about it; that instead of reducing it to symbols capable of verbal expression, they should face it as it was—full of ambiguities, baffling and impenetrable. Sartre replied that anyone who wished, as they did, to arrange the world in a personal pattern must do something more than react; such a person must grasp the meaning of phenomena and pin them down in words. "What made nonsense of our argument was the fact that Sartre was far from understanding London after twelve days' visit, and his résumé of it omitted countless sides of the total picture: to this extent I was justified in rejecting his theory."[2]

Summer: Taking advantage "without scruple" of a 70 percent fare reduction on Italian railways offered by Mussolini to all foreign visitors to the Fascist Exhibition, Sartre and Simone de Beauvoir visited Florence and Venice. Although Simone de Beauvoir was captivated by Italy's charm, Sartre's enjoyment was spoiled by the presence on the streets of black-shirted rank-and-file Fascists and brown-shirted S.S. men.

September: Sartre left for the French Institute in Berlin, where he worked hard, first of all on his story of Roquentin, then reading Husserl and writing his essay "The Transcendence of the Ego," which appeared in *Recherches philosophiques* in 1936.

1. Simone de Beauvoir, *The Prime of Life,* trans. Peter Green (New York: Harper Colophon Books, 1976), p. 114.

2. Ibid., p. 119.

In it he outlined the relationship between the self and the conscious mind and established a distinction between the conscious mind and the psyche. While the conscious mind constituted *per se* an obvious and immediately apprehensible entity, the psyche was a cluster of phenomena which had to be grasped by a process of mental analysis and, like any object of perception, revealed themselves in profile only. Hatred, for instance, was a transcendent quality: it was apprehended by way of *Erlebnissen,* individual experiences, but its actual existence was no more than a probability. One's ego, on the other hand, like the ego of any other person, was by its nature a recognizable phenomenon. This was the foundation of one of Sartre's earliest and most stubbornly held beliefs: the autonomy of the irrational mind.[3]

Sartre enjoyed himself at the institute, not only because to some extent he was able to rediscover the freedom and friendships he had so enjoyed at the École Normale but also because he developed a close and important relationship with "Marie Girard," a young French woman who was married to a resident student "whose zest for philosophy was only equaled by his indifference to passion."[4] Simone de Beauvoir said that "she was an attractive, graceful girl, with a slow smile, and that her pensive, abstracted daydreaming aroused a sympathetic response in Sartre. She felt the same about him. However, they agreed that there could be no future in this relationship, but that its present reality sufficed: accordingly, they saw a good deal of each other." Simone de Beauvoir claimed that she felt no jealousy because Sartre had warned her that he was likely to get involved in such affairs, and having accepted the principle, she found no difficulty in accepting the fact.[5]

Sartre spent the Christmas holidays with Simone de Beauvoir in Paris and Rouen.

3. Ibid., p. 148.
4. Ibid.
5. Ibid., p. 149.

1934

In Berlin, Sartre finished a second version of *Nausea* and wrote "The Transcendence of the Ego." He continued to keep abreast of new writing and was particularly impressed by Faulkner's novels *(As I Lay Dying* and *Sanctuary)* and Kafka's *Trial.* He and Simone de Beauvoir spent a good deal of time discussing these authors in relation to their own ideas when he went back to Paris for the Easter holidays. Simone de Beauvoir maintained that several of the earlier writers, Joyce, Virginia Woolf, and Hemingway among them, had rejected the false objectivity of the realistic novel and chosen to interpret the world by means of a more subjective approach; but the novelty and effectiveness of Faulkner's technique amazed her and Sartre. Not only did Faulkner show great skill in deploying and harmonizing multiple viewpoints, but he seemed to get inside each individual mind, setting forth its knowledge and ignorance, its moments of insincerity, its fantasies, the words it formed and the silences it kept. Sartre and Simone had not hitherto understood Freud, or sympathized with his approach; but the moment someone presented his discoveries in a form more accessible to them, they were all enthusiasm. Previously they had rejected those tools which the psychoanalysts offered to pierce "the dark impenetrable core" set in every human heart. Faulkner skillfully breached the defenses and offered them a glimpse of fascinating depths beyond.[1]

The highest accolade, however, was reserved for Kafka, who, they felt, was personally significant for them: "Faulkner and the rest told us stories remote from our own experience, but Kafka described *ourselves* to us: he openly stated the problems *we* faced, in a world that was without God, yet where our salvation still remained at stake."[2]

July-August: For the summer holidays Simone de Beauvoir traveled by train to meet with Sartre in Hamburg, the starting point for a trip through Germany and Austria and to Prague.

1. Simone de Beauvoir, *The Prime of Life,* trans. Peter Green (New York: Harper Colophon Books, 1976), pp. 149–50.

2. Ibid., p. 151.

Following Camille and Dullin's advice, they went to the passion play in Oberammergau, which pleasantly surprised them, given their dislike of displays of traditional folk culture. Sartre and Simone de Beauvoir split up in Mulhouse, Sartre going off to Alsace to spend a couple of weeks with his family and Simone de Beauvoir traveling to Corsica, wherre she was to experience the delights of camping with Pierre Guille and friends.

October: Sartre returned to his teaching post at the lycée in Le Havre, where Raymond Aron had replaced him during his absence. He had always had extreme misgivings about becoming a teacher, since it involved a whole area of order and discipline that was anathema to him, and this was coupled with a certain resistance to giving up the freedom and carefreeness of youth. Yet various testimonies suggest that he was a good teacher, if somewhat unconventional. "Sartre immediately captivated his students by his gentle authority and his nonconformism. In fact, he was not like a school-teacher, but treated them as young friends and what he said seemed so obvious and so right that we had the impression of discovering the Truth."[3] According to another former student, Albert Palle, Sartre's course was exciting and conducted in an amusing, familiar style. He was a teacher who created relationships with his students quite unlike family or other relationships based on authority, a relationship stripped of the usual barriers.[4] Jacques-Laurent Bost, pupil and son of the Protestant chaplain at the lycée, who became one of Sartre's closest friends, appreciated the free and easy atmosphere of his course. Although Sartre did most of the talking, "in fact he talked his head off . . . nonetheless we never felt inhibited about asking questions or interrupting; there was a sense of total freedom."[5] More specifically, his reputation was greatly enhanced after he got roaring drunk with some of his students following his graduation speech and ended up at the local whorehouse, though he claimed to have no memory of it whatsoever! Sartre came to see that the

3. In *L'Avant-scène théâtre,* nos. 402–3, "Spécial Sartre" (1–15 May 1968), p. 9.

4. In *Liens* (July 1971), p. 11.

5. *Sartre by Himself,* from the text of the film by Alexandre Astruc and Michel Contat, trans. Richard Seaver (New York: Urizen Books, 1978), p. 35.

depression that he suffered in 1935 was partly related to teaching, because, although he took pleasure in talking with his students, he did not relish giving a course, and seeing himself as a teacher, surrounded by other teachers who gave pompous lectures and were strict disciplinarians. He did not like his colleagues, and he did not like the atmosphere of the lycée.[6]

Sartre began a work on the imagination, which Professor Henri Delacroix had commissioned him to write for the Alcan series. It had been the subject of his diplôme d'études supérieures and had won him a prize and a special distinction. He attempted to determine what images are and what their relationship is to the things of which they are images. He found himself most in agreement with the phenomenological view of Husserl, emphasizing that images are not a psychic content but rather a mode of consciousness, distinguished by its intention. He crystallized the first key concepts of his philosophy: the conscious mind as a tabula rasa and its capacity for annihilation *(néantisation)*. He also took a great interest in dreams, dream-induced imagery and anomalies of perception, an interest that was to lead him to experiment with hallucinogenic drugs.

Christmas: He and Simone de Beauvoir decided to try out the latest fashionable sport, skiing, and spent 10 days practicing their turns in the mountains above Chamonix.

1935

February: A former fellow student of Sartre's, Dr. Lagache, who had passed his exams the year Sartre failed and had since trained as a doctor and specialized in psychiatry, suggested that in order to be better equipped to pursue his work on the imagination, Sartre should undertake to have mescaline injections.

---

6. Quoted in Michel Contat and Michel Rybalka's "Chronologie," in the introduction to Jean-Paul Sartre, *Oeuvres romanesques* (Paris: Gallimard, 1981), p. L.

Lagache told him that it could be an unpleasant experience but was not dangerous, and the effects would wear off after a few hours. In fact, Sartre suffered a severe depression accompanied by frightening hallucinations, which lasted for more than six months. Various doctors maintained that such a reaction could not have been caused by the mescaline, but that certain hallucinatory patterns had been set up reflecting a deep emotional malaise, which was itself exacerbated by the fatigue and tension involved in Sartre's extremely arduous work program. As Simone de Beauvoir put it: "Sartre could not resign himself to going on to the 'age of reason,' to full manhood."[1] By her own admission, Simone de Beauvoir had little understanding of Sartre's mental state and in fact found his passivity, his inability to control his emotions, his retreat from "pure mind and radical freedom," to be extremely irksome. It was during this difficult period that Sartre found the company of Olga Kosakiewicz, a student of Simone de Beauvoir's, a great help and comfort. She was to assume a very important place in their lives.

14 July: As a result of the formation of a general left-wing coalition in June of that year, which heralded the Popular Front, and since the rapprochement with the USSR seemed to speak of peace, the Left decided to celebrate its victory with a huge demonstration on Bastille Day. Five hundred thousand people took part in an enthusiastic, flag-waving march, and although Sartre and Simone de Beauvoir were present and shared in the general euphoria, they remained spectators.

Summer: Sartre went off to join his parents on a Norwegian cruise before meeting Simone de Beauvoir for a trip through central France. He was still liable to hallucinatory attacks, but one night, after feeling that he was being trailed by live lobsters, he decided that he would put an end to his madness, and—to all appearances, and much to Simone de Beauvoir's relief—he seemed to regain his earlier cheerfulness.

---

1. Simone de Beauvoir, *The Prime of Life,* trans. Peter Green (New York: Harper Colophon Books, 1976), p. 170.

October: Sartre suggested that he and Simone de Beauvoir prepare Olga Kosakiewicz for a degree in philosophy. She had twice failed to obtain her bachelor of medicine degree, partly because she herself had no interest whatsoever in the subject and was being pushed into it by her parents, with whom she was in a position of tremendous conflict. As a result, she formed a strong dependent attachment to Simone de Beauvoir, who tried to stop her from wasting her talents in boredom and guilt. Although in the beginning Olga seemed to apply herself with vigor to her new studies, she never in fact managed to produce any written work, and the reproaches of Sartre and Simone de Beauvoir only served to send her into a worse state of despair and defeatism. She was allowed to drop her studies, which meant that she began to bloom in the role of companion and friend.

1936

L'Imagination (Paris: Alcan)

Alcan finally published only the first part of Sartre's work on the imagination, which was merely the introductory section of the larger work and was mainly a review of philosophers' attempts to determine what images were. The second part, which was largely rewritten, was not published until 1940, and then by Gallimard, under the title *L'Imaginaire.*

Because another friend began to show an interest in Olga, Sartre developed an obsession about her, needing to know that he was her favored one and, rather more seriously from Simone de Beauvoir's point of view, setting great store by Olga's tastes and judgments, which, unlike Marie Girard's, were highly pronounced. Olga was moody, capricious, inconsistent and egotistical but was, on the other hand, generous and constant in her affections and shared Sartre's contempt for the social vanities and his hankering after the absolute. Given the fact that both Sartre and Simone de Beauvoir were then in their thirties and struggling to free themselves from conventional behavior, social institutions, responsibilities, routine duties and restraints of all sorts, it was no wonder that Olga, the epitome of adolescence and its concomitant rebellious upheavals, completely entranced them, both of them. She seemed to take lack of food and sleep in her stride, and ridiculed rational argument. It was as though she claimed to be free of just that human condition to which others had shamefacedly resigned themselves. As a result, Sartre and Simone loaded her with values and symbols. "She became Rimbaud, Antigone, every *enfant terrible* that ever lived, a dark angel judging us from her diamond-bright heaven." She was reluctant to accept this role and detested this fantastic character, but she was powerless to resist being absorbed into it.[1]

And so Olga became integrated into their communal life, much to the surprise of all their friends. They became a trio rather than a couple, believing that human relationships were a matter of constant fresh discovery, and that no particular kind was *a priori* either especially privileged or beyond the pale: theirs seemed to have come about by itself.[2]

For similar reasons, Jacques Bost, a student of Sartre's, also became a very close friend of theirs. He, too, personified youth for them: he emanated the casual grace of youth, so casual that it bordered on insolence, together with a certain narcissistic fragility: once he spat up a little blood after clearing his throat, and Sartre had to take him off to a doctor in order that he might be persuaded that he wouldn't die at twenty.[3]

And thus they became an inseparable foursome, a "family." Later Olga and Bost were to marry, with Sartre and Simone de Beauvoir as their witnesses. These complicated relationships provided inspiration for Simone de Beauvoir's *L'Invitée (She Came to Stay)*.

Summer: A holiday in Italy—Naples, Rome and Venice—provided Sartre and Simone de Beauvoir with a welcome respite from their various emotional traumas. In Naples, Sartre was taken to a "maison specialisée," where two women, complete

1. Simone de Beauvoir, *The Prime of Life,* trans. Peter Green (New York: Harper Colophon Books, 1976), p. 195.

2. Ibid.

3. Ibid., p. 197

with ivory phallus, nonchalantly mimed the erotic postures portrayed by the frescoes in the Villa of the Mysteries at Pompeii. What had "delighted" Sartre was the feeling of *dépaysement* (homelessness) he had experienced on finding himself all alone "in this garish salon, surrounded by his own reflections, while two women performed, on his behalf, an act that was at once comic and commonplace."[4] He wrote to Olga about the incident and the following year attempted to describe it in a short story entitled "Dépaysement." In Venice, as their trip neared its end and his worries started coming back—the political situation and his relationship with Olga—he suffered a whole night's fear that the lobsters were pursuing him again.

October: Both he and Simone de Beauvoir took up new teaching posts, he in Laon, she at the lycée Molière in Paris. He had been offered a post teaching the "khâgne" students in Lyon but had preferred to take the more modest job teaching the baccalauréat students in Laon, hoping that he would thus more quickly be offered a post in Paris. During the year he went as often as he could to Paris, where they took rooms in the area of le Dôme, in Montparnasse.

Sartre suffered a serious setback when his manuscript entitled "Melancholia"—later to be called *Nausea*—was rejected by Gallimard's reader, Paulhan, who disapproved of Sartre's central purpose: the expression of metaphysical truths and feelings in literary form. Sartre said of this refusal: "This affected me deeply: I had put all of myself into this book and I had worked on it for a long time; in rejecting it, they were rejecting me and my experience."[5]

A somewhat gloomy winter holiday was spent skiing in Chamonix.

---

4. Ibid., p. 217.
5. Unpublished conversations with John Gerassi (1973).

1937

"Le Mur" ("The Wall"), a short story; *La Nouvelle Revue française,* no. 286 (July 1937), pp. 38–62.

"La Transcendence de l'ego: Esquisse d'une description phénoméno-logique" ("The Transcendence of the Ego: An Existentialist Theory of Consciousness"), an essay, *Recherches philosophiques,* vol. 6 (1936–37; printed in August 1937), pp. 85–123.

"The Transcendence of the Ego: An Existentialist Theory of Consciousness" was written in 1934 during Sartre's stay in Berlin. In it he rejected Husserl's notion of a transcendental ego or structured personal consciousness as responsible for the ordering of conscious activity. Consciousness was to be viewed as a free process, not a predetermined, structured entity. He began to develop the idea that consciousness involves the introduction of a psychic distance or Nothingness between the object and itself. "The Transcendence of the Ego" contained in rudimentary form most of the philosophical positions that were to be developed in *Being and Nothingness* and ended with Sartre's anticipating most of his subsequent philosophical work.

"The Wall" was Sartre's first adult short story to be published. He described it later as a spontaneous emotional reaction to the Spanish civil war and not a work of philosophy. It was inspired by an incident in which one of Sartre's friends, Jacques-Laurent Bost, asked for his help in getting accepted as a volunteer to fight in Spain, and it dealt with the dilemma this created for Sartre, who could not refuse this appeal even though he felt the man was militarily and physically unprepared for such an ordeal and would be going to his death. This personal meditation on the possible death of a friend was put into a more general context, and Sartre later admitted that he was more sensitive to the absurdity of such deaths than to the positive elements to be found in the struggle against fascism; he attributed this to the fact that he had no real knowledge of Marxism at that stage.

The problems related to the trio relationship continued to weigh heavily, particularly on Simone de Beauvoir, who became physically ill and required hospitalization, but also on Sartre, whose heart was no longer in it but nevertheless wished to remain on amicable terms with Olga. His spirits were greatly lifted when, thanks to the intervention of Dullin and Pierre Bost, Gaston Gallimard finally accepted "Melancholia" but suggested that the title be changed to *Nausea.*

The Spanish civil war was beginning to make Sartre and Simone de Beauvoir increasingly aware of their own political impotence, especially since they were being supplied with vivid accounts by their friend Fernando Gerassi, who had quickly been promoted, first to captain, then to colonel, and finally to general. He made clear to them what a desperate shortage of trained men, discipline and organization there was in the Popular Army, but they remained sceptical about the attempts of such people as Simone Weil and Colette Audry to help the cause, feeling that their lack of practical skills made them more of a nuisance than a help.

Summer: Sartre traveled to Greece with Simone de Beauvoir and Jacques-Laurent Bost. One village, Emborio—which they visited when they were feeling hot, tired and hungry—was thick with buzzing flies, and the tomato salad that was eventually produced for them was also dotted with dead flies. It was this place that Sartre had in mind when he described Argos in the first act of *Les Mouches (The Flies).*

October: Sartre was appointed to a post at the lycée Pasteur in Neuilly, so he and Simone took rooms at the hotel Mistral, 24 rue Cels in the 14th arrondissement, between the Avenue du Maine and the Montparnasse cemetery. Sartre lived on the floor above Simone; thus, they felt that they had "all the advantages of a shared life, without any of its inconveniences."[1] Sartre worked on his treatise on phenomenological psychology, which he entitled *La Psyché,* of which only an extract was published as *Esquisse d'une théorie des émotions (The Emotions: Outline of a Theory).* In it he developed further his theory of "psychic objectivity," which he had already outlined in "The Transcendence of the Ego." Simone de Beauvoir, with Sartre's

1. Simone de Beauvoir, *The Prime of Life,* trans. Peter Green (New York: Harper Colophon Books, 1976), p. 251.

encouragement, decided to try and work out her relationship
with Olga in the form of a novel, by exploring the theme of
jealousy and the destruction of the Other as the means to independence and salvation. This work was later published as
L'Invitée (She Came to Stay).

Christmas: Again Sartre and Simone de Beauvoir chose to go
skiing, this time in Megève, and this time opting for skiing
lessons, which somewhat accelerated their progress. They also
read Malraux's *L'Espoir (Man's Hope)* with an excitement that
went far beyond any purely literary emotion. He was dealing
with themes that had previously been ignored in literature,
such as the relationship between individual morality and practical politics, or the possibility of maintaining humanist standards in the midst of war.[2]

1938

La Nausée (Nausea), a novel (Paris: Gallimard)
"La Chambre" ("The Room"), a short story in *Mesures,* vol. 3, no. 1
   (January 15), pp. 119–49
"Intimité" ("Intimacy"), a short story in *La Nouvelle Revue française,*
   no. 299 (August), pp. 187–200; and no. 300 (September), pp. 381–
   406
"Nourritures" ("Foods"), an unpublished extract from "Dépaysement"
   ("Homelessness") in *Verve,* no. 4 (September), pp. 115–16
Articles on William Faulkner (no. 293, February, pp. 323–28), John
   Dos Passos (no. 299, August, pp. 292–301) and a review of Paul
   Nizan's *La Conspiration (The Conspiracy)* (no. 302, November, pp.
   842–45) in *La Nouvelle Revue française;* also an article on "La
   structure intentionnelle de l'image" ("The Intentional Structure of
   the Image") in *Revue de métaphysique et de morale,* no. 4 (October),
   pp. 543–609.

Nausea was finally published in the spring of 1938. In essence
it was a fictionalized meditation on Sartre's experiences of the

2. Ibid., p. 257.

past four years: teaching at Le Havre, which is called Bouville (Mudtown) in the novel; the impact of phenomenology and the work of Kafka; and the depression brought on by his experiment with mescaline in February of 1935. It is in the form of a diary kept by one Antoine Roquentin, who describes his feelings of nausea when he discovers that "Things are entirely what they appear to be and *behind them* . . . there is nothing." Sartre later admitted that, faced with the meaninglessness of others, "I pulled off this noble achievement at the age of 30: describing in *La Nausée*—most sincerely, I can assure you—the unjustified, brackish existence of my fellow creatures and vindicating my own."[1]

The novel was very well received by the critics and only just failed to win one of the big literary prizes. Without becoming a best-seller, it nevertheless had a rather substantial success and established Sartre as a writer to be reckoned with. It was Nizan, however, who won the Interallié prize for *The Conspiracy* (reviewed by Sartre in *La Nouvelle Revue française),* in which Nizan calls a detective Sartre. This honor was returned in kind when Sartre put a "General Nizan" in "The Childhood of a Leader." One of Nizan's comments about *Nausea* likened Sartre to Kafka, except that his thinking was "entirely unconcerned with moral problems."[2]

It was at this time that Simone de Beauvoir discouraged Sartre from spending too much time on philosophy, suggesting that although he might contribute a few little niceties to philosophy, he would never be a philosopher and that his true strength lay in writing novels. Consequently, in July, having finished "The Childhood of a Leader," the last of the stories in *The Wall,* he started to plan a new novel, the theme of which was freedom, and gave it the title "Lucifer." This later became *Roads to Freedom.*

The summer holidays were spent traveling in Morocco, which provided the background for an episode in *The Reprieve* and inspired the scenario "Typhus," which, though worked upon in 1943–44 and subsequently changed, was later used in Yves Al-

---

1. Jean-Paul Sartre, *Words,* trans. Irene Clephane (London: Penguin Books, 1967), p. 156.
2. *Ce Soir* (16 May 1938).

legret's film *Les Orgueilleux* in 1953. Throughout this trip Sartre had been keeping his eye on the negotiations that were taking place in Czechoslovakia, fearing that war was inevitable. During the Munich days, expecting to be mobilized at any moment, Sartre, who was very much against war, nevertheless came to the conclusion that Hitler and fascism must be stopped at all costs. Appeasement, he argued, made everyone accessories to all of Hitler's persecutions and exterminations. He began to see that Nizan had been right in his contention that there was no way of avoiding political engagement: to abstain from politics was in itself a political attitude.

Autumn: Sartre began working on *Roads to Freedom,* his zeal fired by the success of *Nausea.* Olga, who was now an enthusiastic drama student at Dullin's Atelier, introduced them to life at the Café de Flore, where they rubbed shoulders with the somewhat bohemian set from the film and theater world. Apparently "their God and oracle, the source of all their opinions, was Jacques Prévert: they worshiped his films and poetry, doing their best to ape his language and attitudes. We too found Prévert's verses and lyrics very much to our taste: his dreamy, somewhat inconsequential anarchism suited us perfectly."[3] Also through Olga, Sartre met Wanda Kosakiewicz, her younger sister, who had recently come to live in Paris; she later acted in most of Sartre's plays under the pseudonym of Marie-Olivier.

Christmas: Again Sartre and Simone de Beauvoir went to Megève, where their skiing continued to improve.

3. Simone de Beauvoir, *The Prime of Life,* trans. Peter Green (New York: Harper Colophon Books, 1976), p. 279.

1939

Esquisse d'une théorie des émotions (The Emotions: Outline of a Theory), an essay (Paris: Hermann)

Le Mur (The Wall) (Paris: Gallimard); this book contained the following short stories: "The Wall" (first published in 1937), "The Room" (first published in 1938), "Erostratus" (not previously published; written in 1936), "Intimacy" (first published in 1938) and "The Childhood of a Leader" (not previously published; completed in July 1938)

"Une Idée fondamentale de la phénoménologie de Husserl: L'Intentionnalité" ("A Fundamental Idea of Husserl's Phenomenology: Intentionality"), an essay, *La Nouvelle Revue française,* no. 304 (January), pp. 129–31.

"M. François Mauriac et la liberté" ("M. François Mauriac and Freedom"), an essay, *La Nouvelle Revue française,* no. 305 (February), pp. 212–32.

Review articles on Elsa Triolet, Vladimir Nabokov, Denis de Rougemont, Charles Morgan and William Faulkner for *La Nouvelle Revue française* and *Europe*

"Portraits officiels" ("Official Portraits") and "Visages" ("Faces"), two short phenomenological essays on the human face, *Verve,* nos. 5–6, pp. 9–12.

Sartre began to be published quite widely, and by choosing to attack such highly respected authors as François Mauriac, he quickly gained notoriety. In his article "M. François Mauriac and Freedom," Sartre delivered a devastating attack on Mauriac's *The End of the Night,* pointing out how his narrative technique revealed and concealed his ethical and metaphysical stance. This idea was later adopted by the structuralists, but at the time it greatly wounded Mauriac, who subsequently blamed Sartre for his lack of productivity: "One of my novels, called *The End of the Night,* had been torn apart by Sartre, who was not only a very young author but the glory of his generation. I won't say that this demoralized me, but just the same it made me think."[1]

The short stories in *The Wall* helped give Sartre a reputation for obscenity, though they are considered by many to be his best work of fiction. Sartre in describing the theme of the col-

1. *France-Soir* (28 February 1969).

lection said that no one wanted to look Existence in the face. Here he presented five little failures—tragic or comic—confronting it, five lives. All their efforts to escape were blocked by a Wall; to flee Existence was still to exist. Existence was a *plenum* man could not leave.[2]

In fact, the book was very successful, having been designated "book of the month" for March 1939 and winning the Roman populiste prize in 1940.

The Emotions: Outline of a Theory, despite its brevity, provides the best introduction to the subsequent major philosophical work *Being and Nothingness.* It lays the ground for the central existentialist doctrine, that people are nothing but what they choose to become, by taking the phenomenological approach to imagination and the emotions, which are viewed as two essential modes of awareness of the world. Emotion arises when people choose to see the world in a particular way—an inferior, magical way rather than according to rational means for attaining ends.

"A Fundamental Idea of Husserl's Phenomenology: Intentionality," written during Sartre's stay in Berlin when he was enthusiastically discovering Husserl's phenomenology, attacked traditional psychology and went on to give an original interpretation of the complex Husserlian idea of intentionality, which Sartre made accessible to a nonspecialized audience.

Of the two essays on the human face, "Visages" is reckoned by some to be one of Sartre's finest pieces of writing. In it he tried to describe phenomenologically the essence of the face, which is summed up in the idea that "the meaning of a face is to be *visible* transcendence."

Now that Sartre was becoming well known, he had the opportunity to meet various writers: Nathalie Sarraute and André Gide had discussions with him about *Nausea,* and at the International Antifascist Conference, which he attended in May, he made the acquaintance of Ilya Ehrenburg, the Soviet culture spokesperson.

The holidays that year were spent in France: at Easter he and Simone de Beauvoir went to Provence, where they spent some time discussing Heidegger, whose *Sein und Zeit* Sartre

2. From the introduction to *Le Mur* (Paris: Gallimard, 1939), as quoted in Michel Contat and M. Rybalka, *The Writings of Jean-Paul Sartre,* trans. R. C. McClealy, 2 vols, Evanston, Ill., Northwestern Univ. Press, 1974, p. 63.

was in the process of reading; in the summer he went to Marseille, where he saw Paul Nizan for the last time, and then on to Juan-les-Pins to Mme. Morel's, where they learned about the ending of the German-Soviet pact.

2 September: Sartre was mobilized and joined the 70th division at the aviation center in Essey-les-Nancy; he was then transferred to Brumath and Morsbronn in Alsace. Being an optimist, he was convinced that the war would be short. Later he was to recount just how decisive the war was in changing his thinking: "The war really divided my life into two. The war began when I was 34, and ended when I was 40, and that marked the passage from youth to maturity. . . . This was the real turning point in my life: before and after."[3] Simone de Beauvoir described their lives as being characterized by a lack of reality. They were sheltered from want and protected against insecurity. Having no children, they had no responsibilities. They were like "elves."[4]

In fact, the war was for Sartre a period of intense work: he continued *The Age of Reason* and filled a series of notebooks.[5] "He kept notes about his life from day to day and kept a sort of account of his past."[6] It was also in these notebooks that he outlined his morality and drafted his philosophical reflections that were to find their definitive form in *Being and Nothingness*. He also did a lot of reading, particularly Kierkegaard, Heidegger and Hegel.

1940

L'Imaginaire: Psychologie phénoménologique de l'imagination (The Imaginary: Phenomenological Psychology of the Imagination), a book (Paris: Gallimard)

3. Jean-Paul Sartre, *Situations,* vol. X (Paris: Gallimard, 1976), p. 180.

4. Simone de Beauvoir, *The Prime of Life,* trans. Peter Green (New York: Harper Colophon Books, 1976), p. 288.

5. *Carnets de la drôle de guerre* (Paris: Gallimard, 1983).

6. *The Prime of Life,* p. 346.

"M. Jean Giraudoux et la philosophie d'Aristote: A propos de *Choix des élues*" ("M. Jean Giraudoux and the Philosophy of Aristotle: Concerning *Duel of Angels*") an essay, *La Nouvelle Revue française,* no. 318 (March), pp. 339–54.

At the beginning of February, Sartre was back in Paris on leave and divulged that he had been thinking a great deal about the postwar period and that he had decided he could no longer remain aloof from politics. His new morality was based on "authenticity," or genuineness, and required each individual to shoulder the responsibility for his or her situation in life; it also required transcending that situation by engaging in a course of action. Any other attitude was an escapist pretense based on insincerity. He could not predict his likely course of political action, but it would involve fulfilling his duty to the younger generation. He wrote a letter to Brice Parain about the idea of generations as a category, like class or nationality, and he also reassured him about his political stance, saying that he would not join a party or follow a leader. He was most concerned that his generation of young men should not come out of the war with "sick consciences."[1]

February 15, the day Sartre finished his leave in Paris, was also the publication day of his work *L'Imaginaire;* it was dedicated to Albert Morel, his former student and son of Mme. Morel. The book was the sequel to the introductory book on the imagination, which he published in 1936, and it started where the earlier work had concluded, stating that the difference between the perception of a chair and the imagining of a chair consists in the mode of consciousness that each represents. Imagination, unlike perception as a mode of consciousness, entailed the creative freedom to envisage what is not the case and so to stand back from the world and frame images. It thus lays the foundation for the philosophy of human nature as systematized in *Being and Nothingness.* One of the first reviews of *L'Imaginaire* was by Daniel Lagache in *Bulletin de la Faculté des lettres de Strasbourg* (1941); this was appropriate, as it was Lagache who had encouraged Sartre to experiment with mescaline so that he could ascertain just what a hallucination was,

1. Simone de Beauvoir, *The Prime of Life,* trans. Peter Green (New York: Harper Colophon Books, 1976), p. 342.

for the purpose of describing different types of consciousness in *L'Imaginaire.*

While on leave in Paris in April for the second time that year, Sartre was greeted with the news that he had been awarded the Roman populiste prize for *The Wall* and his work as a whole. It is said that he used the 5,000 francs prize money to buy a new suit.

23 May: Paul Nizan was killed at the front.

27 May: Sartre wrote to Simone de Beauvoir that he was making good progress in his writing and had nearly finished *The Age of Reason.* He admitted to being completely stupefied by the French defeat.

21 June: On his 35th birthday, Sartre found himself a prisoner of war. First he was imprisoned at Padoux in Lorraine; he was then sent to Baccarat, where he remained until mid-August. From there he was transferred to Stalag XII D at Trèves. This was to be extremely important for him, as he experienced a great sense of comradeship, especially with the Catholic priests who made up a large part of the camp's inmates. He was soon joining them in practicing Gregorian plainsong, while in return he gave talks on Heidegger's philosophy. He even wrote a seemingly religious Christmas play, *Bariona,* which was performed by the prisoners. (In fact, the drama centered on the Roman occupation of Palestine, and his fellow prisoners were quick to see the allusion and applauded this resistance propaganda.) It was a form of collective life he had not known since the École Normale; in a sense, it was once again élitist, but because of the circumstances, it was also very down to earth. Sartre commented that there was nothing quite like going to the toilet in the open, surrounded by your fellow prisoners, for breaking down élitism in whatever form it may exist.[2]

---

2. In *Sartre by Himself,* from the text of the film by Alexandre Astruc and Michel Contat, trans. Richard Seaver (New York: Urizen Books, 1978), pp. 49–50).

1941

"*Moby Dick* d'Herman Melville: Plus qu'un chef-d'oeuvre, un formidable monument" ("Herman Melville's *Moby Dick:* More than a Masterpiece, an Imposing Monument"), an essay; *Comoedia,* no. 1 (21 June)

Various pieces in the journal or report of the resistance group "Socialism and Liberty"

Recently, Sartre had written letters to Simone de Beauvoir expressing confidence in his imminent release from the prison camp. One evening, toward the end of March, she found a note in her pigeonhole at the hotel where she was staying; it was from Sartre, informing her that he was at the Café des Trois Mousquetaires. It was an aptly named rendezvous, even though Sartre's escape from prison was not as dashing as the escapades of the Three Musketeers. He had posed as a civilian, unfit for military service, and on being examined by the camp doctor he had tugged at his eyelid, revealing his near-blind eye in a pathetic manner, and, by way of explanation, saying, "Dizzy spells."[1]

It was enough to secure Sartre his release, and he made his way back to Paris, carrying with him the completed manuscript of *The Age of Reason,* which he had managed to retrieve after it had been confiscated by a German officer.

Sartre returned filled with stern moral principles (he condemned Simone de Beauvoir for buying things on the black market) and determined to form a resistance group of like-minded intellectuals. It was called "Socialism and Liberty" and numbered among its members Merleau-Ponty, Jean and Dominique Desanti, Jacques-Laurent Bost, Jean Cuzin, Jean Pouillon and Simone de Beauvoir. They decided that they were not qualified to manufacture bombs or hurl grenades, and so they concentrated on what they could do best, which was to compile and circulate information in the form of bulletins and pamphlets. In the first bulletin Sartre maintained that if the Germans won the war, as looked possible at that stage, then the

1. Simone de Beauvoir, *The Prime of Life,* trans. Peter Green (New York: Harper Colophon Books, 1976), p. 381.

resisters should make sure that Germany lost the peace. Sartre held meetings with leaders of other groups and with a British intelligence agent, a boyhood friend, Alfred Péron. There was an extraordinary lack of caution in these activities; often they were held in public places such as the terrace of the Closerie des Lilas restaurant or a room in the École Normale, and the resisters would go around with briefcases stuffed full of pamphlets.

After the Easter holidays Sartre went back to his job at the lycée Pasteur, even though his papers were not in order, as he would have to get himself demobilized in the Free Zone, at Bourg, if he wished to regularize his status. Fortunately, the university was not overconcerned about such details. Shortly afterward Sartre had a talk with an education official about his position, and they reached an understanding, as a result of which Sartre was promised the École Normale entrance class at the lycée Condorcet for the following year.

He had been offered a regular literary column in the weekly journal *Comoedia.* The journal was being revived under a new editor; it dealt exclusively with literature and the arts, and the elderly journalist who edited it assured Sartre that it was completely free of German censorship. He used the occasion of his first column to write about a novel that had made a great impression on him, *Moby Dick,* which had just been published in a French translation. When the column actually appeared, Sartre decided the journal was not as independent as he had been led to understand, and, although it was better than some of the collaborationist journals, it still offended against the rule agreed upon by all intellectuals of the resistance: "No writing for Occupied Zone papers." And so he resigned.

Summer: He and Simone decided to spend a holiday cycling around the Free Zone and at the same time called on various figures who might offer guidance and help in developing Socialism and Liberty's contribution to the resistance movement. They met Daniel Mayer in Marseille, Gide in Cabris and Malraux in Saint-Jean-Cap-Ferrat, but to no great effect. Sartre asked Daniel Mayer if he had any broad policy to suggest to the group or any specific tasks to give them; but all that Mayer could suggest was that they write a letter to Léon Blum on the occasion of his birthday. Gide said he didn't see what he could do himself, and Malraux believed any sort of action was useless for the time being, and he was relying on Russian tanks and American planes to win the war. Back in Paris, Sartre found that his group and other groups composed mainly of middle-class intellectuals were proving impotent and unable to coordinate their activities or even communicate with each other. The Communists, who were well organized, viewed them with suspicion; they told one of Sartre's friends that Sartre could only have been released by the Germans if he had agreed to act as an agent provocateur, and they rejected his efforts to make contact with them. Furthermore, the risks were increasing; Sartre's contact, Péron, had been deported, and one of Simone's former students in another resistance group had been arrested and was executed. Throughout October they had interminable discussions about the future of the group and finally decided to disband. Sartre concluded that the one form of resistance open to him was to work on a play, *The Flies,* which would carry his message to the French people, that they should throw off their guilt and assert their right to freedom.

October: Sartre commenced teaching at the lycée Condorcet, where he was to remain until 1944.

At the end of the year he began writing *Being and Nothingness.* He was also writing critical articles for Free Zone journals: *Confluences* and *Les Cahiers du Sud.*

Christmas was spent outside Paris at the house of Mme. Morel in La Pouèze, near Angers. Here Sartre and Simone de Beauvoir were able to eat meat (turkey on Christmas Eve), drink brandy and sit in front of large log fires; it was a welcome relief from the austerities of wartime Paris.

1942

"La Mort dans l'âme" ("Sick at Heart"), extracts from Sartre's war diary, in the journal *Messages,* vol. 5 (10 December 1942); this volume had the title "Exercice du silence" ("Studied Silences") and was published in Brussels, non-paginated.

March: One of Sartre's fellow prisoners in Stalag XII D was released and invited Sartre and Simone to stay with him at his father-in-law's house in Le Havre. They set off on their bicycles on the first day of the Easter holidays. They found that much of Le Havre had been destroyed by British air force bombing. Sartre and his former fellow inmate, Marc Bénard, reminisced about camp life, and especially about a young Catholic priest, Abbé Henri Leroy, who had formed a particularly close friendship with Sartre. Sartre recalled that the priest had become so fond of him that he once declared: "If God were to damn you, I should not accept His heaven."[1] He was very much in agreement with the young priest's belief that the myth of the Incarnation lost all its beauty if it failed to burden Christ with *all* the ills of our human condition. The news of him brought by Marc Bénard was that he had turned down all suggestions that he should try and secure release from the camp, and he was to remain there until the end of the war, ministering to his fellow prisoners. Simone de Beauvoir recalled meeting him after the war, in the company of Sartre and Bénard, and she found him possessed of great charm. He returned to a poor parish in the Cévennes but later left the Church, married and became a bookseller.

In Paris, Sartre and Simone de Beauvoir spent all their time writing in the Café Flore and supplying material and moral support to their "family" of friends, consisting of Olga, Bost, Wanda Kosakiewicz (Olga's sister) and Nathalie Sorokine, a former student of Simone's. Sartre's relations with his own family had improved, especially with his stepfather, who was firmly opposed to all collaboration with the occupying régime.

1. Simone de Beauvoir, *The Prime of Life,* trans. Peter Green (New York: Harper Colophon Books, 1976), p. 405.

Despite spending so much time sitting in the Café Flore, moving between hotels and going on holidays, this was an extremely productive year for Sartre as far as writing was concerned. He finished *The Flies,* began *The Reprieve* and was writing *Being and Nothingness* at the same time. Excerpts from his diary, under the title "Sick at Heart," were published in the journal *Messages* (printed in Belgium). It was also at this time that Sartre had the fruitful idea of writing an existential psychoanalytical study of the author of *Madame Bovary* as a result of reading Flaubert's *Correspondance.*

The summer holiday was again spent cycling in the Free Zone, followed by a visit to Mme. Morel's house. The visit was more of a convalescence, as Sartre and Simone de Beauvoir had arrived at Mme. Morel's exhausted; food had been very scarce, and Sartre had collapsed on arrival and stayed in bed for several days. Toward the end of September, Sartre wrote an article for *Les Cahiers du Sud* on Albert Camus's novel *L'Étranger (The Stranger);* while not completely uncritical of the work, Sartre and Simone de Beauvoir confessed that it had been a long time since any new French writer had moved them so strongly.

October: Sartre wrote to Brice Parain to tell him that *Being and Nothingness* was finished. The work owed something to the philosophy of Heidegger, but Sartre was shocked to hear that a pamphlet was circulating in the Free Zone describing him as a disciple of Heidegger and therefore an advocate of national socialism. The best response to such rumors was to be found in his own writings, such as *The Flies,* but the play had not yet been performed, and a backer was still being sought to fund it, although Barrault had assured him that it would be staged. One attempt to get Dullin to stage it at the Théâtre de la Cité with the backing of a purported millionaire had proved abortive when the man turned out to be a fraud. Nevertheless, Sartre was happy to accept Dullin's invitation to give a course of lectures on the history of the theater, dealing mainly with Greek drama, at Dullin's School of Dramatic Art.

1943

L'Etre et le Néant (Being and Nothingness), a book on phenomenological
   ontology (Paris: Gallimard)
Les Mouches (The Flies), a play (Paris: Gallimard)
"Explication de *L'Étranger*" ("An Analysis of *The Stranger*"), an essay;
   Les Cahiers du Sud, no. 253 (February), pp. 189–206
"Drieu la Rochelle ou la haine de soi" ("Drieu la Rochelle, or Self-
   Hatred"), an article; *Les Lettres françaises* (clandestine), no. 6 (April)
" 'Aminadab' ou du fantastique considéré comme un langage" (" 'Ami-
   nadab,' or The Fantastic Considered as a Language"), an essay; *Les
   Cahiers du Sud,* no. 255 (April), pp. 299–305; no. 256 (May), pp.
   361–71
"Les Chats" ("The Cats"), an excerpt from the forthcoming novel *The
   Age of Reason; L'Arbalète* (Lyon), no. 7 (Summer)
"L'Age de raison" ("The Age of Reason"), excerpt from the forthcoming
   novel of the same title; *Domaine français: "Messages" (French Ter-
   ritory: "Messages"),* Geneva (August), pp. 51–60
"Un Nouveau Mystique" ("A New Mystic"), an essay; *Les Cahiers du
   Sud,* no. 260 (October), pp. 782–90; no. 261 (November), pp. 866–
   86; no. 262 (December), pp. 988–94

Early in 1943 the intellectuals' section of the resistance began
to develop better organization, and certain members of the
Communist intelligentsia invited Sartre to join the Comité National des Ecrivains (CNE). His ironical response was to ask
them if they really wanted a spy in their ranks, but after they
had disclaimed all knowledge of the rumors circulated in 1941,
he agreed to join. He attended the CNE meetings and contributed to *Les Lettres françaises,* providing an article on Drieu la
Rochelle for the April issue.

Dullin kept his promise to put on *The Flies,* and it went into
rehearsal in the spring at the Théâtre de la Cité (formerly Théâtre Sarah Bernhardt), with their friend Olga in a leading role
as Electra. It had managed to escape the censorship of the German authorities and had the approval of the CNE. At the dress
rehearsal, Albert Camus turned up and introduced himself to
Sartre for the first time—the start of a celebrated, though
stormy, friendship. According to Simone de Beauvoir, the atmosphere at the dress rehearsal was extremely tense, as it

seemed impossible to mistake the play's implications: "the word 'liberty,' dropped from Orestes' mouth, burst on us like a bomb."[1] The German critic on the *Pariser Zeitung* made it clear that he saw this as the message, as did Michel Leiris in the clandestine edition of *Les Lettres françaises*. However, most reviewers pretended not to notice such an allusion, and the collaborationist press contented itself with vicious criticisms supposedly justified on purely literary grounds. Public performances did not begin until June, which was almost the end of the season, and there were only 25, although it was to have a second run in October.

The message of liberty was dressed up in the language of Greek tragedy, drawing on historical sources such as Georges Dumézil's *Archaic Roman Religion* and V. Basanoff's *The Truscans and Their Civilization,* which Sartre had read in 1942. In an interview published in *Comoedia* (24 April 1943), he gave only the most abstract philosophical explanation of the play, saying that he wanted to deal with the tragedy of freedom as contrasted with the tragedy of fate, or in other words: "How does a man behave when he has committed an act whose consequences and responsibilities he fully accepts, yet which still horrifies him?" The day after the Liberation he felt freer to state the message more clearly in an interview in *Carrefour* (9 September 1944), admitting that the only reason for putting the words in the mouths of ancient Greeks was to escape the censorship of the fascist regime: the real drama, he said, was that of the (French) terrorist who shoots down Germans in the street and causes 50 hostages to be shot.

The Vichy régime had tried to impose a policy of contrition on the French, making them feel that they were fated to suffer until they had paid for all their sins. *The Flies,* like its philosophical counterpart, *Being and Nothingness,* preached the need to resist such a condition of *bad faith;* everyone had the freedom to choose to escape bad faith. The weakness of this message, as Sartre later admitted, was that the solitary act of heroism, in which this freedom was affirmed, was a means to personal salvation rather than to practical liberation.

L'Etre et le Néant (Being and Nothingness: An Essay on Phenomenological Ontology) was published by Gallimard on 25

1. Simone de Beauvoir, *The Prime of Life,* trans. Peter Green (New York: Harper Colophon Books, 1976), p. 427.

June. Although it grew out of several years' work on philosophy, including Sartre's seminars on Heidegger in the prison camp and his psychological treatise "The Psyché," it was written in only two years and at the same time as he was producing *The Flies* and *The Reprieve.* However, he had jotted down some of the main ideas in the imitation leather notebooks he filled to such good effect during the period of inactivity in the military in late 1939 and had discussed them with Simone de Beauvoir when on leave in April 1940. Its publication in the summer of 1943 could not have come at a worse time, and for a while the work was little discussed and sold few copies. Subsequently it came to be recognized as Sartre's most substantial contribution to pure philosophy, containing, as it did, his most complete statement on human existence, his theory of consciousness, explanations of anguish and bad faith, and the grounds for his ethic of freedom. It set forth an ontology according to which Being was divided into Being-in-itself and Being-for-itself. In contrast to Being-for-itself, Being-in-itself was nonconscious being, which is complete in itself and does not depend on consciousness. Being-for-itself required human consciousness, and Sartre agreed with Husserl in maintaining that all consciousness is consciousness *of* something. Consciousness was to be defined by its negating or nihilating activity, in which it distanced itself from Being-in-itself and from other Beings-for-themselves, and in so doing became aware of what it is *not*. It was the consciousness of the fact that things have no meaning in themselves, that they are Nothing, and that existence has no meaning except that which we choose to bestow on it that constituted man's freedom. This was also the source of man's anguish (Angst)—the consciousness of freedom. Bad faith *(mauvaise foi)* was the attempt to avoid that anguish by evading the realization that one is responsible for one's life because one is absolutely free, and so pretending to oneself that one is not "in" what one is doing.

15 July: Sartre joined Simone de Beauvoir on holiday. He arrived at Uzerche station carrying two tool bags and with a rubber tire slung over one shoulder—Simone had written to him saying her bicycle had a flat tire and asking him to bring an inner tube. He also gave her the news that he had been signed up by Pathé to write scripts and was receiving a large retainer for his services; on the strength of this he was considering giving up teaching. During the holiday he worked on *The Reprieve,* which was almost lost when a heavy storm washed the manuscript from his bicycle saddlebag into the gutter. Much time was spent drying it out and putting it together again. On his return to Paris, he set it aside temporarily in order to write a new play, originally entitled "Les Autres" ("Others"), but subsequently *Huis clos (No Exit* in America, and *In Camera* in Britain). Marc, the husband of Olga Barbezat, a rich businessman and publisher of the journal *L'Arbalète,* had offered to back a play if it had a small cast of about three, one of whom should be his wife and another Wanda Kosakiewicz. The idea intrigued Sartre, and he envisaged it as a situation in which a small group of people are shut up in a cellar during a lengthy bombardment; he then had the inspired notion of placing them in hell for all eternity. An extract—under the original title, *Les Autres*—was published in *L'Arbalète* in 1944. The play had been written in two weeks. At an early stage, Sartre asked Camus to play the part of Garcin and to take charge of the production, and some rehearsals were held on that basis, but it was not to work out.

Sartre published two important essays. The first, which appeared in the April and May issues of *Les Cahiers du Sud,* was a critical study of the fantastic in literature, focusing on the work of Maurice Blanchot and comparing him to Franz Kafka. The second, with the title "Un Nouveau mystique" ("A New Mystic"), also appeared in *Les Cahiers du Sud,* toward the end of the year, and dealt with Georges Bataille's *The Experience Within.* He criticized Bataille's rather mystical anthropological notions and some ideas derived from Emile Durkheim's sociology and Freud's psychoanalysis. However, he was soon to become friendly with Bataille and others in his circle, such as Michel Leiris and Raymond Queneau. Indeed, Leiris and his wife Zette soon became the most intimate friends of Sartre and Simone de Beauvoir.

This was the year in which Sartre and Simone de Beauvoir were first confronted with the label "existentialist," which Gabriel Marcel had recently coined.

1944

Tribute to Jean Giraudoux, in *Comoedia* (5 February); reprinted in *Voici la France de ce mois,* no. 49 (March), pp. 10–11

"Aller et retour" ("Departure and Return"), article in *Les Cahiers du Sud,* no. 264 (February), pp. 117–33; no. 265 (March), pp. 248–70

"La Littérature, cette liberté" ("Literature, That Freedom"), article in *Les Lettres françaises* (clandestine), no. 15 (April), p. 8; unsigned

"Un Film pour l'après-guerre" ("The Kind of Movie that We Need When the War Is Over"), article in *Les Lettres françaises* (clandestine), no. 15 (April), pp. 3–4; unsigned

Huis clos, pièce en un acte *(No Exit,* A Play in One Act), published under the title *Les Autres (The Others), L'Arbalète,* no. 8 (Spring), pp. 37–80; it appeared for the first time under the title *Huis clos* in 1945, published by Gallimard

"L'Espoir fait homme" ("Hope Makes a Man of You"), article in *Les Lettres françaises* (clandestine), no. 18 (July), p. 2; unsigned

"A propos du *Parti pris des choses*" ("Concerning *A Prejudice for Things*"), article in *Poésie 44,* no. 20 (July–October), pp. 58–77

"L'Insurrection" ("The Uprising"), article in *Combat* (28 August)

"Naissance d'une insurrection" ("Birth of an Uprising"), article in *Combat* (29 August)

"Colère d'une ville" ("A City's Wrath"), article in *Combat* (30 August)

"Toute la ville tire" ("The Whole City Is Shooting"), article in *Combat* (31 August)

"Espoirs et angoisses de l'insurrection" ("Hopes and Fears of the Uprising"), article in *Combat* (1 September)

"La Délivrance est à nos portes" ("The Rescuers Are at Our Gate"), article in *Combat* (2 September)

"La République du silence" ("The Republic of Silence"), article in *Les Lettres françaises* (first legal issue), no. 20 (9 September), p. 1

"23 septembre 1938" ("September 23, 1938"), an extract from *The Reprieve; Les Lettres françaises* (28 October)

"Dullin et l'Espagne" ("Dullin and Spain"), article in *Combat* (8 November)

"Paris sous l'occupation" ("Paris During the Occupation"), article in *La France libre* (London), no. 49 (15 November), pp. 9–18

"A propos de l'existentialisme: Mise au point" ("A More Precise Characterization of Existentialism"), in *Action,* no. 17 (29 December), p. 11

Jean Giraudoux died on 31 January, and Sartre published a generous tribute to him in *Comoedia* on 5 February. Giraudoux's philosophy was very different from Sartre's own, and so the tribute was even more impressive when Sartre wrote that, despite the fact that events seemed to have proved Giraudoux's philosophy of harmony to be false, nevertheless the humanistic values he offered still remained as "an opportunity which is possible" or "a regret which is still beautiful." Also in February, Sartre was able to participate in paying tribute to another writer whose work he admired—Mouloudji, whose book *Enrico* won the Pléiade prize; Sartre was on the jury and strongly supported Mouloudji's cause.

Mouloudji, who later became better known as a singer, was one of those who performed at the social gatherings that Sartre and Simone de Beauvoir were beginning to attend in the circle composed of former surrealists such as Leiris and Queneau; others who attended included Georges Bataille, Georges Limbour, Armand Salacrou, Camus and Picasso. Sometimes the gathering would take on the character of a public literary occasion, as on 19 March, when there was a reading of Picasso's play *Le Désir attrapé par la queue (Desire Caught by the Tail)* in the Leirises' drawing room. Camus compèred the proceedings; Sartre played one of the main parts, "Round End," and Simone de Beauvoir was "The Cousin." These three regarded it as a great lark. For many of the others who attended, especially admirers of Picasso, it was considered an important and serious literary and theatrical event. Barrault was there from the world of the theater, along with many others, and Braque was one of the painters in attendance. Sartre and his friends stayed all night—defying the curfew in spirit if not technically. Subsequently they had more social meetings with Picasso and also more such fêtes or parties. One of these they organized was on 5 June in the apartment of Dullin and Camille, and when they left it early in the morning, they were greeted with the news that the Allied landings had taken place in Normandy. Some of Camille's fellow tenants thought Sartre and his friends must have had advance notice of the landings, as they were celebrating the event the night before.

In May, Sartre met Jean Genet for the first time. He came over to the table in the Café Flore, where Sartre was sitting with Camus and Simone de Beauvoir, and said brusquely, "You Sartre?" Despite Genet's hard appearance and aggressive expressions, Sartre became very attached to him and felt they held many beliefs in common, especially their idea of liberty or freedom.

The première of *Huis clos (No Exit)* took place on 27 May at the Théâtre du Vieux-Colombier, under the direction of Raymond Rouleau. When Sartre first wrote the play in 1943, at the suggestion of Marc Barbezat, the idea was that it should go on tour as curtain-raiser for a road show organized by Barbezat in the Free Zone. Sartre asked Camus to direct it and play the part of Garcin, and in the first rehearsals, held in Simone de Beauvoir's room, the other parts were played by Olga Barbezat, Wanda Kosakiewicz and Chauffard, a former student of Sartre's. The tour fell through after they ran into financial difficulties and when Olga Barbezat was arrested. The play was then accepted by Annet Badel, an industrialist, who had just become director of the Théâtre du Vieux-Colombier, and professional actors were hired. Camus felt that he was not qualified to direct professional actors on the Paris stage, and so he withdrew. Only Chauffard remained of the original cast. It was an instant success (even though to begin with it had to share the bill with a light comedy) and became a classic of the Paris stage. In Britain it was banned by the censor (but was nevertheless performed in private clubs under the title *Vicious Circle);* it was a great success, however, in the United States, where it received the Donaldson Prize for the best play performed in New York in 1946–47. A few days after the Paris opening, there was a public debate at the theater about the play, with Sartre giving a short lecture and then entering into discussion with Cocteau, Camus and Barrault, and others. It was clear that the play contained an important and highly subtle philosophy that could easily be misunderstood. Sartre sought to elucidate the message in his oral preface to the later recording of the play by Deutsche Grammophon Gesellschaft, in which he said that "Hell is other people" had always been misunderstood. It had been thought that what he meant by that was that our relations with other people are always poisoned, that they are invariably hellish relations. But what he really meant was something totally different. He meant that if relations with someone else were twisted, vitiated, then that other person could only be hell. This was because other people were basically the most important means individuals had for their knowledge of themselves. When they thought about themselves, when they tried to know themselves, basically they had to use the knowledge of them which other people already had. One judged oneself with the criteria other people had developed and had given us for judging ourselves. Into whatever one said about oneself someone else's judgment always entered. Into whatever one felt within oneself someone else's judgment entered. Which meant that if one's relations were bad, one was situating oneself in a total dependence on someone else. And then one was indeed in hell because of being too dependent on the judgment of other people. But that did not mean that one could not have relations with other people. It simply brought out the vital importance of all other people for each one of us.[1]

The other points that Sartre said he wanted to make were that the people in the play differed from us in being dead, and death symbolized the condition of those victims of others' judgments who were so cowardly as not to try to break out of the habits that brought on the judgments and who accepted the judgments as inevitable. Since we are alive, we are free to break out of the circle of living death, and if we choose not to act to change that situation, then that, too, is an act of free will.

In mid-July, Camus told Sartre that a member of the *Combat* movement had been arrested and had confessed names to the authorities. Camus advised his friends to move from their addresses. Sartre and Simone de Beauvoir first moved in with the Leirises and then moved out to Neuilly-sous-Clermont. On 11 August the newspapers and radio announced that the Americans were on the outskirts of Chartres, and so Simone and Sartre mounted their bicycles and returned to Paris so as not to miss the Liberation. When the resistance movement began to take over the key buildings, Sartre and other members of the National Theater Committee occupied the Théâtre-Français. He had been asked by Camus to write a series of articles about the Liberation for *Combat,* and this he proceeded to do with the help of Simone de Beauvoir.

9 September: In the first nonclandestine issue of *Les Lettres françaises,* the front page carried Sartre's article "La République du silence," which began with the famous phrase: "We have

1. Quoted in Michel Contat and Michel Rybalka, *The Writings of Jean-Paul Sartre,* trans. R. C. McCleary, 2 vols., Evanston, Ill., Northwestern Univ. Press, 1974, p. 99.

never been more free than under the German Occupation."

It was in September that the group was established to constitute the managing committee of a new journal, *Les Temps modernes,* which was to be the main organ for promoting the ideas of Sartre and his friends in the immediate postwar period. The committee included Raymond Aron, Simone de Beauvoir, Michel Leiris, Maurice Merleau-Ponty, Albert Ollivier, Jean Paulhan and Sartre. André Malraux was asked to participate but refused. Now that Sartre had a regular income from the theater and from his scriptwriting for Pathé, he was able to devote himself entirely to writing and took unlimited leave from the university. He did not actually resign until the 1960s.

The writing proceeded rapidly, and in November he finished *Le Sursis (The Reprieve)* and sent it to the publishers Gallimard at the same time as the novel *L'Age de raison (The Age of Reason)*.

Camus offered Sartre an assignment in December. It was to go to the United States and write a series of articles for *Combat* during the following year. He accepted.

29 December: The Communist weekly *Action* published Sartre's article "A More Precise Characterization of Existentialism." It was a response to Communist criticisms and accusations that suggested that he was a disciple of the philosopher Heidegger (whose work was praised by the Nazis) and that existentialism diverted people from the class struggle. Sartre's main thrust was that a man's freedom lay not in doing whatever he wanted, but in choosing to accept his lot with resignation or to rebel against it.[2]

2. *Action,* 29 December, 1944.

1945

L'Age de raison (The Age of Reason), a novel, vol. 1 of the trilogy Les
  Chemins de la liberté (Roads to Freedom), (Paris: Gallimard)
Le Sursis (The Reprieve), a novel, vol. 2 of Les Chemins de la liberté
  (Paris: Gallimard)
Huis clos (No Exit), full text of the play (Paris: Gallimard)
"Un Collège spirituel" ("A Spiritual School"), an excerpt from a study
  of Baudelaire; Confluences, no. 1 (January–February), pp. 9–18
A series of newspaper articles on the United States in Combat and Le
  Figaro from January to July
"L'Homme ligoté: Notes sur le 'Journal' de Jules Renard" ("Man in
  Chains: Notes on Jules Renard's Journal"), Messages II, 1944, but
  not printed until April 15, 1945
"New Writing in France: The Resistance Taught that Literature Is
  No Fancy Activity Independent of Politics," article Vogue (July), pp.
  84–85
"La Libération de Paris: Une Semaine d'apocalypse" ("The Liberation
  of Paris: An Apocalyptic Week"), article Clartés, no. 9 (August 24),
  p. 1
"Qu'est-ce qu'un collaborateur?" ("What Is a Collaborator?"), article
  La République française, vol. 2, no. 8 (August), pp. 5–6; no. 9 (September), pp. 14–17
"Présentation" ("Introduction"), article Les Temps modernes, no. 1
  (October), pp. 1–21
"La Fin de la guerre" ("The End of the War"), article in Les Temps
  modernes, no. 1 (October), pp. 163–67
"La Nationalisation de la littérature" ("The Nationalization of Lit-
  erature"), article in Les Temps modernes, no. 2 (November), pp. 193–
  211
"La Liberté cartésienne" ("Cartesian Freedom"), extracts from an in-
  troduction to Descartes' works, Labyrinthe (Geneva), no. 14 (No-
  vember), p. 7
"Portrait de l'antisémite" ("Portrait of the Anti-Semite"), essay in Les
  Temps modernes, no. 3 (December), pp. 442–70

Like Camus, Sartre refused the Légion d'honneur, on grounds
of principle that were to remain consistent throughout his life,
as shown by his later refusal of the Nobel prize.

12 January: Sartre left for the United States with a party of
French journalists on board a military plane—there were few

civilian flights. The invitation to the French journalists had been made because the United States wanted its war effort to be better known in France. Camus had asked Sartre to go as the *Combat* correspondent, but it was agreed that he would also write for *Le Figaro*. Camus was disappointed with the first reports because Sartre seemed to send the lighter, more entertaining pieces to *Le Figaro* and to reserve for *Combat* the heavier and drier pieces that had cost him more effort to write. An example of the contrast was the entertaining article in *Le Figaro* describing Sartre's impressions of American cities, whereas *Combat* the next day received a careful study of the Tennessee Valley Authority. In all, some 32 articles were written. The first article, dated 22 January and published in *Le Figaro* on 24 January, caused a stir, as Sartre seemed to accuse the State Department of supplying money to bring out a newspaper among the French exiles in the United States that harmed the French cause, because it criticized the Gaullist faction in the struggle between the various political groups among the exiles during the war years. When the *New York Times'* Paris correspondent condemned Sartre for attacking the very foundations of Franco-American friendship, Sartre sent a letter, which the *New York Times* published on 1 February, in which he said the correspondent had distorted the spirit of his article, and he reiterated his belief in Franco-American friendship and stated that he had not intended to question it. The articles show that Sartre found much to admire in American life and its people, which is not surprising in view of his long-standing enthusiasm for American novels, films and jazz. However, he did offer some strong political criticisms and pointed to the contradictions in American culture regarding individualism and conformism, egalitarian social relations but inequalities of power, and a racial problem that would only be solved when the American proletariat—black and white—recognized that their interests in opposition to the ruling class were the same.

Socially, Sartre's stay in America was a great success. In New York he again met Stépha and Fernando Gerassi, who introduced him to Alexander Calder. He also met André Masson, Yves Tanguy, Fernand Léger, Claude Lévi-Strauss, André Breton, Howard Fast, Richard Wright and many others. Among the others was a young woman with whom he fell in love and with whom he was to have a relationship that caused Simone de Beauvoir a great deal of concern—Dolores V. He spent much of his time in New York in her company; she was half-separated from her husband and unsettled in her life. By the time he left to return to Paris in May, they had decided that they would spend two or three months together every year.[1]

Along with the other French journalists, Sartre was introduced to President Franklin D. Roosevelt, only a few days before his death, and was much struck by his personality. There was a visit to Hollywood (where he ran into Henriette Nizan), which he enjoyed writing about. And he attended a private showing of *Citizen Kane,* about which he wrote a highly critical article.

On his return to Paris, he and Simone de Beauvoir threw themselves into the social life of the city, mixing with the fashionable set (le Tout-Paris). He then went on his own to stay with his mother (his stepfather had died during the winter). In August he and Simone had a month's holiday at Mme. Morel's house, La Pouèze. This was followed by a conference in Belgium, organized by the Dominicans through the publishers Cerf, at which Sartre responded to Gabriel Marcel's application of the label "existentialist" to him by saying: "My philosophy is a philosophy of existence; I don't even know what Existentialism is."[2]

By the fall of that year, the word and topic of existentialism were everywhere and unavoidable. The first two volumes of *Roads to Freedom* were published in September; the first issue of *Les Temps modernes* appeared on 29 October, and Sartre's "Introduction" caused a stir in the literary world; Simone de Beauvoir's play *Les Bouches inutiles,* with its seemingly existentialist message, was produced on 29 October. Many articles about them appeared in the press. "In the end, we took the epithet that everyone used for us and used it for our own purposes. So that, without having planned it, what we launched early that fall turned out to be an 'Existentialist offensive.' "[3]

Sartre found himself, within a few weeks, a national celebrity. He discussed the phenomenon in an article, "La nationalisation de la littérature," in *Les Temps modernes,* where he commented:

1. Simone de Beauvoir, *Force of Circumstance,* trans. Richard Howard (London: Penguin Books, 1968), p. 77.

2. Ibid., pp. 45–46.

3. Ibid., p. 46.

"It is not pleasant to be treated as a public monument during one's lifetime."

The same phenomenon was in evidence on 28 October, at a conference at the Club Maintenant in Paris, where Sartre gave a lecture that became almost a legendary event in the short history of existentialism. The subject was "Is Existentialism a Humanism?" and so many people tried to attend that women fainted in the overcrowded room and the speaker could hardly be heard. The lecture had to be repeated in private so that discussion could take place. Existentialism had become a popular cult.

Because Sartre was becoming a public monument, he was a convenient target for criticism. The Communists renewed their attacks on him. Although he made efforts to conciliate them and agreed to a meeting with some of his Communist critics, arranged by his former pupil Jean Kanapa, he found himself embroiled in arguments with Garaudy and Mougin. Garaudy published a violent attack entitled "A False Prophet: Jean-Paul Sartre" in *Les Lettres françaises* on 28 December.

The other source of attack was those who were scandalized by the morality or subject matter of the two volumes of the novel *Roads to Freedom*. The plan for *Roads to Freedom* was conceived in the summer of 1938, and Sartre informed Simone de Beauvoir at that time that the theme was to be freedom. He saw it as a sequel to *Nausea,* and he thought of the character Mathieu as a continuation of Roquentin in the earlier work. The development is that this character discovers freedom and is a hero who takes action. The first volume centers on the personal problems of a group of individuals who are set in a stagnating France during the interwar period. The second, *The Reprieve,* aimed to recapture the sense of disarray that seized many of these people during the Munich crisis, when they could no longer think of themselves simply as individuals but were part of a "detotalized totality." While writing *The Reprieve,* Sartre had the idea for the third volume. This was originally to be called "The Last Chance," but it became *Troubled Sleep* in 1949, and the earlier title was transferred to a projected fourth volume, which was never published, although some of it appeared in *Les Temps modernes.*

The reception of the first two volumes in 1945 was mixed. They created something of a literary sensation and a scandal at the same time. Some critics deplored Sartre's morals and the fact that there was a story of abortion at the center of *The Age of Reason*. Sartre replied that Mathieu's real sin lay less in his suggestion that Marcelle get an abortion than in his having committed himself to living with her for eight years without loving her. Even worse was the sin of falsity and deceit in their relationship, because the affair was not really a shared undertaking—there was no true commitment.

The final controversial publication of this tumultuous year was "Portrait of the Anti-Semite" in *Les Temps modernes*. In this case the controversy was conducted mainly in private, in that concerned Jewish friends prevailed on Sartre to cut out 50 pages devoted to Jewish authenticity and inauthenticity. Because the published article had a good reception in progressive Jewish circles, Sartre subsequently put out the complete version as a book, with the title *Reflections on the Jewish Question* (American title: *Anti-Semite and Jew*). Sartre likened the inauthentic Jew to the worker who wished to deny his condition as a worker by acting like a bourgeois instead of demanding to be liberated as a worker. The authentic Jew was one who took responsibility for his Jewishness, asserted that he was a Jew and demanded his full rights, not just as a man but also as a Jew.

1946

L'Existentialisme est un humanisme (Existentialism Is a Humanism), revised text of a lecture (Paris: Nagel)

Morts sans sépulture (usually translated as *The Victors*), a play in three acts (Lausanne: Marguerat)

La Putain respectueuse (The Respectful Prostitute), a play in two acts (Paris, Nagel)

Réflexions sur la question juive (Reflections on the Jewish Question), an essay (Paris, Morihien); referred to hereafter by the American edition title, *Anti-Semite and Jew*

Prefaces to the *Écrits intimes (Intimate Writings)* of Baudelaire and to a volume of selections from Descartes

Introduction to *Les Mobiles de Calder (Calder's Mobiles)*, a show catalog, and to Gjon Mili's text for his photography exhibition: "Jean-Paul Sartre présente Gjon Mili"

"Manhattan: The Great American Desert," an article, *Town and Country* (May), p. 65 ff.

"Matérialisme et révolution" ("Materialism and Revolution"), an article, *Les Temps modernes,* no. 9 (June), pp. 1–32

"Forgers of Myths: The Young Playwrights of France," an article, *Theater Arts* (New York), vol. 30, no. 6 (June), pp. 324–35

"American Novelists in French Eyes," translation by Evelyn de Solis of a lecture given by Sartre at Yale in 1946; *Atlantic Monthly,* vol. CLXXVIII, no. 2 (August), pp. 114–18

"Présentation" ("Introduction" to a special issue on the United States), *Les Temps modernes,* nos. 11–12 (August–September), pp. 193–198

"La Guerre et la peur" ("War and Fear"), an article, *Franchise (Notebooks of a France Reborn),* no. 3 (November–December)

"Ecrire pour son époque" ("We Write for Our Own Time"), an article, *Erasme* (The Hague), nos. 11–12, pp. 454–60

"Prose et langage" ("Prose and Language"), an article, *Vrai* (Brussels), no. 51 (21 December)

"Une Confèrence de Jean-Paul Sartre" ("A Lecture by Jean-Paul Sartre"), excerpts in *Fraternité* (31 December)

Sartre spent the first part of the year in New York, having had himself invited to give lectures at some American universities, but also with the purpose in mind of pursuing his relationship with Dolores, the young woman he had met the year before. On his return in April, he talked to Simone de Beauvoir with such gaiety about his time spent with Dolores that Simone could not refrain from finally asking him who meant most to him. His reply—"M. (Dolores) means an enormous amount to me, but I am with you"[1]—did little to dispel her fears, but he subsequently clarified that, since they had always taken actions to be more truthful than words, he chose to invoke the evidence of a simple fact, a response that went a long way in reassuring her.

Shortly after his return Sartre came down with the mumps and had to stay in bed for a couple of weeks. He worked on some "American sketches," which he subsequently abandoned.

Toward the end of May, the publisher Albert Skira organized a series of lectures on existentialism to be given by Sartre, first in Geneva, then in Zurich and finally in Lausanne, where he

1. Simone de Beauvoir, *Force of Circumstance,* trans. Richard Howard (London: Penguin Books, 1968), p. 78.

met André Gorz, who later portrayed Sartre vividly in his book *Le Traître (The Traitor).*[2]

At this time Sartre was getting a lot of publicity, not only for his published works but also for his life-style. He used to spend much of his time in the Café de Flore or the Pont-Royal, primarily in order to work but also to meet with his friends, such as Michèle and Boris Vian, Raymond Queneau, Michel Leiris, Giacometti, Nathalie Sarraute and Bost. In response to a study of Sartre by Roger Troisfontaines *(Le Choix de J.-P. Sartre,* Paris: Aubier-Montaigne [1946]), where he tries to render Sartre suspect by focusing on his love of the café, which Troisfontaines presents as an intrinsically evil place, Sartre explains that what draws him to the café is the indifferent atmosphere where other people exist without caring about him and without his bothering about them. Whereas a wife and children creeping around so as not to disturb him would bother him, the constant activity in a café is like a movement of his consciousness, and nothing more.[3]

L'Existentialisme est un humanisme (Existentialism Is a Humanism), the text of his lecture given at the Club Maintenant in 1945, proved very popular as a simple introduction, but it was much criticized for its simplifications, and Sartre himself came to reject it. Unfortunately it provided his many critics with ready ammunition, since in popularizing the claims of existentialism, this article came close to making a travesty of them.

Of the two introductory essays Sartre published that year, on Baudelaire and on Descartes, the one on Baudelaire managed to cause quite a stir in literary circles: Sartre was criticized for having dealt with the man rather than with the "fact of being a poet," a criticism that was later used to challenge Sartre when, in speaking of Genet, he chose to valorize the poet above the man. In trying to reconstruct Baudelaire's experience, Sartre focused on the idea of original choice and concluded that, since Baudelaire "is the man who has chosen to see himself as

2. (Paris: Seuil, 1958), pp. 245–48.

3. Sartre's response to the 1st edition of Troisfontaines's book was included in the 2nd edition in 1946, and is quoted in Michel Contat and Michel Rybalka, *The Writings of Jean-Paul Sartre,* trans. R. C. McCleary, 2 vols., Evanston, Ill., Northwestern Univ. Press, 1974, p. 149.

if he were another . . . his life is nothing but the story of that failure." Descartes, on the other hand, was claimed by Sartre as the only Frenchman to have had a great effect on his thinking, and in this essay he gave a clear account of what he considered to be Descartes's strengths and weaknesses: Descartes understood, long before Heidegger, that freedom was "the sole basis of being" and that free will was bound to negativity; but since he had not been able to "conceive of this negativity as productive," he had attributed to God the role that properly belongs to man.

The two plays that Sartre wrote and had performed that year, *The Victors* and *The Respectful Prostitute,* managed to stir up criticism from both sides: the right-wing press censured *The Victors* for reviving old hatreds, and the left-wing press reproached Sartre for depicting members of the resistance as cowards and traitors. As for *The Respectful Prostitute,* "the Communists thought it a pity that Sartre had shown his public a Negro trembling with fear and respect, instead of a real fighter,"[4] whereas others criticized it for being an outrage to decent morality and a "vulgar defamation of the great American democracy."[5]

The Victors had been written at the end of 1945, at a time when the ex-collaborators were beginning to reappear in public life. Sartre wished to refresh people's memories. He had thought a lot about torture, and particularly the relationship between the torturer and his victim. He was once again dealing with the dilemma between ethics and *praxis.* The character Lucie retreated stubbornly into her individualistic pride, while the militant Communist, presented by Sartre as in the right, aimed at effectiveness.[6]

Sartre's own subsequent evaluation of the play was highly critical. He was quoted as saying that the play was a failure and that it was a very grim play, lacking in surprise. "It would have been better to make a novel or a film of it."[7]

The Respectful Prostitute, which was written in a few days in 1946 so that it could be performed with *The Victors,* involved

4. *Force of Circumstance,* p. 123.

5. F. Dupont, *Le Figaro* (21 November 1946).

6. *Force of Circumstance,* p. 121.

7. *Les Cahiers libres de la jeunesse,* no. 1 (15 February 1960), pp. 2–4.

Sartre in all kinds of trouble. The idea for the play came from a famous case, reported by Vladimir Pozner in *Les Etats désunis (The Dis-United States),*[8] in which nine blacks were accused of raping two prostitutes and were condemned as a result of their testimony to death in the electric chair. The affair had international repercussions and was made more complicated by the fact that the two prostitutes, affected by various pressures put on them, changed their testimony several times. Sartre wanted to portray and condemn the racism that this case revealed but found himself charged with anti-Americanism. Although efforts to ban the play were not successful, the management of the subways insisted that the word *putain* be censored from all publicity, and so the play was henceforth known as *La P. . . . . respectueuse.* In the United States, despite wrangles with the censors in many towns, particularly Chicago, the play, produced by the "Respectful Company" in a mutilated translation, was highly successful. This adaptation, however, was indirectly the source of serious financial difficulties for Sartre. One clause of the contract specified that the company reserved the rights to a movie version. In 1951 Sartre, wanting to do a favor for one of his friends, Marcel Pagliero, authorized him to film a French version of the play. Arguing on the basis of its contract, the Respectful Company brought a suit against Sartre, succeeded in blocking his American rights and forced him to pay a very large sum in compensation.

June: Sartre and Simone de Beauvoir went on a lecture tour of Italy, where they enjoyed their easy relationship with Communist intellectuals. At home Sartre's relations with the Communist Party were becoming increasingly strained, especially after the publication of his article "Matérialisme et révolution," in which he formulated his fundamental objections to the prevailing Stalinist orthodoxy of dialectical materialism, particularly the notion of a dialectic of nature, and affirmed his belief in freedom as the constituent structure of action. He attacked the dogmatism of French Communist intellectuals and singled out for personal criticism Roger Garaudy, who had condemned Sartre in his article "Un faux prophète: Jean-Paul Sartre" ("A

8. (Paris: Denoël, 1938).

False Prophet: Jean-Paul Sartre") in *Les Lettres françaises* (28 December 1945).

It was at this time that Sartre began to feel that he might need help with his correspondence, and since Jean Cau, who was studying for the École Normale entrance exams, needed work, Sartre decided to take him on. However, it seems that his mail was still not in fact that voluminous, and Simone de Beauvoir recounts how, on first meeting with his secretary, Sartre had to hunt through his pockets in order to root out two or three meager envelopes.[9] Sartre feared that Jean Cau might be using up time instead of saving it, but in fact, in October, when Sartre moved into the new apartment in the rue Bonaparte with his mother, Cau succeeded in bringing some order into his life, and he remained Sartre's secretary until 1957. About this move Sartre said in his "Conversations with John Gerassi" (unpublished, 1972): "Until then I had always lived in a hotel, worked in a café, eaten in a restaurant: possessing nothing was important to me. It was a way towards personal salvation; I would have felt lost—as Mathieu did—if I had my own apartment, with furniture, and my own possessions." Nevertheless he did attach meaning and importance to his piano, which he played regularly after dinner before getting back to his work.

The political situation of extreme polarization between the United States and the USSR meant that on a personal level, both among friends and at work, relationships turned on where one stood. There was, for instance, a big rift in *Les Temps modernes'* team: Raymond Aron became more anti-Communist, and Albert Ollivier moved toward the Right in sympathy with the newly created Gaullist Union, and they both left and began to write for *Combat;* Merleau-Ponty took over the joint management with Sartre of *Les Temps modernes,* but it was an uneasy alliance; Sartre and Camus had serious differences of opinion, Sartre accusing *Combat* and Camus of being too concerned with moral issues at the expense of political ones; and Koestler, who said of Sartre, "You are a better novelist than I am, but not such a good philosopher," accused Sartre and even Camus of seeking to compromise with the Soviets. During one evening

9. *Force of Circumstance,* p. 102.

in November when discussions between Koestler, Camus and Sartre became particularly heated, Camus said (of Sartre and Simone de Beauvoir), "What we have in common, you and I, is that for us individuals come first; we prefer the concrete to the abstract, people to doctrines, we place friendship above politics."[10] Only a few months later they were to have an argument that ended their friendship. It was the day after this evening that Sartre had to give a lecture at the Sorbonne, under the aegis of Unesco, on "The Writer's Responsibility," and since he had to stay up all night in order to prepare it, he dosed himself with amphetamines, a habit he had recently acquired to help him cope with particularly demanding pieces of work.

November: Sartre and Simone de Beauvoir traveled to Holland, which provided the starting point for Sartre's definition of art in "Q'est-ce que la littérature?" ("What Is Literature?"). They also went to the Psychological Institute run by Van Lennep and underwent graphological analysis and projective testing, which were still very much in their infancy. On their return to Paris, they went to Calder's exhibition of mobiles, for which Sartre wrote the preface to the catalog, describing in an almost poetic way the "strange beings, halfway between matter and life," that mobiles are.

December: Sartre gave a lecture in Paris under the auspices of *Fraternité* and the *Alliance Against Racism* on the problem of minorities in America and in the same month became an active member of the French League for a Free Palestine, writing several texts and appeals in *La Riposte*.

10. Ibid., p. 118.

1947

Baudelaire (Paris: Gallimard); previously published as an introduction to *Ecrits intimes: Fusées, Mon coeur mis a nu, Carnet, Correspondance (Intimate Writings: Rockets, My Heart Laid Bare, Notebook, Correspondence)*

Les Jeux sont faits (The Chips Are Down), a movie script (Paris: Nagel)

Situations, Vol. I (Paris: Gallimard), 16 critical essays arranged in order of publication, 1938–45:
"*Sartoris*, by William Faulkner"
"John Dos Passos and *1919*"
"*The Conspiracy*, by Paul Nizan"
"A Fundamental Idea of Husserl's Phenomenology: Intentionality"
"M. François Mauriac and Freedom"
"Vladimir Nabokov: 'Mistrust' "
"Denis de Rougemont: *Love and the Western World*"
"On *The Sound and the Fury*: Time in the Work of Faulkner"
"M. Jean Giraudoux and the Philosophy of Aristotle: Concerning *Duel of Angels*"
"An Analysis of *The Stranger*"
"*Aminadab*, or The Fantastic Considered as a Language" (on Maurice Blanchot)
"A New Mystic" (on Georges Bataille)
"Departure and Return" (on Brice Parain)
"Man and Things" (on Francis Ponge)
"Man in Chains: Notes on Jules Renard's 'Journal' "
"Cartesian Freedom"

Théâtre: Les Mouches, Huis clos, Morts san sépulture, La Putain respectueuse (Theater: The Flies, No Exit, The Victors, The Respectful Prostitute), (Paris: Gallimard)

"La Responsabilité de l'écrivain" ("The Writer's Responsibility"), a lecture; published in *Les Conférences de l'U.N.E.S.C.O.* (Paris: Fontaine)

"Sculptures à n dimensions" ("N-Dimensional Sculpture"), introduction to a show by David Hare

Les Faux Nez (The False Noses), a movie script, *La Revue du cinéma*, no. 6 (Spring), pp. 3–27.

"Qu'est-ce que la littérature?" ("What Is Literature?"), *Les Temps modernes*, no. 17 (February), pp. 769–805; no. 18 (March), pp. 961–88; no. 19 (April), pp. 1194–1218; no. 20 (May), pp. 1410–29; no. 21 (June), pp. 1607–41; no. 22 (July), pp. 77–114.

"Le Cas Nizan" ("The Nizan Case"), *Les Temps modernes*, no. 22 (July), pp. 181–84.

"La Tribune des *Temps modernes*" ("The *Temps modernes* Tribune"), radio broadcasts

January: Simone de Beauvoir left for a lecture tour of the United States in the knowledge that, during her absence, Dolores would be going to Paris to spend time with Sartre and that she, Dolores, was determined to do everything she could to make him ask her to stay. Simone de Beauvoir admitted to feeling great anxiety and even panic during this separation, and it was toward the end of her stay in America, in May, after Sartre had asked her to remain away a bit longer because of Dolores's continued presence in Paris, that she began her affair with the writer Nelson Algren, which was to last for four years.

February: Sartre began publication of "What Is Literature?" in *Les Temps modernes,* in which he finally broke with the Communist Party, stating that "The policy of Stalin's Communism is incompatible with the honest exercise of a writer's trade." He took the Communist Party to task "for the precedence it gave to scientism, for its oscillations between conservatism and opportunism, and for a utilitarianism which degraded literature to the status of propaganda."[1] He also responded to an attack on him published in *Pravda* in which existentialism was said to teach that "all historical processes are absurd and fortuitous, and every ethic a lie; that there are neither peoples nor society; only personal interest and profit according to the principle, *carpe diem.*" He wrote a spirited defense of Nizan, whose name was being sullied by the Communist Party as being an informer. The success of this defense in clearing Nizan's name did nothing to endear Sartre to the Communists, and he began to realize that, since he was suspect on all sides, he was condemning himself to a future without a public. Nevertheless, he accepted this isolation willingly, refusing to give up his basic right to free research, which, had he joined the Communist Party, he knew he would have to do. He maintained that he was being singled out for attack because, since his position was so close to theirs, he was actually stealing their clientèle.[2]

At the end of May, Sartre gave a lecture on Kafka to raise money for the French League for a Free Palestine and two days

1. Simone de Beauvoir, *Force of Circumstance,* trans. Richard Howard (London: Penguin Books, 1968), p. 140.

2. In *Sartre by Himself,* from the text of the film by Alexandre Astruc and Michel Contat, trans. Richard Seaver (New York: Urizen Books, 1978), p. 65.

later talked on "Consciousness and Knowledge of Self" at the French Philosophical Society. He strongly supported Jean Genet's candidacy for the Pléiade Prize for his plays *The Maids* and *Deathwatch,* and although his candidate was eventually successful, the deliberations were not without animosity. In July he and Simone de Beauvoir went to London, where he gave a press conference for the opening of *The Respectful Prostitute* and *The Victors.* It was shortly after this that Dolores returned to the United States, leaving Sartre and Simone de Beauvoir somewhat uncertain about their relationship, but their easy companionship was soon restored after the summer spent traveling together in Denmark, Sweden and Lapland. Nevertheless, on their return to Paris, Simone de Beauvoir left almost immediately for Chicago, where she spent two weeks with Nelson Algren and planned to travel with him the following spring to Guatemala and Mexico.

September: Sartre addressed film buffs during the First International Congress of Filmology, held at the Sorbonne, when his movie *Les Jeux sont faits (The Chips Are Down),* produced by Jean Delannoy "faithfully but without genius," was screened. Although the film dealt with elements that first appeared in "The Room," such as the theme of sequestration, and bears some resemblance to *Huis clos (No Exit),* which was actually written at about the same time, Sartre himself said in an interview with Paul Carrière[3] that it was very much not an existentialist play, being suffused with determinism throughout.

Autumn: On the initiative of his former colleague from Le Havre, Lucien Bonafé, the Paul Ramadier government suggested to Sartre that he hold a weekly forum on the radio, helped by friends and colleagues on the staff of *Les Temps modernes.* The first broadcast, on 6 October, was entitled "We Must Campaign Against Believing that War Between the U.S. and the U.S.S.R. Is Inevitable." In it Sartre urged his listeners to reject the Cold War politics of the two blocs, observing that to become part of one or the other would only aggravate the conflict between them. The second broadcast, on 20 October, was entitled "De Gaulle and 'Gaullism' as Seen by Jean-Paul

3. *Le Figaro* (29 April 1947).

Sartre (and the *Temps modernes* Staff)" and again denounced the belief in the inevitability of war on which Gaullist politics was based. Bonafé, in the course of the discussion, compared de Gaulle to Hitler, and Pontalis spoke of de Gaulle's scorn for the masses. Not surprisingly this broadcast evoked an immediate response from de Gaulle's supporters, two of whom, Henry Torrès and de Bénouville, replied to Sartre on the radio and in the press in the following terms: "M. J.-P. Sartre is talking about General de Gaulle in an indecent way, and his comparison of the liberator of our country, the restorer of our freedom and our republic, to Marshall Pétain, not to mention the comparison to Hitler, is impermissible and worthy of public scorn."[4] Many insults followed in the right-wing press, and old enmities resurfaced: Albert Ollivier, a former member of the *Temps modernes* staff, called those who took part in the broadcast "virtual fascists," and Paul Claudel commented: "M. Sartre attacks General de Gaulle's looks; is he so proud of his own?"[5] Aron had sided with de Bénouville and thus precipitated the quarrel that had been brewing between him and Sartre even since he, Aron, had been writing for *Le Figaro* and sympathizing with the Rassemblement du peuple français (R.P.F.). The third broadcast, on 27 October, entitled "J.-P. Sartre Talks About Anticommunism at the *Temps modernes* Tribune"—in which, according to Simone de Beauvoir, they "portioned out [their] criticisms and reservations in such a way as to make the common struggle possible"[6]—nevertheless provoked a very strong response from the Communist Party press, and Sartre was referred to as Ramadier's "court jester."[7] In December, when Ramadier was replaced by Schuman as minister, the series was suspended. What Sartre had intended to discuss in the next broadcasts was an intellectuals' manifesto on the international situation, appealing for peace and the creation of a neutral and socialist Europe. Sartre and Camus were still more or less in agreement, at least in their dislike of the Rassemblement du peuple français and Gaullism, but it was at this time that

4. *Combat* (22 October 1967). Quoted in Michel Contat and Michel Rybalka, *The Writings of Jean-Paul Sartre,* trans. R. C. McCleary, 2 vols., Evanston, Ill., Northwestern Univ. Press, 1976, p. 179.

5. *Carrefour* (29 October 1947).

6. *Force of Circumstance,* p. 148.

7. *Action* (5 November 1947).

Koestler decided to throw his lot in with the Rassemblement du peuple français, and his friendship with Sartre came to an end.

In December, Sartre wrote the introduction to a David Hare exhibition catalog. David Hare was an active member of the surrealist group and a friend of André Breton and had published several pieces in *Les Temps modernes*. His exhibition was called "N-Dimensional Sculpture."

The Christmas holidays were spent at La Pouèze, at Mme. Morel's, with Simone de Beauvoir, where they attempted to recover from all the mudslinging of the past year, confident in the knowledge that even if Mme. Morel did not share their political opinions, there, at least, it did not matter. "We were always happy to see her, both for her own sake and because she was a link with our lost past."[8] Sartre began work on *Les Mains sales (Dirty Hands)*.

1948

L'Engrenage (In the Mesh), a movie script (Paris: Nagel)

Les Mains sales (Dirty Hands), a play in seven acts (Paris: Gallimard)

Situations, Vol. II (Paris: Gallimard); the volume includes essays written between 1945 and 1947:

"Introduction to *Les Temps modernes*"

"The Nationalization of Literature"

"What Is Literature?"

"Orphée Noir" ("Black Orpheus"), an introduction to *Anthologie de la nouvelle poésie nègre et malgache de langue française (Anthology of New Black and Malagasy Poetry in the French Language)*, by Léopold Sedar Senghor

Preface to *Portrait d'un inconnu (Portrait of a Man Unknown)*, by Nathalie Sarraute

"La Recherche de l'absolu" ("The Search for the Absolute"), article on Giacometti, the introduction to the catalog for the Giacometti exhibition at the Pierre Matisse Gallery in New York, January 1948

"Conscience de soi et connaissance de soi" ("Consciousness of Self and Knowledge of Self"), a paper read to the Société française de philosophie (French Philosophical Society) meeting on 2 June 1947

Various articles relating to the Revolutionary Peoples' Assembly (RDR)

8. *Force of Circumstance*, p. 153.

February: Sartre went to Berlin to participate in a discussion of *The Flies,* which was performed at the Hebbel Theater. Sartre tried to show that there were parallels between Germany in 1948 and France in 1943, that the feelings of guilt about the past must give way to the sense of responsibility and freedom that would make for a fruitful future. The response of the bishop of Berlin to Sartre's play was to reiterate that repentance was the only way to true freedom. During this visit Germany made a very "lugubrious" impression on Sartre and Simone de Beauvoir.

On his return to Paris, Sartre joined the managing committee of the movement known as the Revolutionary People's Assembly (RDR) and signed the announcement of its foundation, "Appel du Comité pour le Rassemblement Démocratique Révolutionnaire" ("Appeal from the Committee of the Revolutionary People's Assembly"). The appeal was made public at the end of February and gained wide publicity. Essentially, the movement sought a middle way of democratic socialism between the opposing blocs of Soviet communism and American capitalism. The appeal followed the same lines as the earlier "First Call to International Opinion," which had come out in November 1947. It called for an international, democratic socialist solution to political and economic problems. A press conference was held on 10 March, with Sartre, Jean Rous and David Rousset representing the RDR. The first large meeting was held at the Salle Wagram on 19 March, at which Sartre took up one of the themes he had been prevented from developing when controversy brought to a premature end the series of radio broadcasts, "Tribune of *Les Temps modernes,*" in 1947. It dealt with attacks of those who condemned workers for "sordid materialism," and it interpreted hunger as a demand for freedom and an expression of class solidarity. At a meeting of the RDR in the Salle des Sociétés on 11 June, there were brawls with members of the Gaullist RPF, who tried to disrupt the meeting. Despite Sartre's intense involvement in the RDR, he was to quit the movement in disillusionment in October 1949. In an interview several years later, he stated that he had had nothing to do with the founding of the RDR, which was the work of Rousset and Altman, and that it was a tiny group outside the main lines of historical development.

At about this time, Sartre handed over the management of

Les Temps modernes to Merleau-Ponty, who joined the RDR sometime later but never participated very actively. Sartre instead worked for *La Gauche R.D.R.*, the mouthpiece of the movement.

2 April: *Les Main sales (Dirty Hands)* was performed for the first time at the Théâtre Antoine, under the direction of Simone Berriau, staged by Pierre Valde, with some "friendly supervision" from Jean Cocteau, whom Sartre saw often at this time. François Perier was a great hit in the role of Hugo, and the play as a whole was a huge success, especially once the right-wing press had decided that it could safely proclaim it as anti-Communist. Guy Leclerc, writing in *L'Humanité* (7 April 1948), said, "Hermetic philosopher, nauseating writer, scandalous playwright, third-rate demagogue: such are the stages of M. Sartre's career." Sartre himself said that he had not intended it to be a political play; it became one simply because he had chosen members of the Communist Party as its protagonists. Much later, in 1964, the Italian translator of the *Critique de la raison dialectique,* Paolo Caruso, in an interview with Sartre, tried to point out to him that he, Sartre, had underestimated the psychological mechanism by which *Les Mains sales* came to be labeled as anti-Communist. Hugo is in the wrong right up to the end of the play, but, for the audience, "the way that the final speeches give the whole of the rest of the play a meaning that justifies Hugo and condemns the revolutionary party is dramatically very effective indeed." Furthermore, the audience does identify more with Hugo, the bourgeois would-be revolutionary, than with Hoederer. Hoederer is almost an embodied ideal, *the* revolutionary for whom the audience feels admiration, but the human drama is Hugo's from beginning to end, and it is through his eyes that the audience perceives the world, and it is his fate that captivates them. Hugo comes from the bourgeois world, but, as Caruso points out, the reasons why Hugo abandoned his class are the most genuine thing about him, which is why the right-wing press hesitated in order to see what the Communists' verdict would be before claiming the play's morality as its own.[1] Sartre was greatly annoyed when

---

1. In Jean-Paul Sartre, *Sartre on Theater,* ed. Michel Contat and Michel Rybalka, trans. Frank Jellinek (New York: Pantheon Books, Random House, 1976), p. 214.

his play was used as a Cold War weapon and subsequently, in 1952, decided to permit its performance only with the agreement of the Communist Party in the country where it was to be performed. Sartre himself was not present for the opening night: he was giving a lecture to a Masonic lodge, having been led to believe that the Masons would give serious support to the RDR.

During June and July, Simone de Beauvoir returned to the United States to embark on a trip to Guatemala and Mexico with Nelson Algren, while Dolores came over from New York to spend time with Sartre. These relationships appeared to be getting complicated and demanding, and it was with some relief that Sartre and Simone de Beauvoir set off together for a trip through Algeria in August.

October: Sartre—along with Camus, Breton, Mounier and Richard Wright—set up a "council of solidarity" with Gary Davis, a pacifist, who declared that he was giving up his American citizenship to become a citizen of the world. There was much support for this "World Government Movement," particularly from Camus's editorials in *Combat,* but by the end of the year Sartre had disassociated himself from this movement, regarding it as moralizing, naive and ineffective.

30 October: By order of the Holy See, all of Sartre's works were put on the Index. In New York *Les Mains sales,* translated as *Red Gloves,* was performed in a sadly butchered, badly translated form and given an anti-Soviet dimension, while in Helsinki, the Soviets took official steps to get the authorities not to show the play, since they considered it to be "propaganda hostile to the U.S.S.R."

December: Sartre and *Les Temps modernes* became embroiled in an argument with Malraux, and the latter put pressure on Gallimard to stop publishing *Les Temps modernes*. From then on the journal was published by Julliard.

1949

La Mort dans l'âme (Sick at Heart) (Paris: Gallimard); published under
the title *Troubled Sleep* in the United States and as *Iron in the Soul*
in Britain, vol. 3 of *Les Chemins de la liberté (Roads to Freedom)*

Situations, vol. III (Paris: Gallimard); this volume includes 12 pieces,
in French, published between 1944 and 1948 and divided into five
sections:

1. On the war and the occupation:
   "The Republic of Silence"
   "Paris During the Occupation"
   "What Is a Collaborator?"
   "The End of the War"
2. On the United States:
   "Individualism and Conformism in the United States
   "American Cities"
   "New York, Colonial City"
   "Introduction" (to a special issue of *Les Temps modernes* on
   the United States)
3. "Materialism and Revolution"
4. "Black Orpheus"
5. "The Search for the Absolute" (on Giacometti)
   "Calder's Mobiles"

Entretiens sur la politique (Discussions of Politics), with David Rousset
and Gérard Rosenthal (Paris: Gallimard)

Articles in *Combat* (on Georges Lukács, on racial oppression in the
United States), *Le Figaro littéraire* (a reply to an attack by François
Mauriac), *Politique étrangère* (on the defense of French culture by
defending European culture), *Peuple du Monde* (on the World Cit-
izens' Movement), *Bulletin de la N.R.F.* (introduction to *The Thief's
Journal,* by Jean Genet), *Franc-Tireur* (on Haiti) and *Les Temps
modernes* (excerpts from volume 4 of *Roads to Freedom,* entitled
"Drôle d'amitié" ("Strange Friendship"))

13 January: *Combat* published an interview with the Hun-
garian Marxist, G. Lukács, under the title "Existentialism Indirectly Justifies Capitalism," in which Lukács justified his
having renounced his own early works as being outmoded He-
gelianism and at the same time claimed that Sartre had not
succeeded in bridging the gap between the Heideggerianism of
Being and Nothingness and the Kantianism of *Existentialism*

Is a Humanism. Sartre replied to the criticisms in an interview published in *Combat* on 20 January, under the title "Jean-Paul Sartre Criticizes George Lukács for Not Being a Marxist." Sartre denied that he had changed his philosophy, although he claimed the right to do so if the development of his thinking required it. A real philosopher should feel no need to renounce his earlier works as his thinking develops—Marx certainly did not. Lukács's use of the term *denounce* was symptomatic of a way of thinking that was not free; it came from a medieval and religious attitude, suitable to scholastic philosophy. The polemic became more bitter in the 3 February issue of *Combat,* when Lukács denied Sartre the moral right to comment on Marxism and characterized him as a "mediocre academic." In the same issue, in an interview entitled "The Earth Does Not Turn for Lukács," Sartre criticized Lukács for not having had the courage to make a statement like Galileo's "but it does turn" when faced with pressure to forsake his convictions. The reason, Sartre suggested, was that for Lukács "the earth doesn't turn any more."

Sartre came under much vituperative criticism from the Communists, who considered him to be a serious public enemy: Fedeev, at the Wroclaw Congress, had referred to him as a "jackal with a fountain pen"; Ehrenburg said that, after *Les Mains sales,* he felt nothing but contempt for Sartre; and Kanapa, who was in charge of *La Nouvelle critique,* devoted much time and attention to attacking existentialism in general and Sartre in particular.

In March, Sartre and Simone de Beauvoir went to the south of France, to Cagnes, in order to be able to work in peace: he was working on his "Morale" and the fourth volume of *Roads to Freedom,* to be called "The Last Chance"; she was finishing the second volume of *The Second Sex.* It was a pleasant time for both of them, but Sartre was feeling uneasy about the possibility of Dolores coming to live in France. He was apparently "trying to dissuade her."[1]

24 April: Sartre gave a lecture on "Defending French Culture by Defending European Culture" at the Centre d'études de politique étrangère, subsequently published in *Politique étrangère*

---

1. Simone de Beauvoir, *Force of Circumstance,* trans. Richard Howard (London: Penguin Books, 1968), p. 184.

(June 1949). In it he examined the relations between American and French cultures, which he argued were nonreciprocal because of America's political, economic, demographic and military hegemony. Furthermore, European culture was inherently pessimistic and a reflection on the problem of evil, whereas American culture was optimistic, technical, practical and scientific. French culture, he maintained, could only survive by being integrated within a European culture founded on an economic and political European union, powerful enough to withstand the pull of the United States and the USSR.

May: Sartre and Mauriac became embroiled in public argument about philosophy and its relation to politics, as a result of the publication of *Discussions of Politics.* Mauriac suggested that Sartre should give up politics and study mathematics, to which Sartre replied, "The less a man knows what he's talking about, the more zestful he becomes: this is what happens to M. Mauriac when he tries to talk politics." Furthermore, since Mauriac had said earlier that he would back Sartre's candidacy for the French Academy, Sartre's retort at this juncture was to say: "I find in certain members of the Academy so much bitterness, so much arrogance and, beneath a forced humility, such a consciousness of being superior to everyone else that it is definitely not the place I'll go to learn about equality."[2] Their controversy was to continue for many years.

Rousset returned from a trip to America that had completely seduced him. He and Altmann began to proclaim America as a trade-union culture where the workers governed the country, and, much to Sartre's dismay, the R.D.R. took on a fervently pro-American tendency. In June, at his own expense, Sartre called an extraordinary general meeting of the R.D.R., which pronounced its opposition to Rousset; shortly afterward the R.D.R. split up, with Sartre finally resigning in October. It was a severe blow to him, a definitive lesson in realism: he concluded that movements could not be created. "Circumstances merely appeared to be favourable to the association. It did answer to an abstract need, defined by the objective situation, but not to any real need among the people. Consequently they did not support it."[3]

2. *Le Figaro littéraire,* May 7, 1949.

3. Unpublished notes of Sartre, quoted in *Force of Circumstance,* p. 187.

16 June: *Combat* published an extract from the large work on
ethics that Sartre had been working on for some time but that
was never completed. The extract was from a chapter on "Revolutionary Violence," and it had the title "Le Noir et le blanc
aux Etats-Unis" ("Black and White in the United States"). It
analyzed the relationship of oppressors to the oppressed, using
the example of racism in the United States. Oppression was
not deliberate nor obvious to the oppressor but was often hidden
and acquiesced in because the inferiority of blacks to whites
seemed to be a natural fact. ". . . [I]n order for the oppressor to
get a clear view of an unjustifiable situation, it is not enough
for him to look at it honestly; he must also change the structure
of his eyes. As long as he looks at it with his conceptualist
framework, he will judge it to be right and just."

Later in June, Sartre came up with some friendly criticisms
of the World Citizens' Movement, which was being promoted
by the American Gary Davis and had received support from
Camus and many others in Europe. Sartre accused it of utopian
idealism in its project for a world government. The criticism
appeared as "Jean-Paul Sartre ouvre un dialogue" ("Jean-Paul
Sartre Opens a Dialogue") in *Peuple du Monde,* a supplement
to *Combat,* 18–19 June.

During the summer months, Sartre and Simone de Beauvoir
went their separate ways, she to Italy, Tunisia, Algeria and
Morocco with Nelson Algren, and he to Guatemala, Panama,
Curaçao, Haiti and Cuba with Dolores. In Haiti he was greatly
interested in everything to do with the voodoo cult; in Havana
he visited Ernest Hemingway. In October they went back to
Cagnes together but were saddened to see that the gossip col-
umnists were beginning to follow them even during their quiet
retreats.

On their return to Paris, *La Mort dans l'âme (Troubled Sleep),*
the third volume of *Roads to Freedom,* was published. The novel
was less successful than its predecessors, partly because it was
a sequel rather than a conclusion, but most critics considered
it to be the best in the series. The first part covers chronolog-
ically the period from 15 June to 18 June 1940 and concludes
by leaving Mathieu in a particularly desperate situation; the
second part describes the first days of captivity of a group of
French soldiers, which includes the militant Communist, Bru-
net, and a certain Schneider, who is suspected of being an in-

former. But it is in these conditions that Mathieu experiences his first taste of pure freedom and, subsequently, of solidarity. He learns that one never saves oneself alone: individual freedom is indissolubly linked to the freedom of others (this as he and his comrades shoot wildly and hopelessly at the advancing Germans). *Troubled Sleep* left the reader in doubt as to whether Mathieu was dead or alive. "Drôle d'amitié" ("Strange Friendship"), which would have been volume 4 of *Roads to Freedom,* appeared in serial form in the November and December issues of *Les Temps modernes,* but "The Last Chance," of which this was but an extract, was never finished. In this final volume, Mathieu, tired of being free "for nothing," finally commits himself to working for the resistance, is arrested and dies under torture—a hero, not in essence but because he *made himself* a hero. According to Simone de Beauvoir, the third volume was a failure because the critics at the time gave it very poor reviews: the Right was shocked because Sartre depicted officers deserting their troops, while the Communists "were indignant because the French people, civilians and soldiers alike, were shown as passive and apolitical."[4]

During their usual winter stay at La Pouèze, Sartre worked on a preface to the works of Genet that Gallimard had asked him to do, while Simone de Beauvoir finished her translation of Algren's novel.

1950

Preface to *L'Artiste et sa conscience: Esquisse d'une dialectique de la conscience artistique (The Artist and His Conscience: Sketch for a Dialectic of the Artistic Consciousness),* by René Leibowitz

"Faux savants ou faux lièvres?" ("Which Are False, the Wise Men or the Elephants?"), preface to *Le Communisme yougoslave depuis la rupture avec Moscou (Yugoslavian Communism Since the Break with Moscow),* by Louis Dalmas

Preface to *La Fin de l'espoir (The End of Hope),* by Juan Hermanos

Preface to *Portrait de l'aventurier: T. E. Lawrence, Malraux, Von Salomon (Portrait of the Adventurer: T. E. Lawrence, Malraux, Von Salomon),* by Roger Stéphane

4. *Force of Circumstance,* p. 204.

"Les Jours de notre vie" ("The Days of Our Life"), an article; *Les Temps modernes,* no. 51 (January), pp. 1153–68

Reply to a questionnaire, "Is Neutrality Possible?" in *L'Observateur,* no. 9 (June 9), p. 31

"Jean Genet, ou Le Bal des voleurs" ("Jean Genet, or the Thieves' Ball"), a series of six articles; *Les Temps modernes,* no. 57 (July), pp. 12–47; no. 58 (August), pp. 193–233; no. 59 (September), pp. 402–43; no. 60 (October), pp. 668–703; no. 61 (November), pp. 848–95; no. 62 (December), pp. 1038–70

"The Chances of Peace," excerpts from a long letter-article addressed to the American people; *The Nation* (30 December), pp. 696–700

Undoubtedly the most important political statement to appear under Sartre's name in 1950, in the eyes of many people, was "Les Jours de notre vie" ("The Days of Our Life"), published under his name and that of Merleau-Ponty in the January issue of *Les Temps modernes.* It protested the existence of the Soviet concentration camps. However, the article had been drafted by Merleau-Ponty alone, although Sartre had agreed to publish the details about the camps when the information was brought to him by Roger Stéphane in November 1949. Simone de Beauvoir commented that the article displeased everyone, or almost everyone, but especially the Communists, who redoubled their criticism of Sartre.

Sartre abandoned his work on ethics at this time because he felt that "the moral attitude appears when technical and social conditions render positive forms of conduct impossible. Ethics is a collection of idealistic tricks intended to enable us to live the life imposed on us by the poverty of our resources and the insufficiency of our techniques."[1] Although he was working with Merleau-Ponty on *Les Temps modernes,* the magazine was going through a slack period, and Sartre himself was little involved in political activity. Simone de Beauvoir commented: "four years before we had been everyone's friends, now we were looked upon by everyone as enemies."[2]

Sartre was reading a lot of history and economics; he reread Marx; and he worked on a preface to Genet that began to take

1. Unpublished notes of Sartre, quoted in Simone de Beauvoir, *Force of Circumstance,* trans. Richard Howard (London: Penguin Books, 1968), p. 210.

2. Ibid., p. 209.

on the dimensions of a major work, which was published in part in six issues of *Les Temps modernes*. At the same time he started a book on Italy, to be called "Queen Albemarle and the Last Tourist," which—according to Simone de Beauvoir—"was intended to be the *Nausea* of his maturity, as it were; in it he gave a capricious description of Italy, its present structure, its history and its countryside, and also meditated on what it means to be a tourist."[3] He wrote several hundred pages of it but never had the inclination or the time to revise them and only published tiny fragments of it later. It is evident that he had moved closer to both psychoanalysis and Marxism, and it seemed to him at that time that the possibilities of any individual were strictly limited by his situation. The individual's liberty consisted in not accepting his situation passively but, by the manner of his existence, interiorizing and transcending it in order to give it meaning.[4]

In the spring, at Leiris's suggestion, Sartre and Simone de Beauvoir decided to make a trip to the Sahara and to Black Africa to find out and publish the facts about the repression of the leaders of the Révolution démocratique africaine (RDA). Unfortunately, the trip was a failure: Sartre developed a high fever and was quite sick, but, worse than that, he was unable to make any political contact with the RDA because they had received strict instructions from the French Communists to have nothing to do with him. Sartre was very upset by this rejection.

On his return to Paris he quarreled with Dolores, who, against Sartre's wishes, had come to live in France, and they eventually separated. At that time, too, Simone de Beauvoir went to Chicago to spend two months with Nelson Algren, but their relationship was also nearing its end, with Algren already talking of remarrying his ex-wife.

Of the four prefaces that Sartre wrote and published that year, his "Faux savants ou faux lièvres?" ("Which Are False, the Wise Men or the Elephants?") was undoubtedly the most contentious. In it he revealed his sympathies for Titoism, which was being harshly attacked by the USSR and the French Communists, and went on to a discussion of the theoretical aspects

3. Ibid.
4. Ibid.

of Tito's stand, focusing on the reciprocal relationship between subjectivity and objectivity. He maintained that the dogmatic Marxism of the Stalinist bureaucrats had, by eliminating subjectivity or by equating it with failure, error or treason, made itself incapable of understanding the historical fact of a successful opposition. This line of argument was not well received by the Communists, but his support for Tito won him much sympathy in Yugoslavia. In his preface to the profoundly pessimistic message of Juan Hermanos's *La Fin de l'espoir (The End of Hope)*, Sartre took a stand against the Franco régime, though he was particularly aware of his own political impotence. Sartre's preface to Stéphane's *Portrait de l'aventurier (Portrait of the Adventurer)* permitted him to muse on the qualities of the adventurer, qualities he thought might be used to good effect by the militant, a theme to which he returned in *Le Diable et le bon Dieu*.

In his preface to René Leibowitz's work about the committed musician, *L'Artiste et sa conscience: Esquisse d'une dialectique de la conscience artistique (The Artist and His Conscience: Sketch for a Dialectic of the Artistic Consciousness)*, Sartre argued that since music in itself has no ideological content, because it produces *sense* rather than *signification,* the musician's commitment resides in his overall involvement in the contradictions of his time.

The Korean war brought out major differences between Sartre and Merleau-Ponty, which were particularly important as far as the content of *Les Temps modernes* was concerned, since not a single article was devoted to this issue. Merleau-Ponty, who at this time was virtually running the magazine, was becoming, according to Simone de Beauvoir, totally apolitical. Sartre, on the other hand, although "drifting in uncertainty,"[5] continued to express his dislike and distrust of the polarization between the USSR and the United States. In June *L'Observateur* printed Sartre's response to a questionnaire it had sent out to prominent figures in France on the subject "Is Neutrality Possible?" His judgment was that France should adopt a policy of neutrality in order to remove the justification for America's undertaking a war against Russia in the name of the defense of Free Europe. He expressed similar judgments

5. Jean-Paul Sartre, *Situations,* vol. IV (Paris: Gallimard, 1964), p. 240.

in a letter-article published in the American journal *The Nation* (30 December) in response to the question "Is it possible to negotiate an agreement with Russia without sacrificing the democratic principle?" Sartre replied that as neutrals, determined to resist all aggression, the European nations would be more useful to the cause of peace than as military allies. He added some remarks on the reasons why America kept finding itself under attack from world opinion. The Communists always followed the principle of putting themselves on the side of the exploited and oppressed, except where Russian interests required a different position. By contrast, the Americans, when they held power in Korea, for example, had not pushed through agrarian reforms in the south and therefore found themselves defending a population that was extremely dubious about its "protector." He argued that the best way for America to regain world confidence was to take a "calculated risk": risking not war but peace.

It was during this period that Sartre and Simone de Beauvoir began to spend evenings listening to music in her apartment. With Boris Vian, writer and jazz trumpeter, to guide her, she bought a phonograph and assembled a record library that went from Monteverdi to Berg, Beethoven, Ravel, Stravinsky and Bartok, with a strong preference for jazz: Charlie Parker, Duke Ellington and Dizzy Gillespie.

1951

Le Diable et le bon Dieu (The Devil and the Good Lord), a play in 3 acts and 11 tableaux (Paris: Gallimard)

"Gide vivant" ("The Living Gide"), a tribute to André Gide, written after his death in February 1951; *Les Temps modernes,* no. 65 (March), pp. 1537–41

A major part of 1951 was taken up with the writing and production of *Le Diable et le bon Dieu.* Sartre was working on it when he and Simone de Beauvoir went off to the ski slopes of Auron during the Christmas holidays: Sartre decided to forego the skiing, not only so that he could get on with his work but also so that he might avoid the public gaze. Back in Paris, Simone Berriau put the play into rehearsal before Sartre had even finished the last few scenes. Already it was far too long, and so the daily rehearsal saw Sartre under pressure from Simone Berriau, not only to finish it as quickly as possible but also to make several cuts. Small wonder that tensions abounded: Louis Jouvet, who had been forcefully chosen by Simone Berriau to produce the play, loathed Sartre's blasphemies and was clearly uncommitted to the play's message; several arguments ensued, and Jouvet was to die of a heart ailment later in the year. Neither did Sartre always see eye to eye with Pierre Brasseur, who was playing the difficult role of Goetz: in fact, on opening night Sartre was at such loggerheads, not only with Jouvet and Brasseur but also with Simone Berriau, that he was not invited to the celebratory supper at Maxim's. (On the positive side, Sartre's friendship with Camus, which was being sorely tried, had a brief period of renewal.) The ostentation of the means employed to stage the play (the program proudly mentioned the 19,400 hours of work required to effect the décors and the costumes) all added to the keen anticipation that surrounded opening night.

The inspiration for *Le Diable et le bon Dieu* came from a play by Cervantes, *The Lucky Rascal,* but as recounted to Sartre by Jean-Louis Barrault in 1943, when they had both been teaching at Charles Dullin's school. The play was set in the 16th century, during the Peasants' Revolt. Like the main character in Cervantes' play, Sartre's hero, Goetz, does evil at the start and then, on the cast of a die, decides to devote himself just as resolutely to good. But he discovers that, regardless of whether he does good or evil, the results are the same and the same disasters befall him, because in both cases his acts are determined by relations with God rather than by relations with men. Between the Devil and the Lord, Goetz chooses man, and—unlike Hugo, the young bourgeois idealist in *Les Mains sales*—comes to understand the imperatives of concrete action.

Le Diable et le bon Dieu opened at the Théâtre Antoine on 7 June 1951, with settings by Félix Labisse and the following cast for the main parts: Goetz—Pierre Brasseur, Heinrich—Jean Vilar, Hilda—Maria Casarès, Catherine—Marie-Olivier, Nasty—Henri Nassiet, Karl—R.-J. Chauffard. The opening was the event of the theatrical season, and the play, which caused a scandal in Catholic circles, was a very big hit: it ran continuously until March 1952 and was revived in September of the same year for a special series of 30 performances.

In sharp contrast, earlier that year, in January, *The Flies* had reopened at the Vieux-Colombier with Olga Kosakiewicz, only recently cured of a serious illness, playing the role of Electra, which she had originally created, and Hermantier as director. Unfortunately, Olga had not yet recovered complete control of her powers, and Hermantier was not a good director, with the result that the play was a total flop, Simone de Beauvoir describing the performance as "execrable."

1 February: *Les Nouvelles littéraires* published an interview with Sartre in which, for a change, he was presented sympathetically. About his influence on the young he said that the people who condemned him for perverting the young had an interest in concealing the fact that the causes of the corruption were social. Because they were blinded by a personalist bourgeois culture, they focused on the individual when in fact the causes were general. And, as they wished to remain ignorant of collective factors, they made a writer their scapegoat. Questioned about the existentialists' stress on the base bodily functions, he replied that the reason why existentialists mentioned even the most humble functions of the body was that one must not forget that the spirit descends into the body, or, in other words, the psychological into the physiological. He did not speak about these things for his amusement but because in his view a writer ought to grasp man whole.[1]

In late February, Sartre wrote a tribute to André Gide on the occasion of his death: "Gide vivant" ("The Living Gide"), which appeared in the March issue of *Les Temps modernes*. Sartre had first met Gide in 1939. Two years later, after his return from captivity, Sartre founded a group of resistance intellectuals and went off to find Gide in the south of France in an effort to establish contacts with writers living in the Free Zone. They saw each other three or four times after the war, and it appears that Sartre felt a real friendship for Gide, who

---

1. "Rencontre avec Jean-Paul Sartre," interview by Gabriel d'Aubarède, *Les Nouvelles littéraires* (1 February 1951).

had described *The Respectful Prostitute* as "a kind of master-piece," a comment that greatly endeared him to Sartre.

Sartre's rapprochement with the Communist Party started at about this time. In an interview with *Paris Presse/L'Intransigeant* (7 June 1951), he explained that one's real enemy is always the one who is closest, and that since he was inspired by a rather broad Marxism, he was viewed with enmity by the Stalinist Communists, whose ethic he nevertheless regarded as conformist and petty-bourgeois. However, he went on to say that "Until the new order arrives, the Communist Party represents the proletariat as far as I can see, and I cannot see how that would change in the near future. ... It is impossible to take an anti-Communist position without being against the proletariat." He therefore decided to publicly disassociate himself from the movie version of *Dirty Hands,* directed by Fernand Rivers, which had met with very violent Communist protest, since it was clearly being used as a propaganda device.

July: Sartre and Simone de Beauvoir traveled to Norway, Iceland and Scotland, where in each case they admired the beauty of the landscapes but were less enamored of the life-styles. Scottish austerity appalled them. They experienced difficulty finding rooms, and also found it was impossible to work in them because there was no table and no desk lamp. "If you want to write, go into the writing room," they told Sartre. He had to put his papers on the bed-table or just use his knees. Their meal hours were no less strict; once when they were waiting for a boat at ten in the morning in driving rain, not one hotel would serve them so much as a cup of coffee or a piece of bread: it was too late for breakfast and too early for lunch. Their hearts sank at the grimness of the towns.[2]

In the winter of that year, Sartre took on some new colleagues at *Les Temps modernes:* Marcel Péju, Claude Lanzmann, Guy de Chambure and Bernard Dort. Lanzmann and Péju particularly helped Sartre "repoliticize" the magazine, and "it was they more than anyone else who oriented it toward that 'critical fellow-travelling' which Merleau-Ponty had abandoned."[3] Si-

2. Simone de Beauvoir, *Force of Circumstance,* trans. Richard Howard (London: Penguin Books, 1968), p. 260.

3. Ibid., pp. 263–64

mone de Beauvoir commented that the weekly meetings of *Les Temps modernes'* staff were the only bright spot in a very depressing period of their lives. Nationally and internationally things were going from bad to worse, with war between the United States and the USSR an ever-present possibility, and personally things seemed bleak and unpromising. Sartre continued to work with great determination but in an isolated way. Whilst revising his political position, he was pursuing at the same time an exhausting inner development and time-consuming studies. Simone missed his old insouciance and the golden age when they had always had so much time to go on strolls through Paris, and spend evenings at the cinema.[4]

1952

Saint Genet, comédien et martyr (Saint Genet, Actor and Martyr), (Paris: Gallimard)

Preface to the *Guides Nagel, Les Pays nordiques,* a travel guide.

"Sommes-nous en démocratie?" ("Are We in a Democracy?"), an article; *Les Temps modernes* no. 78 (April), pp. 1729–33.

"Les Communistes et la paix" ("The Communists and Peace"), two articles; *Les Temps modernes* no. 81 (July pp. 1–50, and nos. 84–85, October–November), pp. 695–763.

"Un Parterre de capucines" ("A Garden of Capucines"), an article; *L'Observateur* (24 July), pp. 16–17.

"Reponse à Albert Camus" ("Reply to Albert Camus"), an article; *Les Temps modernes* no. 82 (August), pp. 334–53.

Various texts relating to the Congress of Vienna

Sartre's rapprochement with the Communist Party began to take a concrete form. He realized that he could no longer stay aloof. He realized that he was a victim of and an accomplice in the class struggle: a victim because he was hated by an entire class; an accomplice because he felt both responsible and powerless. He discovered the class struggle through the "slow dismemberment that tore us away from them (the workers) more

4. Ibid., p. 267.

and more each day . . . . I believed in it, but I did not imagine that it was total . . . . I discovered it *against* myself.¹ So when Claude Roy and Jean Chaintron asked Sartre to participate in the campaign for Henri Martin, a Communist sailor imprisoned for distributing leaflets condemning the French military action in Indochina, he was only too ready to assist, and in January he presented a demand to President Auriol for Martin to be pardoned. He also agreed to collaborate with the Communists on a book about the Henry Martin affair.

Spring: Sartre went on a trip to the south of France with Bost, Michèle Vian and Simone de Beauvoir. Michèle had separated from Boris, and Sartre, who had always found her attractive, had become intimately involved with her. Simone liked her very much; in fact everyone always liked her because she never seemed to put herself first. "Gay and rather mysterious, very discreet and yet very much there, she was a charming companion.² Sartre and Michèle then went off to spend three weeks in Italy. During this period he was working on his study of Mallarmé.

Sartre's radicalization took another step forward a few months later when he learned of the arrest of Jacques Duclos, one of the leaders of the Communist Party, who participated in the demonstrations against NATO and General Ridgeway, who was coming to take over from Eisenhower as head of SHAPE. The police discovered two pigeons in the trunk of Duclos's car and construed them to be homing pigeons used to plot with the Soviets rather than accepting his statement that they were in fact intended for his Sunday lunch. This, and the Henri Martin affair, coupled with the reading of Henri Guillemin's *Coup du 2 décembre,* were the basic elements in Sartre's radicalization. He claimed that the exposures by Guillemin gave him an insight into "just how much shit can be crammed into a middle-class heart." It was at this time that he became a fellow traveler of the Communists. He was not completely radicalized, however, for if he had been it would have taken him

1. Sartre's unpublished notes, quoted in Simone de Beauvoir, *Force of Circumstance,* trans. Richard Howard (London: Penguin Books, 1968), pp. 272–73.
2. Ibid., p. 270.

even further left, beyond the Party itself. But it was nonetheless a step in that direction.[3] (*Sartre by Himself,* 1972, p. 72)

With this renewed hatred for the bourgeoisie, Sartre felt that if he did not express what he felt, he would choke. He wrote, day and night, the first part of "The Communists and Peace," which appeared in the July edition of *Les Temps modernes,* a month before his "Reply to Camus." These two pieces of writing had the same implication: the postwar period was over. There could be no more postponements, no more conciliations were possible. They felt forced into making clear-cut choices. Despite the difficulty of his position, Sartre still felt he had been right to adopt it. "His mistake up to that point had been, he thought, to try to resolve the conflict without *transcending* his situation.[4] For four years, with the exception of writing *Kean,* Sartre's ctivities were to be almost entirely dominated by politics.

"Friendships and rejections became a matter of passion," since, in Sartre's eyes, they mirrored the class struggle. With the publication of *L'Homme révolté (The Rebel)* by Camus in 1951, in which Camus expressed philosophical, ethical and political views very opposed to Sartre's, their already tempestuous relationship came to the breaking point. Sartre, out of friendship for Camus, had not wanted the review for *Les Temps modernes* to be too unkind, but, in the event, the one written by Francis Jeanson in May 1952 was extremely biting and accused Camus of rejecting "history" and of emulating the moralizing, ineffectual attitude of the "noble soul."[5] Camus was incensed by the criticism and more particularly by the fact that it appeared as a betrayal of their friendship, since not Sartre, but Jeanson, had been chosen to lead the attack. Camus therefore replied directly to Sartre, addressing him as "M. le Directeur"[6] in a cold and curt tone, saying that he was tired of getting "lessons in effectiveness from professional critics who never put

3. *Sartre by Himself,* from the text of the film by Alexandre Astruc and Michel Contat, trans. Richard Seaver (New York: Urizen Books, 1978), p. 72.

4. *Force of Circumstance,* p. 274.

5. "Albert Camus ou l'âme révolté" ("Albert Camus, or The Rebel Soul"), pp. 2077–90.

6. *"Lettre au directeur des Temps modernes"* ("Letter to the Editor of *Les Temps modernes"),* (30 June 1952), *Les Temps Modernes,* no. 82 (August), pp. 317–33.

any more than their armchairs on the line of history." Sartre, feeling he had to defend Jeanson, replied even more harshly. Jeanson inveighed yet again against Camus in another article, "Pour tout vous dire" ("To Tell You the Whole Truth").[7] All of this was accompanied by widespread publicity of a sensational kind. Their friendship was over, and Sartre and Camus never saw each other again. Despite the *ad hominem* comments, the articles were of a high quality and typified the polarization that existed in postwar French intellectual life.

Simone de Beauvoir's inevitably partial account of the relationship between Sartre and Camus is interesting. According to her, the reason why the friendship seemed to explode so violently was because for a long time not much of it had remained. The political and ideological differences which already existed between Sartre and Camus in 1945 had intensified from year to year. In her view, Camus was an idealist, a moralist and an anti-Communist; forced to yield to History, he attempted to secede from it; whilst sensitive to men's suffering, he imputed it to Nature. Sartre, by contrast, had laboured since 1940 to repudiate idealism, to wrench himself away from his original individualism, to live in History. Sartre's position was close to Marxism, and he desired an alliance with the Communists. Although Camus was fighting for great principles, usually he refused to participate in the particular and detailed political actions to which Sartre committed himself. Sartre believed in the truth of socialism, whereas Camus became a more and more resolute champion of bourgeois values; *The Rebel* was a statement of his solidarity with them. When a neutralist position between the two power blocs had become impossible, Sartre drew nearer to the U.S.S.R.; Camus, who hated the Russians, although he did not like the United States, went over to the American side.[8]

Conor Cruise O'Brien, in his study of Camus, pointed out that wherever there was a public capable of being interested in the Sartre-Camus controversy, that public was encouraged to see in Camus, not in Sartre, "the exemplar of the truly independent intellectual." The account of the controversy best known in America is the essay "Sartre versus Camus, a Political

7. *Les Temps modernes* no. 82 (August 1952), pp. 354–83.
8. *Force of Circumstance*, pp. 271–72.

Quarrel" (originally published in 1952) by Nicola Chiaromonte, which allowed no merit whatever to Sartre's side in the controversy and accused Sartre of being an amateur Communist, intellectually dominated by the Marxist-Leninist-Stalinist mentality, guilty of moral smugness and intellectual arrogance, and spreading "the intellectual confusion by which the Communist Party benefits." But Chiaromonte's account amounted to United States government propaganda. He was at that time director of *Tempo Presente,* the Italian magazine supported by the Congress for Cultural Freedom, which was covertly subsidized by the Central Intelligence Agency.[9]

In his two articles on "The Communists and Peace"—the third was not written until a year and a half later—Sartre defended the Communist Party against various accusations made by the Right and the non-Communist Left. He was concerned to find out the extent to which the Communist Party was the *necessary* expression of the working class and the extent to which it was the *exact* expression of it. In the second article he tried to explain why the workers' strike on 4 June failed: their discouragement came from their feeling of powerlessness and isolation as individuals; the Communist Party with its revolutionary praxis would transform them into a powerful, united *class,* conscious of their common interest. His stand caused wide repercussions on the left, particularly among the staff of *Les Temps modernes.* Merleau-Ponty was in violent disagreement, and resigned after the appearance of the third article the following year.

Saint Genet, Actor and Martyr, though difficult to classify, is a major work. It was received with the usual fanfare and, in some circles, horror. As a philosophical essay, it is situated between *Being and Nothingness* and *Critique of Dialectical Reason,* in that it uses both existential psychoanalysis and a Marxist method of analysis; and as a critical literary essay, it comes between *Baudelaire* and the "Flaubert" that was to come. In contrast to his work on *Baudelaire,* Sartre treats the man, Genet, and his work as an indissoluble whole, within which, by a dialectical process, the work produces the man as much as it is produced by him. Sartre greatly admired Genet—who was a thief, sophist and pederast—as "one of the heroes of our time" for having freed himself from the weight of his past, for having

9. Conor Cruise O'Brien, *Albert Camus* (New York: Viking Press, 1970), pp. 73–74.

made something out of what other people had made of him. His aim in the book was to "retrace in detail the history of a liberation . . . . to show that psychoanalytic interpretation and Marxist explanation have their limits, and that freedom alone can account for a person in his totality . . . ."[10]

Summer: Sartre began to get interested in the Peace Movement's activities, and he took part, as an individual, in the People's Peace Congress, organized in Vienna from 12 to 19 December by the World Council for Peace. He spoke in favor of peaceful coexistence based on East-West exchanges, reunification of Germany without changing the economic régime of the two zones, peace in Indochina and admission of China to the United Nations. Also in the fall of 1952 he signed the National Writers' Committee's "Manifesto Against the Cold War." The time for abstention was past.

It was at this point that Sartre's life-style changed. He had become a celebrity and could no longer hang around in cafés, or do whatever he wanted, or say what he felt like. He was obliged to hire a secretary to answer some of his letters, and sort out who he could see and not see. Simone de Beauvoir viewed the change as a loss—"the loss of a certain happy-go-lucky attitude he'd always had. But it was a necessary loss. And the change never carried over into his psychology."[11]

1953

L'Affaire Henri Martin (The Henri Martin Affair), a commentary (Paris: Gallimard)

"Mallarmé, 1842–1898," a critical article in *Les Écrivains célèbres,* vol. 3, ed. Raymond Queneau, pp. 148–151.

"Ce que j'ai vu à Vienne, c'est la paix" (What I Saw in Vienna Was Peace), text of Sartre's speech at the Congress of Vienna; *Les Lettres françaises* 1–8 January.

10. Jean-Paul Sartre, *Saint Genet, Actor and Martyr* (New York: G. Braziller, 1963), p. 536.

11. Comment by Simone de Beauvoir in the text of the film *Sartre by Himself,* p. 75.

"Réponse à Claude Lefort" ("Reply to Claude Lefort"), the third article on "The Communists and Peace"; *Les Temps modernes* no. 89 (April) pp. 1571–629.

For Sartre this was a year of intense political debate, alleviated by the writing of only one "literary" piece: an adaptation of Dumas's *Kean* on the suggestion of Pierre Brasseur, who wished to play the title role. This he wrote in the summer in Rome "in a few weeks, and with a great deal of enjoyment."[1] For once the rehearsals went off without any problems, and on 14 November the play had its première at the Théâtre Sarah-Bernhardt and was a huge success.

15 January: Sartre attended the inaugural lecture of Maurice Merleau-Ponty at the Collège de France, but by May their political disagreements were becoming so strong that Merleau-Ponty threatened to resign from the editorial board of *Les Temps modernes* over the publication of an article by Pierre Naville, of whom Merleau-Ponty disapproved. Sartre tried to stop him from leaving, but they were already too far apart: "We accused each other of abusing power, I suggested an immediate meeting, I tried all ways of making him change his mind: he was immovable. I did not see him for a few months; he never again appeared at the *Temps modernes* and was never involved in it again."[2]

At about the same time that Sartre was wrangling with Merleau-Ponty, a new controversy arose between Sartre and Mauriac about the question of anti-Semitism in the USSR. Mauriac had accused Sartre of remaining silent on the issue,[3] to which Sartre replied that he was about to discuss the problem in *Les Temps modernes* but that he had no intention of speaking about it merely to win *Le Figaro's* esteem and would instead address himself to "his friends on the Left, whether they be Communists or not, Jews or not, because the problem concerns them first of all, and for them alone takes the form of a drama. They alone,

1. Simone de Beauvoir, *Force of Circumstance,* trans. Richard Howard (London: Penguin Books, 1968). p. 310.

2. Jean-Paul Sartre, *Situations,* vol. IV (paris: Gallimard, 1964), p. 260.

3. *Le Figaro* (17 March 1953).

and not M. Mauriac, have the right to ask me what I think, and they're the only ones I want to ask about their thoughts."[4]

One of Sartre's articles that had helped precipitate Merleau-Ponty's resignation was his "Réponse à Claude Lefort," who was a friend of Merleau-Ponty, an intellectual with a Trotskyist background and a regular collaborator of *Les Temps modernes.* Lefort had criticized Sartre's conception of the revolutionary praxis of the working class and of the role of the party. The debate centered on the differences between those who held to "spontaneism" and those who held to "democratic centralism" within the international labor movement. At this point Sartre supported Lenin's Bolshevik theses. Sartre's reply elaborates and expands the ideas that he had already expressed in "The Communists and Peace."

Sartre had been greatly impressed by the Congress of Vienna the previous year and wished to convince people of its importance. He said that there had been only three extraordinary experiences in his life since he became a man, three "which suddenly gave me hope again: the Popular Front of 1936, the Liberation, and the Congress of Vienna."[5] He went on to show how the press mystified people and provoked their mistrust by presenting the congress as Communist-inspired. He gave examples of lies by the press and how several incidents were deliberately misinterpreted by the correspondents for the bourgeois press. In response to arguments that tried to minimize the importance of what had been accomplished in Vienna, Sartre maintained that what had been important was not so much the final resolutions but more the contacts, discussions and the fraternity between men of different beliefs. "So I testify that the Congress of Vienna is, and, in spite of all the slander, will remain a historic event."

In May he made a speech at a meeting of the Peace Movement during a debate at the Mutualité on the war in Indochina. Sartre tried to show that the government's intention of internationalizing the war at a time when negotiations had begun to end the Korean conflict made French policy one of the principal causes of international tension, which risked causing worldwide conflict.

4. *L'Observateur* (19 March 1953).

5. "Ce que j'ai vu à Vienne, c'est la paix" ("What I Saw in Vienna Was Peace"), *Les Lettres françaises,* (1–8 January 1953).

Although Simone de Beauvoir was now living with Claude Lanzmann, she and Sartre still made a point of spending at least part of every summer together. Having spent July in Rome, which was to become his annual summer retreat, Sartre went off to spend the following month in Amsterdam with Simone de Beauvoir, and during their wanderings in the countryside, he was able to show her the remains of the stalag where he had been a prisoner. Simone de Beauvoir felt grave doubts about her capacity to hold on to her relationship with Sartre at this time, especially since she was spending so much time with Lanzmann but also because Sartre was intensely involved in his political activities, a development that she did not wholeheartedly welcome. She said of the situation that at first she had been afraid that Lanzmann would not be able to accept her relationship with Sartre; but eventually Lanzmann was taking up so much room in her life that she began to wonder if her understanding with Sartre would suffer in consequence. The life Sartre and she led together was no longer quite the same. He had never before been so absorbed by his political activity, his writing, all his work; in fact he was overworked. She was profiting from her rediscovered youth; she gave herself to each moment as it came. She was sure that they would always remain intimate friends, but wondered whether their destinies, hitherto entwined, might eventually separate. Later she was reassured. The equilibrium she had achieved, thanks to Lanzmann, to Sartre, and to her own vigilance, was durable and endured.[6] Lanzmann, it should be said, greatly approved of Sartre's new commitment to politics, which he considered to be more essential than literature. He was not one of the ones, who, on the publication of *L'Affaire Henri Martin* in October, suggested that Sartre would be better employed working on his "ethics" or on his novel.

L'Affaire Henri Martin was not in fact published until after Martin's release. The book contained a number of articles and documents detailing the whole matter, edited by Sartre with a 100-page commentary by him. According to Contat and Rybalka: "Sartre's is a model text of a kind which numbers few successes—the polemical commentary on present history. A model of style in the first place, swift and effective; incomparable too in its lively or sarcastic irony; but a model also of the

6. *Force of Circumstance*, p. 309.

strict honesty of a defender trying to convince and never over-whelm . . . ."[7]

Toward the end of the year, Sartre had the idea of writing an autobiography. "Having been thrown in to the atmosphere of action, I suddenly clearly saw the kind of neurosis which had dominated all my previous work."[8] "It took me a long time to understand the importance of my childhood, and not only be-cause of my resistance to psychoanalysis; basically this resist-ance pointed up the importance of psychoanalysis: it was my childhood that I was rejecting."[9] Later, in 1962, Sartre decided to undergo psychoanalysis, out of intellectual curiosity, with J. -B. Pontalis, but in view of his close personal relationship with Sartre, Pontalis declined.

1954

Kean, an adaptation in five acts of *Kean ou Désordre et génie (Kean, or Disorder and Genius),* a comedy by Alexandre Dumas (Paris: Gallimard)

Preface to *D'une Chine à l'autre (From One China to the Other),* by Henri Cartier-Bresson and Jean-Paul Sartre

"Opération 'Kanapa' " ("Operation 'Kanapa' "), an article; *Les Temps modernes,* no. 100 (March) pp. 1723–28.

"Les Communistes et la paix" ("The Communists and Peace"), III, an article, *Les Temps modernes,* no. 101 (April), pp. 1731–819.

"Les Peintures de Giacometti" ("The Paintings of Giacometti"), a piece written for a show at the Maeght Gallery (14 May–15 June 1954); *Maeght Gallery Review,* no. 65, and *Les Temps modernes,* no. 103 (June) pp. 2221–32.

"Julius Fucik," an article; *Les Lettres françaises* (June 17–24,)

"La Bombe H, une arme contre l'histoire" ("The H-Bomb, a Weapon Against History"), *Défense de la Paix,* no. 38 (July), pp. 18–22.

7. Michel Contat and Michel Rybalka, *The Writings of Jean-Paul Sartre,* 2 vol., trans. Richard C. McCleary (Evanston, Ill.: Northwestern University Press, 1974), p. 280.

8. Interview in *Le Monde* (18 April 1964).

9. "Conversations with John Gerassi" (unpublished, 1973).

"Le Impressions de Jean-Paul Sartre sur son voyage en U.R.S.S."
("Jean-Paul Sartre's Impressions on His Trip to the USSR"), comments gathered by Jean Bedel in five articles in *Libération* (July
15–22).

For Simone de Beauvoir 1953 had ended well: on a personal
level her relationship with Claude Lanzmann was flourishing,
and on an international level there seemed to be a movement
toward détente: communism had triumphed in China, and Mao
Tse-tung was about to become president of the new People's
Republic; the Korean war ended; Ho Chi Minh let it be known
that he was prepared to negotiate; Nagy had just abolished the
concentration camps in Hungary; to sympathizers, the USSR
appeared to be developing toward a greater political and intellectual democracy; and when Malenkov announced that the
USSR possessed the H-bomb, the likelihood of a world conflict
seemed to be removed for some time to come, on the assumption
that a "balance of terror" was better than terror without any
balance.

But for Sartre, this was the beginning of one of the most
difficult periods of his life, which was to last until 1959, when
ill health, the direct result of fatigue and overwork, overtook
him. Internationally, 1954 failed to live up to the hopes of the
previous year: France, supported by America, rejected Ho Chi
Minh's advances, and on 13 March the battle for Dien Bien
Phu was joined; America exploded a bomb on Bikini, and the
witch hunts in America showed no signs of abating.

In February, Sartre, on the invitation of Elsa Triolet, participated in a conference of writers from East and West at
Knokke-le-Zoute in Belgium, and it was as a result of this that
he was invited by the Russian writers to visit Moscow in May.
But he had a lot of work to do before then: he was writing the
preface to Cartier-Bresson's book of photographs, *D'Une Chine
à l'autre,* and the third part of "The Communists and Peace,"
which was published in April, and he was to participate in the
World Council for Peace in Berlin in May. He was already suffering from high blood pressure, and his doctor had prescribed
a long rest in the country; "he did no more than take a few
drugs,"[1] since he did not particularly like the countryside. He

1. Simone de Beauvoir, *Force of Circumstance,* trans. Richard Howard (London:
Penguin Books, 1968), p. 316.

commented to Francis Jeanson at about this time that for the first three days (in the countryside) he was incapable of sleeping, the silence made him dizzy, and he felt as if he were perpetually floating.[2]

24 May: Sartre set off for Berlin en route to Moscow, having as yet had no time to prepare his speech. Entitled "The Universality of History and Its Paradox" and later published as "The H-bomb, a Weapon Against History," this speech, prepared on the plane, dealt with the appearance of weapons capable of demolishing the Earth and, on the other hand, the intervention in world affairs of countries that had been colonialized and that, in order to gain independence, were starting national wars against which atomic bombs were powerless.

26 May: Sartre arrived in Moscow, the start of a four-week gruelling round of talks, sightseeing, meetings, visits, journeys, banquets. He was, for example, supposed to spend 48 hours in Samarkand, during which he had expressed a wish to spend one of the two days on his own. The officials were surprised at this request, since "beauty doesn't cease to be beauty just because there are forty people looking at it at once"[3] and attributed it to his bourgeois individualism. In the event the trip was cut to a single day. Various notables escorted Sartre to look at palaces and mosques dating from the reign of Tamburlaine, with the whole trip punctuated by long and detailed accounts of each building. "Then the interpreter spread his arms and shooed everyone away: 'And now, Jean-Paul Sartre wishes to be alone.' They all moved off, and Sartre was left standing there, waiting until he could decently join them."[4]

But the toughest challenges to Sartre's stamina came during the festive occasions, at banquets, where there were always heavy drinking bouts. At Simonov's *dacha* there was a four-hour banquet, 20 toasts in vodka, and his glass was continually filled with Armenian vin rosé and Georgian red wine. One of the guests said of him, "He must be a good man, because he

---

2. Francis Jeanson, *Sartre dans sa vie* (Paris: Editions du Seuil, 1974); note, p. 206.

3. *Force of Circumstance,* p. 319.

4. Ibid., p. 320.

eats and drinks sincerely"—high praise, which Sartre felt he had to live up to. Similarly, after his visit to Tashkent, an engineer challenged him to a vodka duel; "his challenger then accompanied him out to the airport, where he sank into a heap on the asphalt, a great moment of triumph for Sartre, who then managed to get to his seat and immediately sank into a leaden sleep."[5] The very next day he was invited to a lunch with Simonov in Moscow, where again the wine flowed freely and again his ability to withstand alcohol was seen as a singular virtue. At the end of the meal Simonov presented Sartre with a drinking horn "of imposing dimensions" full of wine: "Empty or full, you shall take it with you," and Sartre did what was expected of him. That afternoon and night his heart would not stop pounding, and the following day, since he felt unable to attend a meeting with a group of philosophers that had been arranged for him, a doctor was called, and he was immediately admitted to a hospital, where he remained for 10 days.

On his return to Paris, Sartre was clearly far from well: he gave a long and enthusiastic interview about his trip to the USSR to *Libération* but did not feel up to checking it over afterward. This was published as five separate articles, generally of a low level and lacking Sartre's usual critical sense. As a result, he became embroiled in a controversy over the USSR with Hélène and Pierre Lazareff, who had traveled there at about the same time as Sartre but returned with very unfavorable impressions. His reply, which was published in *Libération* on 22 July, was written from Italy, where Sartre was taking a much-needed rest in the company of Michèle Vian, which may explain the more detached, even playful tone that he tried to bring to the debate.

Later in the summer, toward the end of August, Sartre and Simone de Beauvoir traveled to Germany, Austria and Czechoslovakia. His initial fatigue and feeling of disgust for the whole business of writing—"Literature is a lot of horseshit," he told Simone[6]—gave way to a gradual recovery of morale, when, in Salzburg, he began to write again. Their trip ended in Vienna, where, without Sartre's permission, a production of *Les Mains sales* was about to be presented. Since he had already decided

5. Ibid.
6. Ibid., p. 323.

that this play could not be produced without the permission of the local Communist Party, he protested and explained his position to a press conference.

In the fall *The Mandarins,* by Simone de Beauvoir, was published, winning her the prestigious Goncourt prize. She took great pains to avoid press publicity after the announcement, granting only one interview, to *Humanité-Dimanche,* to explain that her novel was not hostile to the Communists. With her prize money, she was able to buy an apartment, and she and Lanzmann moved in together. The one thing that tormented Simone de Beauvoir particularly strongly during this period was the sudden realization that Sartre would die. It was something she had never faced up to; in order to counter it, she invoked her own disappearance from the world, which, though it filled her with terror, also reassured her. However, the threat was still the same; whether it was in twenty years, or tomorrow, he was going to die. "A black enlightenment!"[7]

Of the works published in 1954, *Kean* was perhaps closest to Sartre's heart, dealing as it did with the theme of the traitor, the bastard, who, in order to escape his resentment against society, becomes an actor, whose role is to reveal the posturings and falsehoods of the society that nurtured him. At another level it treats the myth of the actor, the actor who does not know when he is acting, who does not know who he is. With Brasseur, the actor, playing Kean, the actor, the audience was treated to a mystifying game of mirrors reflecting the underlying theme of the "actor trap." Sartre said of his own role that he had little to do "except scale some rust and air out some mustiness, just clean up a little so that the audience's full attention will be brought to bear on the extraordinary sight of an actor whose role is to play himself."[8] Francis Jeanson commented that Sartre himself was the traitor par excellence, who always refused to be taken for anybody, least of all himself.[9]

December: Sartre was made vice-president of the France-USSR Association, and although he was unable to attend the

---

7. Ibid., p. 319.
8. "About Kean" from the program notes (8 November 1953).
9. *Sartre dans sa vie,* p. 173.

congress in person, he sent a message in which he stressed the need for Franco-Soviet friendship. He was to write a number of articles on this theme for the review *France-U.R.S.S.*

1955

Nékrassov, a play in eight acts; first published in *Les Temps modernes,* nos. 114–117 (June–Sept.); published in book form by Gallimard in 1956.

Various articles about the USSR (in *France-U.R.S.S.,* no. 115 [April] pp. 4–5, and no. 121 [October] pp. 3–4 and interviews about China in *France-Observateur* [1 December and 8 December] and *New Statesman and Nation* [3 December]); an interview article about the theater (in *Théâtre populaire,* no. 15 [September–October] pp. 1–9.

Sartre par lui-même, ("Sartre By Himself") by Francis Jeanson (Paris: Seuil)

North African colonialism was coming under heavy pressure, which brought about considerable realignment on the French political scene. The left hesitated between supporting the FLN and the MNA in Algeria: Francis and Colette Jeanson took the view that the FLN, which demanded independence for the Algerian people, best represented the Algerian majority, and the editorial policy of *Les Temps modernes* became, at the beginning of 1955, one of support for the FLN against the MNA. Later in the year, in May, the *Temps modernes* team published a special issue on "The Left" in an attempt to elucidate the meaning behind the much-misunderstood label, with articles by Claude Lanzmann, Jean Pouillon, Marcel Péju and Claude Bourdet. Simone de Beauvoir wrote an article in which she attempted to define the principles professed by the Right, which were, in her eyes, nothing more than the defense of privileges by the privileged.

Sartre was still occupied with pursuing his friendship links with the Soviet Union and, later in the year, with China. In February he gave a speech at a meeting in the Salle Pleyel organized by the France-USSR Association to commemorate the victory of Stalingrad, in which he urged France to strengthen its ties with the USSR: "Only one attitude is possible—gratitude and friendship—towards a people who have shed their blood to save their future—and the future of the universe—and who have proved by their sacrifices that they meant to make history, not submit to it; towards a people who were for a half a century, each time Germany threatened the peace, always there at our side."[1] This speech, somewhat hyperbolic in tone, marked the height of Sartre's pro-Soviet position. About his relationship with the French Communists during these years he was to say later, in 1972: "I was dealing with men who considered as comrades only people of their party, who, armed with instructions and interdictions, regarded me as a temporary fellow traveler, and, looking prematurely into the future, anticipated the moment when I would have disappeared from the mêlée, co-opted by right-wing forces."[2]

Having been converted to the dialectical method, Sartre was concerned to reconcile it with his basic existentialism and was working very hard toward this end. Roger Garaudy suggested that they put their respective methods to the test by taking a concrete case study—Sartre suggested Flaubert—and analyzing it from an existentialist and a Marxist viewpoint. Sartre worked on an elaborate study for three months, but it was so carelessly put together that there was no question of its being published. He was also working on his autobiography, sifting through his childhood years for reasons that had prompted him to become a writer.

Nékrassov, which had its première at the Théâtre Antoine on 8 June, having already suffered several delays due to changes in the text and tempestuous rehearsals, was not a great success and ran for only 60 performances. It dealt in a satirical way with the methods used by the press to put out anti-Communist propaganda and, as such, met with very violent press reaction. On opening night, a tract handed out by a group called "The Free Center for Russian States" condemned the play as a "mystification of a lounge lizard who never fought anywhere

1. *France-U.R.S.S.*, no. 115 (April, 1955), pp. 4–5. Quoted in Michel Contat and Michel Rybalka, *The Writings of Jean-Paul Sartre,* 2 vol., trans. Richard C. McCleary (Evanston, Ill: Northwestern University Press, 1974), p. 314.

2. Michel Contat and Michel Rybalka, "Chronologie," in the introduction to Jean-Paul Sartre, *Oeuvres romanesques* (Paris: Gallimard, 1981), p. LXXIV.

and whose hands have been dirty ever since he shook those of the executioners of the Russian people." According to Sartre, some newspapers even refused to accept the publicity notices for his play, and those critics who did attend ripped it to shreds. Jean Cocteau, however, defended it in a letter published in *Libération:* He said that Sartre's play was something new. It shook up all the comfortable little commitments everyone had settled into by using Sartre as a reference. In *Nékrassov* he made fun of the people who didn't listen to and hear him properly. But it was with grace, and ease, without there being a shadow of spitefulness in "this *opéra-bouffe,* this end-of-the-century review. I imagine that *The Marriage of Figaro* was the same sort of escapade.[3]

June: Sartre and Simone de Beauvoir attended the Congress of the Peace Movement in Helsinki, where they were both impressed by the strength of the bond that united such disparate peoples in the quest for peaceful solutions. In his speech Sartre called for a new kind of peace, which would be "an indissoluble whole, an indestructable bond between a certain kind of international relations and a certain kind of political and social relations within nations"; he asked for aid to be given by the two great powers to developing nations without any intention to enslave; and he expressed the hope that the increasing consciousness of colonialized peoples should be a factor for peace. During the meetings Sartre had discussions with Ilya Ehrenburg, who asked Sartre not to be too critical of the United States, since conciliation was now the order of the day. It was also here that for the first time Sartre met Lukàcs, with whom, in 1949, he had had a particularly bitter public debate. Of their meeting Sartre had this to say: "Two philosophers who argue almost always do so at the lowest level. I don't like discussing ideas because they serve no purpose: each one sticks to his own position. In philosophy particularly, discussions are sterile: writing is essential. Men are generally inferior in life to what they are in their books."[4]

In June, Merleau-Ponty, who was becoming increasingly irritated by Sartre's pro-Soviet position, published *Les Aventures*

3. *Libération* (20 June 1955).
4. "Chronologie," p. LXXV.

de la dialectique (Adventures of the Dialectic), one chapter of which, entitled "Sartre and Ultra-Bolshevism," brought out the differences between the two philosophers. For once, Sartre remained silent under attack, but Simone de Beauvoir replied forcefully, if not virulently, in an article entitled "Merleau-Ponty and Pseudo-Sartrianism," in which she tried to clarify Sartre's application of the dialectical method.

At about this time Sartre and Simone de Beauvoir met Claude Lanzmann's 22-year-old sister, Evelyne Rey, an actress with a provincial repertory company that was performing *The Three Sisters* in Paris. Both of them liked her a lot, and shortly afterward she took over the role of Estelle in *Huis clos* when it was revived at the Théâtre de l'Athénée, later playing the role of Johanna in *Les Séquestrés d'Altona* (1959) and Estelle again in the televised version of *Huis clos* in 1965, just a few months before her death.

6 September: Sartre and Simone de Beauvoir set off on a two-month visit to China. Earlier in the year, in June, they had gone to see the Peking Opera in Paris, and they had read what Chinese authors they could find in translation, but, nevertheless, they found the country fundamentally foreign to them. And since none of their writings were known in China, mutual ignorance, as well as political constraints, inhibited all personal exchanges. But nothing detracted from their total admiration of a country intent on eradicating poverty: "the immensity of the victories won in only a few years over the scourges that had once held sway in China—dirt, vermin, infant mortality, epidemics, chronic malnutrition, hunger; the people had clothes and clean housing, and something to eat."[5] They were received at the highest official levels: by the vice-minister, Chen-Yi, and by Mao Tse-Tung, but, much to their disappointment, they were not able to enter into any protracted discussions with them. On their way back to France, they stopped off in Moscow, where Sartre participated in a congress of Soviet critics and Simone de Beauvoir was able to appreciate at first hand the Russian hospitality that had so overwhelmed Sartre the year before. Back in Paris, Sartre agreed to write an essay on his trip to

5. Simone de Beauvoir, *Force of Circumstance,* trans. Richard Howard (London: Penguin Books, 1968), p. 345.

China but, in the event, gave up the idea soon afterward. Happily, Simone de Beauvoir took up the suggestion and wrote *The Long March,* which was published in 1957. In addition to working on his autobiography, Sartre was also adapting a film scenario called *The Witches of Salem* from Arthur Miller's play *The Crucible.*

1956

Les Sorcières de Salem (The Salem Witches), a film script drawn from Arthur Miller's play *The Crucible, Les lettres françaises,* Aug. 2–8.
Various articles in *Les Temps modernes:* "Le Réformisme et les fétiches" ("Reformism and Fetishes"), no. 122 (February), pp. 1153–64 "Réponse à Pierre Naville" no. 123 (March–April), pp. 1510–25; "Le Colonialisme est un système" ("Colonialism Is a System"), no. 123 (March–April), pp. 1371–86. An interview-article condemning Soviet intervention in Hungary: *L'Express,* supplement to no. 281 (9 November). The text of a debate entitled "The First East-West Dialogue in Venice Between Merleau-Ponty, Sartre, Silone and the Soviet Writers," *L'Express* (19 October)

World events in 1956 made it difficult for left-wing views to be given a fair hearing: in March the new premier, Guy Mollet, granted independence to Tunisia and Morocco and described the Algerian War as "cruel and lunatic." But a month later he gave in to the army and the million *pieds-noirs,* intensified the war and launched a home front propaganda campaign that attempted to portray Algeria's Moslem majority as wishing to keep their links with France and the rebellion as the result of an Islamic conspiracy promoted by the Arab League and Egypt's Gamal Nasser. *L'Humanité* published accounts of French army atrocities, which the government tried to suppress, and journalists who pursued this line of inquiry were deemed traitors. Keeping Algeria French was seen to be a matter of honor, dignity and grandeur.

Between March and June the number of French soldiers in Algeria doubled, from 190,000 to 380,000, and the entire population of the country was caught up in a great tide of chauvinism and racism. Simone de Beauvoir commented: "If Poujade suddenly lost his importance, it was because everyone in France had become a Poujadist."[1] Sartre wanted the Peace Movement to condemn the war, but this action was considered inopportune, since the Soviet Union feared a French defeat would turn Algeria into an American zone of influence, and the French Communist Party was afraid to appear less nationalistic than the other parties and waged only a muted attack against the government. Protests there were: meetings, strikes, demonstrations and obstructions to the departure of troop trains were organized. Sartre spoke out at an antiwar meeting at the Salle Wagram on 27 January, and *Les Temps modernes* took a position in favor of those who demonstrated their refusal to fight in North Africa. But such was the general climate of opinion that Sartre and Simone de Beauvoir felt very keenly their sense of isolation and powerlessness, knowing that they were out of step with the rest of their countrymen.

In February, Sartre became involved in a polemical discussion with Pierre Hervé, Guy Besse and Pierre Naville about Communist Party ideology and de-Stalinization. Pierre Hervé, a Communist intellectual, in a work entitled *La Révolution et les fétiches,* had for the first time since the death of Stalin dared to criticize the official ideology of the party, particularly for its lack of democratic discussion and its dogmatism. His point of view was violently attacked by the Communist press, especially by Guy Besse, and on 14 February Hervé was expelled from the Communist Party by the Political Bureau. Four days before this expulsion, Sartre published an article in *Les Temps modernes,* moderate in tone, but nevertheless taking them both to task, Hervé for his muddled inadequacies and Besse for his methods of criticism, and, while deploring the stagnation into which Marxism had fallen, he emphasised how important Marx's thought had always been for him. Men of his age he said, were well aware of the fact that, even more than the two world wars, the all-important thing in their lives had been a perpetual confrontation with the working class and with the ideology of the working class which afforded them an irrefutable vision of the world and of themselves. For them, Marxism was

1. Simone de Beauvoir, *Force of Circumstance,* trans. Richard Howard (London: Penguin Books, 1968), p. 352.

not merely a philosophy, it was the climate of their ideas, the environment that nourished them, it was the movement of what Hegel called the Objective Spirit.[2]

Pierre Naville subsequently attacked Sartre in *L'Observateur* for equating Marxism with the Communist Party, a charge that Sartre then strongly denied in an article entitled "Réponse à Pierre Naville,"[3] in which he also tried to explain the meaning of the de-Stalinization announced at the 20th Party Congress. Defending the Communist Party, he said, "I am far from claiming that the Party has never been wrong. I am only saying that on the whole, its stands have been correct." This statement was to ring hollow a few months later when Sartre was to criticize the Soviet intervention in Hungary. At this time, in March, during the legislative elections, Sartre decided for once to exercise his democratic rights and voted for the Communist candidate in his arrondissement.

March: Sartre met Arlette El Kaim, a 19-year-old Jewish Algerian who was living in Versailles, where she was preparing for the competitive examination for entrance to the École Normale Supérieure in Sèvres. She had written to him in connection with her dissertation on the subject of injustice with some questions arising from her reading of *L'Être et le Néant*. As always, Sartre was very responsive and encouraging to young writers, and after a short correspondence, they met. She very soon became his mistress but was not approved of by Simone de Beauvoir, and when, two years later, it was rumored that Arlette was pregnant and that Sartre had been prepared to marry her, the relationship between Sartre and Simone became extremely tense. As it happened, some eight years later, in March 1965, when Arlette was faced with the threat of deportation, Sartre took the decision, very much without Simone's agreement, to make Arlette his adopted daughter. Arlette published short stories in *Les Temps modernes,* and between 1960 and 1965 she collaborated on a film review journal. In the early 1980s, after Sartre's death, the rivalry between Arlette and Simone was rekindled as disputes over the ownership and publication of Sartre's unpublished work became apparent.

2. Quoted in *Force of Circumstance*, p. 354.

3. *Les Temps modernes* no.123 (March–April 1956), pp. 1510–25.

At the end of March, Sartre attended a colloquium in Venice organized by the European Culture Society, an organization founded in 1950 with the aim of bringing together scientists, artists, writers and intellectuals from East and West European countries. Here Sartre again met Merleau-Ponty after a three-year separation, and they became involved in a discussion about the philosophical problems raised by the "thaw" in East-West relations: Merleau-Ponty wondered whether the new Soviet line implied that they were abandoning the "intellectual line of the cold war, according to which the intellectual life is not a dialogue, but a struggle" and whether the thaw was going to provide the basis for a "new universalism." His point of view was that this was possible only at the price of a very "deep and consubstantial change" in the Soviet régime. Sartre pointed out that there needed to be a similar thaw within the non-Communist half of mankind and that bourgeois Western culture was just as determined by the economic structure as was Marxism. Sartre wished to look for a universal, not in the sense of seeking ideas valid in both systems but rather in the sense of asking the Communists to discuss ideas from the Marxist point of view, seeing what they might accept, in the same way that Western thinkers should try to understand ideas from their ideological point of view: a universality through opposition rather than an unopposed universality. At this juncture in their lifelong polemical discussions, Merleau-Ponty accepted Sartre's view that it was the West that needed to "thaw."

Sartre continued to work on his autobiography and a screenplay adaptation of Arthur Miller's *The Crucible,* which dealt with the 1690 witch hunt and trial in Salem, Massachusetts. It was released in April 1957, with Yves Montand and Simone Signoret in the principal roles and directed by Raymond Rouleau, but it was not a huge success: Sartre was considered to have made the speeches too long-winded, and Rouleau was criticized for his over-static direction. He also worked on his study of Flaubert and undertook to do another film script, this one set during the French Revolution, whose main character was to be Joseph Lebon, a commissioner sent by the Public Safety Committee to the Northern Army and guillotined after Thermidor for brutality and excess of violence. Simone de Beauvoir was working very hard on *The Long March* at this time: she would work at home in the mornings and then at Sartre's place in the afternoons.

The summer and early part of the fall were spent traveling with Michèle Vian, Simone and Claude Lanzmann in Italy, Yugoslavia and Greece. In Italy they enjoyed "warm and open-hearted" discussions with Italian Communists—discussions that they felt contrasted starkly with the often prickly relationship that they had with the French Communist Party. But it was in Rome, on 24 October, that they learned of the Soviet intervention in Hungary, an action that threw Sartre and many Soviet sympathizers into the depths of despair. On his return to France, Sartre gave an interview to P. Viansson-Ponté for *L'Express* in which he unreservedly condemned Soviet aggression in Hungary, said that he was "regretfully but completely" breaking off all relations with his friends in the Soviet Union and even more roundly attacked the policies of the French Communist Party. He signed several petitions to the same effect, resigned from the France-USSR Association but decided to remain in the CNE (National Writers' Committee), and the Peace Movement, where he sponsored a resolution demanding the withdrawal of Soviet troops. In November he again put himself on the line, this time in condemning the Israeli-Franco-British intervention in Suez.

Despite this very serious break with the Soviet Union and the orthodox Communists, which seemed to place in jeopardy all the careful bridge building of the last four years, Sartre nevertheless soon came to see that things really had changed. As Simone de Beauvoir put it, the Russians had decided not to alienate the sympathizers who had refused to accept Budapest; for example, Vercors, one of those who had protested, still received an invitation to visit Russia in 1957. It seemed to be a new and important development, that people could attack the USSR on a specific point without being considered as traitors. This moderate attitude allowed them to work side by side with the French Communist Party on the issue that was most burning for them all: Algeria.[4]

4. *Force of Circumstance*, p. 377.

1957

"Le Fantôme de Staline" ("The Ghost of Stalin"), an article, *Les Temps modernes* nos. 129–31 (November–December 1956, January 1957), pp. 577–697.

"Brecht et les classiques" ("Brecht and the Classical Dramatists"), for the program of the Théâtre des Nations, "Hommage international à Bertolt Brecht" ("An International Tribute to Bertolt Brecht"), (4–21 April)

"Vous êtes formidables" ("You Are Really Something"), an article, *Les Temps modernes,* no. 135 (May), pp. 1641–47.

"Jean-Paul Sartre on His Autobiography," interview by Olivier Todd; *The Listener* (6 June), pp. 915–16.

"Questions de méthode" ("Search for a Method"), an essay, *Les Temps modernes,* nos. 139–140 (September and October), pp. 658–98.

"Le Séquestré de Venise" ("The Prisoner of Venice"), a study on Tintoretto; *Les Temps modernes* no. 141 (November), pp. 761–800.

Having severed relationships with the Soviet Union and the French Communist Party over Hungary, and feeling somewhat shattered and disillusioned by the apparent naiveté of his earlier expressed confidence in Soviet positions, Sartre worked ever more obsessively on solving his own contradictions and attempting to understand how Marxism had become so ossified that it could no longer tolerate unfettered analysis of real situations. In his article "Le Fantôme de Staline" ("The Ghost of Stalin"), he conclusively attributed the Russian repression of Hungary to a provisional victory of the non-de-Stalinized faction of the ruling bureaucracy of the USSR and reaffirmed that the only way to help the progress of communism was to help it de-Stalinize itself.

In Poland there seemed to be signs that a new, more pragmatic Marxism was being tried under Gomulka: forced collectivization was ended; censorship was lifted; and in the arts, the doctrine of "social realism" was abandoned. Sartre was told at a Polish embassy dinner that his works were particularly appreciated in Poland and was invited to Warsaw for the Polish première of *Les Mouches* in January. For the Polish journal *Tworczosc,* he wrote a major article entitled "Marxism and Existentialism," which was published later in the year in *Les*

Temps modernes, with some adaptations for the requirements of French readers, under the title "Questions de méthode" ("Search for a Method"). This article became the core of *La Critique de la raison dialectique.* The central question of the article is whether we have the means of establishing a structural and historical science of the origins, developments and beliefs of man. In the first part of this three-part essay, Sartre begins by situating existentialism in relation to Marxism: the former is a "provisional enclave" inside Marxist philosophy brought into being by the failure of 20th-century Marxism to account for the lived dimension of human phenomena it claims to explain. Because Marxism had become stunted and rigidly dogmatic, it could not allow dialectic reasoning to turn on itself and examine its own historical determinism and its own knowledge. The second and third parts of the essay are mainly devoted to criticism of the "lazy" Marxism, which erects a certain number of a priori claims into an established body of knowledge. Existentialism, on the other hand, seeks to be no more than a heuristic method that borrows its principles from Marxism and takes them as "regulative ideas" or "indicators of tasks" rather than as concrete truths. "Only the project, as the mediation between two objective phases, can account for history, that is, for human creativity." By drawing on examples from the French Revolution and the case of Flaubert, Sartre shows, on the one hand, that dialectical Marxism must incorporate the contributions of American sociology to understand history and itself and, on the other, that it must integrate Freudian psychoanalysis to comprehend the individual as a whole.

The situation in Algeria continued to trouble a minority of French people, the majority hoping that the problem would go away. Evidence of torture was being published, but, as Simone de Beauvoir put it, because the whole country was an accomplice to it, the plot to conceal it succeeded. Those who did speak were not listened to, the others shouted louder to drown them out, and if people did hear a few rumours in spite of themselves, they quickly forgot them. The crimes that Servan-Schreiber described seemed to have had no effect on public opinion: "Arabs shot down 'for the fun of it,' prisoners brutally murdered, villages burned, mass executions, etc. No one turned a hair."[1]

1. Simone de Beauvoir, *Force of Circumstance,* trans. Richard Howard (London: Penguin Books, 1968). p. 380.

Sartre on several occasions protested against the torture and
the war in Algeria. He was asked by *Le Monde* in April to comment on the pamphlet "Des rappelés témoignent" ("Reservists
Testify)," in which young soldiers had described the tortures
they had witnessed in Algeria, but his piece, entitled "Une en-
treprise de démoralisation" ("An Effort to Demoralize"), was
judged to be too violent for publication. It was subsequently
published in slightly modified form in *Les Temps modernes* in
May, under the title "Vous êtes formidables" ("You Are Really
Something"), the title of a radio program popular at the time.
In June, Sartre used this article as the basis of a speech protesting the war at a Peace Movement meeting.

It was in the spring of 1957 that Francis Jeanson became
involved in clandestine activities in support of the FLN (National Liberation Front). Although he and Sartre had disagreed
with each other over their reactions to the Soviet intervention
in Hungary (Jeanson considering Sartre to have had too in-
transigent an attitude), nevertheless Sartre, even during this
period when relations were cold and even nonexistent between
them, judged Jeanson to have committed himself in good faith,
although he could not yet bring himself to follow the same
course of action.

In the summer Jean Cau gave up his position as Sartre's
secretary; publicly no reason was given for the break. A blanket
of discretion was and has been drawn over this particular relationship. His position was filled in September by Claude Faux,
a member of the Communist Party, who remained as Sartre's
secretary until 1963.

Sartre and Simone de Beauvoir spent a month together in
Rome and Capri, where—as a restful change from the *Critique
de la raison dialectique*—he wrote the preface to *Le Traître (The
Traitor),* by André Gorz, entitled "Des rats et des hommes" (Of
Rats and Men"), and worked on a study of Tintoretto for Gallimard's lavish coffee-table series on Renaissance painters. The
latter was published under the title "Le Séquestré de Venise"
("The Prisoner of Venice"), which appeared in the November
issue of *Les Temps modernes* but was never completed for Gallimard because Sartre decided that he did not like the style.

Francis Jeanson's estimate of Sartre's state of mind at this
point in his life was that he, Sartre, felt isolated and impotent,
incapable of committed political action, unproductive. His essay

"Of Rats and Men" Jeanson judged to be one of Sartre's finest, the only one with truly tragic dimensions. In it Sartre likened men to bewildered rats who run around in a strange maze, in which they are both experimenters and guinea pigs, both colonizers and colonized—rats hopelessly prey to certain demands made by man: prisoners, condemned for life to the exercise of an intelligence that offers them no way out. The obsessive theme was that of *prisoners,* as in "Le Séquestré de Venise" and, in 1959, *Les Séquestrés d'Altona.*

10 December: Sartre was a witness for the defense of Ben Saddock, who had shot Ali Chehkal, the former vice-president of the Algerian Assembly and one of the most notable Moslem collaborators. The argument for the defense was that Saddock's action was caused by the conditions of life imposed on his fellow Algerians; Sartre, in deliberately moderate tones, explained that young men could not be expected to display the same patience as their elders because all they knew of France was a bloodstained face and that Saddock's act was a political murder and not a terrorist attack. In the event, it was with relief that Sartre learned of the verdict: life imprisonment, not the death penalty. "We were happy for Saddock first of all, but it was also a comfort to find that there were still men in France capable of judging an Algerian according to their conscience."[2]

1958

"Une Victoire" ("A Victory"), first published in *L'Express* (6 March), a response to *La Question,* by Henri Alleg

"Des Rats et des hommes" ("Of Rats and Men"), pp. 11–47, preface to *Le Traître (The Traitor),* by André Gorz (Paris: Seuil).

"Nous sommes tous des assassins" ("We Are All Assassins"), an article; *Les Temps modernes,* no. 145 (March), pp. 1574–76.

"Le Prétendant" ("The Pretender"), an article; *L'Express* (22 May)

"Les Grenouilles qui demandent un roi" ("The Frogs Who Wanted a King"), an article; *L'Express* (25 September)

2. Ibid., p. 395.

This was what Simone de Beauvoir described as an "intolerable" year: France came close to civil war over the Algerian question; Sartre, in order to do all the work that he wanted to do, kept dosing himself with corydrame, an amphetamine, and narrowly missed having a heart attack; and Simone de Beauvoir's liaison with Claude Lanzmann came to an end, leaving her with no defense against her rising dread of old age and mortality. And suddenly Sartre's financial situation changed with the arrival of a tax assessment of 12 million francs ($266,000). Although he was earning a lot of money at this stage in his life, he was also spending a lot: besides his mother, a number of people depended on him financially; he gave money away all the time; and his constant traveling was expensive. He liked to carry a lot of cash on him, sometimes as much as a million francs, and he tipped excessively, saying that since waiters lived exclusively from tips, it was up to him to see that they lived well.

Fortunately a project materialized that promised a handsome financial reward: 25 million francs. John Huston asked Sartre to write the screenplay for a movie about Freud, concentrating on the period before he became famous, when his ideas had led him into hopeless error. It was agreed that the screenplay should end with Freud discovering the Oedipus complex. Sartre was greatly attracted by the project and added it to the pile of works awaiting completion: Tintoretto; *La Critique;* and a play (to be called *Les Séquestrés d'Altona (The Condemned of Altona),* which was to be an illustration of a theme in *La Critique,* of the "serial otherness" of individuals making history, even if it is not the history they set out to make, and of the responsibility of the soldier who goes too far.

6 March: *L'Express* published Sartre's comments on a work entitled *La Question,* by Henri Alleg, a member of the Algerian Communist Party and one-time editor of the newspaper *Alger républicain,* who, having gone "underground" in November 1956, had been arrested in June 1957 by the parachutists of the 10th Airborne Division and placed in solitary confinement for a month at El-Biar. His book tells of the conditions of his detention and deals with the problem of torture in Algeria. Sartre's article denounced torture in no uncertain terms, discussed the ethical questions raised by it and went on to consider the dialectic between the torturer and his victim, a situation that had preoccupied him since the occupation and that he had already explored in *The Victors.* Because of Sartre's article, this issue of *L'Express* was confiscated by the authorities, and, three weeks later, so was *La Question,* for being "part of an attempt to demoralize the army with the aim of damaging the national defense." In April, Sartre, along with André Malraux, Roger Martin du Gard and François Mauriac, sent an "Official Message" to the president of the republic protesting the attacks on freedom of speech and the confiscation of Alleg's work, demanding an explanation of the facts he reported and calling on the government to condemn unequivocally the use of torture. From this date, seizures, particularly of *Les Temps modernes,* became increasingly frequent.

The events of May and June, when civil war seemed most imminent, which led to General de Gaulle's seizure of power and the setting up the Fifth Republic, filled Sartre and Simone de Beauvoir with despair and loathing. They took part in demonstrations—there was a massive anti-Gaullist procession from the Nation to the Place de la République on 28 May—and Sartre earlier in that week had published an article in *L'Express* attacking de Gaulle's dictatorial designs with the words: "The solitude of this man immured by his own grandeur will not allow him, under any circumstances whatsoever, to become the head of a Republican state. Or, what amounts to the same thing, will not allow any state of which he is the head to remain a Republic." On 30 May, Sartre gave a press conference about the violation of human rights in Algeria. But he was generally so depressed about the whole political situation that, for the most part, he chose to bury himself in a fury of work. Simone de Beauvoir said of his state that at the end of an afternoon of frantic work he would be exhausted; all his powers of concentration would suddenly relax, his gestures would become vague, and quite often he would get his words all mixed up. They spent their evenings in her apartment; as soon as he drank a glass of whiskey the alcohol would go straight to his head. "That's enough," she would say to him; but for him it was not enough; against her will she would hand him a second glass; then he'd ask for a third; two years before he'd have needed a great deal more; but now he lost control of his movements and his speech very quickly, and she would say again: "That's enough." Two or three times she flew into violent tempers, and smashed a

glass on the tiled floor of the kitchen. But she found it too exhausting to quarrel with him. And she knew he needed something to destroy himself a little.[1]

Simone de Beauvoir herself was in an equally depressed state,
which was aggravated by her separation from Lanzmann, but,
unlike Sartre, she found it impossible to concentrate on her
work. So in mid-June they left for Italy—Venice, Spoleto and
Rome—for a much-needed rest. There they stayed until mid-
September.

September: *L'Express* editor Servan-Schreiber flew to Rome
to ask Sartre to write three articles appealing for a "no" response to de Gaulle's call for a constitutional referendum on
28 September, which, if passed, would create the Fifth Republic.
In the end he wrote only two, because of fatigue and ill health.
The first one was drafted in Rome and denounced the blackmail
on which the referendum was based. Simone de Beauvoir and
Servan-Schreiber undertook to edit the piece for him, but Sartre
felt it was dull. The second one he wrote on his return to Paris
and, despite considerable weariness, worked at giving it more
life, spending 28 hours at a stretch on it. Again Simone de
Beauvoir edited it, this time with a more successful outcome.
At the same time he prepared a speech for a meeting against
the referendum, at which Roger Garaudy and André Mandouze
also spoke, and, despite having given Simone de Beauvoir the
impression that he had worked himself into a state of complete
numbness, it appears that he spoke very well.

De Gaulle won his referendum by a massive 80 percent "yes"
vote, and Sartre and Simone de Beauvoir felt profoundly disillusioned. "It's a sinister defeat because it's not merely the
defeat of a party or of an idea, but a repudiation by eighty per
cent of the French people of all that we had believed in and
wanted for France. A repudiation of themselves, an enormous
collective suicide."[2] Sartre's condition worsened: he had splitting
headaches and recurring dizzy spells; he began to lose his sense
of balance and started to stutter. Simone Berriau finally persuaded him to see a doctor, who told him that he had a fatigued

1. Simone de Beauvoir, *Force of Circumstance,* trans. Richard Howard (London:
Penguin Books, 1968). pp. 397–98.

2. Ibid., p. 461.

left ventricle of his heart and that rest was the only cure. Simone Berriau immediately put off *Altona* until the following fall, but Sartre still needed to be forced to stop working, seemingly unconcerned that his life was in danger.

Simone de Beauvoir said of that year that Sartre had only just missed having a heart attck. He had put his health to a terrible test for a long time, not so much because of the exhaustion his desire to make "full use" of himself was inflicting on him as because of the tension he had set up inside himself. To think against oneself was all very well—it had fertile results—but in the long run it tore one to pieces. By forcibly smashing a way through to new ideas he had also done damage to his nerves. Above all it was the defeat of the Left and de Gaulle's accession to power that had really stunned him.[3]

1959

Les Séquestrés d'Altona (The Condemned of Altona), a play in five acts; *Les Temps modernes,* no. 164 (October), pp. 584–656; no. 165 (November), pp. 813–74. Published in book form in 1960 (Paris: Gallimard).

In the spring of 1959, the mounting evidence about the existence of prison camps in Algeria became inescapable. In order to cut down the opposition, the army had herded together thousands of peasants, behind barbed wire, in so-called redistribution centers, where they lived in appalling conditions. According to one report, published in April and addressed directly to a government minister, there were said to be at least a million such people: "On an average, 550 out of every thousand inmates were children, and one of those 550 was dying every two days; since many of the women and old men were also unable to withstand the conditions, it may be estimated that these camps killed more than a million people in three years."[1] Sartre, in May, finally

3. Ibid., pp. 463–64.

1. Simone de Beauvoir, *Force of Circumstance,* trans. Richard Howard (London: Penguin Books, 1968), pp. 468–469.

decided that he could no longer stand on the sidelines and responded with alacrity to Francis Jeanson's request for help in
his clandestine network that supported the FLN (National Liberation Front). In the beginning the underground paper *Vérité
pour . . .*, edited by Francis Jeanson, had dealt with the economic
and political causes of the war, but now, in order to make public a means of action that should theoretically remain underground, it was advocating desertion and support of the
FLN. Sartre therefore granted Jeanson an interview that
appeared under his own name in order to provoke the army
to seek an indictment against him for aiding and abetting
the enemy.

One political event that year that brought encouragement to
Sartre was Fidel Castro's seizure of power in Cuba. There had
been mass killings under the dictator, Batista, and Castro,
having been welcomed ecstatically by the population of Havana,
agreed to a trial that resulted in 220 death sentences, a fact
hastily seized upon by the press in France and used to discredit
the revolutionary régime.

Sartre's health gradually began to improve. He finished *La
Critique de la raison dialectique,* and during the summer spent
in Rome with Simone de Beauvoir, each benefited from the other's often fiercely expressed criticism, she for *The Prime of Life,*
which she was just beginning, and he for *Les Séquestrés d'Altona* (The Condemned of Altona), which he all but finished by
the end of August. On his return to Paris he became very occupied with the rehearsals, which were accompanied by the
usual tantrums and near disasters, but this time Sartre, after
the failure of *Nékrassov,* admitted to being very anxious about
this new play's reception. In the event, the play had its première
on 24 September, at the Renaissance Theater, and was a great
public success. Serge Reggiani as Frantz won almost unanimous
approval, though the production and settings were sharply
criticized. Flaws there are, mainly in acts 1 and 3, which contain
some heavy or obscure passages, but it is generally reckoned,
along with *Huis clos* and *Le Diable et le bon Dieu,* as one of
Sartre's three major plays, rich in meaning, tight in construction and taut in dialogue.

Les Séquestrés d'Altona is thus titled because the soldier hero,
Frantz, has imprisoned himself in a windowless room since
World War II in the family mansion in Altona, a suburb of

Hamburg, and because the entire aristocratic family is imprisoned and paralyzed by its contradictions, failures and solitude. In the beginning of the play the audience is led to believe that Frantz was killed years ago, having been mentioned as a war criminal at the Nuremberg trials. Then the secret of the house of Altona is revealed: Frantz is alive and for 15 years has remained locked inside his room, looked after by his sister. He is obsessed by the torture he committed on the Russian front, haunted by the Nuremberg judgment and decides to assume his own and his country's destiny in the face of history's judgment. His guilt is translated into a madness in which Frantz addresses tape-recorded pleas of innocence to future centuries in a courtroom of crabs. Commenting on the theme of the play, Sartre said: "I believe that the tribunal of history always judges men according to standards and values which they themselves could never imagine. We can never know what the future will say of us . . . . The point is that we know we shall be judged, and not by the rules we use to judge ourselves. And in that thought there is something horrific."[2] Although the setting was transferred to Germany, and the play dealt with a German family, clearly the theme had relevance to the draftee returning from Algeria, where he may have taken part in inhuman acts, half-accomplice, half-victim. Sartre did not wish the play to be limited spatially and temporally to the France of that time, realizing that it would thus fall into socialist realism, "the very negation of theater," but rather wanted to show that no one in a historical society that becomes a repressive society is free of the risk of torturing someone.

Greatly relieved by the warm reception of his play, Sartre flew off to Ireland at the end of September to talk to John Huston about *Freud*. Sartre's script was far too long—seven hours of it—and although he tried to pare it down, other difficulties about interpretation arose between them that led to a break: Huston returned to the script written 10 years earlier by Kaufman, but Sartre was paid his contractual half million dollars. As a result of this exercise, he was more critical of the shortcomings of psychoanalysis, its lack of dialectics, "its inability to make phenomena derive from each other in such a way as

2. Quoted in Kenneth Tynan, *Tynan Right and Left* (New York: Atheneum Publishers, 1967).

to make each forward step conditioned on the previous one while at the same time containing and superseding it."[3]

Although Sartre's involvement in Huston's film on Freud was not brought to full fruition, his thinking led him on to one of his major works, in which he tried to apply a dialectical Marxist-Freudian method: his study of Flaubert.

1960

Critique de la raison dialectique (Critique of Dialectical Reason), printed with a preceding separate essay, *Questions de méthode (Search for a Method)*, (Paris: Gallimard)

Foreword to *Aden Arabie*, by Paul Nizan (Paris: Maspero).

"Albert Camus," *France-Observateur* (7 January)

"Ideología y revolución" ("Ideology and Revolution"), (in Spanish); *Lunes de Revolución*, no. 51 (March)

"L'Artiste est un suspect . . ." ("The Artist Is a Suspect"), text for André Masson's "Vingt-deux dessins sur le thème du désir" ("Twenty-two Sketches on the Theme of Desire"); text published in part in *L'Arc*, no. 10 (Spring), pp. 19–22.

"Jean-Paul Sartre vous présente *Soledad*" ("Jean-Paul Sartre Presents *Soledad*"), program notes to *Soledad*, a three-act play by Colette Audry, Théâtre de Poche (April)

"Un Texte inédit de Sartre" ("An Unpublished Text by Sartre"), excerpts from a lecture on the theater; *Premières*, vol. 11, no. 9 (June), pp. 1–2, 8

"Ouragan sur le sucre: Un Grand Reportage à Cuba de Jean-Paul Sartre sur Fidel Castro" ("Storm over Sugar: A Major Report on Fidel Castro from Cuba by Jean-Paul Sartre"), a series of 16 articles in *France-Soir* (28 June–15 July)

"M. Jean-Paul Sartre dresse un parallèle entre Cuba et l'Algérie" ("M. Jean-Paul Sartre Draws a Parallel Between Cuba and Algeria"), *Le Monde* (1 September) a report of a lecture given by Sartre at the Brazilian Institute of Advanced Studies, Rio de Janeiro (31 August)

Letter to the Military Tribunal during the Jeanson trial, published in *Le Monde* (22 September)

---

3. Axel Madsen, *Hearts and Minds: The Common Journey of Simone de Beauvoir and Jean-Paul Sartre* (New York: William Morrow, 1977), p. 209.

The year began badly with the death on 4 January of Camus, killed in a car crash. Sartre and Simone de Beauvoir spent the evening with Bost, reminiscing about Camus, mainly in terms of their early comradeship before the arguments and estrangement.

It was a year notable for the publication of Sartre's second major philosophical work, *Critique of Dialectical Reason,* and for political controversy over his trip to Cuba and his stand against oppression of those who opposed France's policies in Algeria.

Just as the first philosophical opus, *Being and Nothingness,* had been many years in the making, so, too, the *Critique* emerged from the major reconsideration of Marxism that he had begun early in the 1950s. Simone de Beauvoir reported that by 1956 Sartre had been converted to the dialectical method and was attempting to reconcile it with his basic existentialism. The first occasion to present his ideas came when he was invited to submit a paper on the situation of existentialism in 1957 for publication in a Polish journal; a revised version of the paper was then published under the title "Questions de méthode" in *Les temps modernes* (September 1957). Although this clear essay was subsequently published in the same book as *Critique of Dialectical Reason* in France (but kept separate in the English version), the two works are very different in length and style. The *Critique* was written in great haste, without revision, and is very long (835 pages in English). The Algerian War and the controversy surrounding it was at its height, and Sartre's way of coping with it was to bury himself in his work.

He protected himself by working furiously at his *Critique de la raison dialectique*. But it was not a case of writing as he ordinarily did, pausing to think and make corrections, tearing up a page, starting again. Now, for hours at a stretch, he raced across sheet after sheet without re-reading them, as though absorbed by ideas that his pen, even at that speed, couldn't keep up with. To maintain this pace he chewed corydrame capsules, of which he managed to get through a tube a day.[1]

1. Simone de Beauvoir, *Force of Circumstance,* trans. Richard Howard (London: Penguin Books, 1968), p. 397.

His intention in the *Critique* was to synthesize his own existentialist approach with an undogmatic Marxism and to provide in this first volume (the second volume was never finished) a philosophical anthropology that would furnish an ontological basis for Marxism. Marxism was the preferred philosophical framework, and existentialism had a place within it. In his preface, Sartre expressed the intention of the work as being to raise the question of whether we now possess the materials for constituting a structural, historical anthropology. This question was located within Marxist philosophy, for—as he made clear— he regarded Marxism as the untranscendable philosophy for our time, and he believed that the ideology of existence, along with its "comprehensive" method, was an enclave within Marxism itself, both produced and then rejected by Marxism.[2]

Since *Being and Nothingness,* much of Sartre's philosophical language and focus had changed. There are real continuities, but the encounter with Marxism had worked a transformation. In an important interview with the English journal *New Left Review* in 1969, he was to express incredulity that in the earlier work he had been so impressed by his wartime experience of heroism that he had taken it to represent the human condition. After the war he found the crucial experience was that of the conditioning of society. In the *Critique* he began to develop a method that would enable us to understand the development of a person—a psychological biography—in conjunction with the structures of society and the movement of history (a method demonstrated in his massive study of Flaubert). In the *Critique* Sartre argues that if we really want to understand a person, we must seek to know him "totally as an individual and yet totally as an expression of his time." The aim of dialectical reason is not only to understand the development and meaning of a particular life but also to apprehend the movement of history. The method, which he borrowed from an article by the sociologist Henri Lefebvre, entitled "Perspectives de sociologie rurale" ("Perspectives of rural sociology"), was called "the progressive-regressive method" by Sartre. In Sartre's 1938 essay "The Emotions," he had used both the method of psychological regression and that of phenomenological progression, but he

2. Jean-Paul Sartre, *Critique of Dialectical Reason,* trans. Alan Sheridan-Smith (London: NLB [New Left Books], 1976), p. 822.

had not managed to combine them. Regression remained characteristic of those external, analytic inquiries that begin with data gathered from objects and work back to causes and explanations; whereas progression was characteristic of internal, synthetic enterprises that begin with intentions held by subjects and work out to actions and significations.

What Sartre gained from Lefebvre's discussion of a method for rural sociology was an idea of how to put these two processes together end to end, as it were, so that at the point of conjuncture or articulation there would be the existential subject. The joint progressive-regressive method could provide the only adequate means of dealing with history because it makes the explanatory-causal chain (which is not in itself deterministic) pass *through* human agents. He quoted Engels, saying, "Men themselves make their history but in a given environment which conditions them." Sartre then explained this in terms of his method: Men make their history on the basis of real, prior conditions (among which he included acquired characteristics, distortions imposed by the mode of work and of life, alienation, etc.), but it was *the men* who make it and not the prior conditions. Otherwise men would be merely the vehicles of inhuman forces which through them would govern the social world.[3]

The regressive analysis entailed drawing on sociology and psychoanalysis to specify the structures that mediate between the individual and history (the latter encompassing the dynamic development of society in general); such structures included political groups, systems of beliefs, families, industries, cities, etc. But these disciplines needed to pursue their investigations in a hyperempirical way, avoiding premature abstract theorizing. They must avoid the Marxist temptation of "totalizing too quickly" and of replacing real groups, such as the Gironde, by insufficiently determined collectivities like "the bourgeoisie." The progressive analysis would focus on what the individual made of himself or herself in the given circumstances by virtue of making choices and undertaking projects. Sartre saw his own major work on Flaubert as an application of these methods— a total characterization of a life with respect both to what pro-

3. Jean-Paul Sartre, *The Problem of Method,* trans. Hazel E. Barnes (London: Methuen, 1964), p. 87.

duced it and to what it produced—its historical determination and its existential project.

Among the key concepts that figure in the *Critique* are: *praxis*—"the activity of an individual or group in organizing conditions in the light of some end"; *project*—a chosen way of being, expressed in praxis; *practico-inert*—matter in which praxis is embodied; *scarcity*—the contingent impossibility of satisfying all the needs of an *ensemble* (any collection of individuals, however related); *series*—an ensemble, each of whose members is determined in *alterity* (a relation of separation, opposed to reciprocity), which is in contrast to a *group,* where relations are based on reciprocity; *fused group*—a newly formed group, directly opposed to seriality, and unstructured; *pledged group*—a group that develops from a fused group through an organized distribution of rights and duties enforced by a pledge; *institution*—a group that develops from a pledged group through ossification of its structures and the emergence of sovereignty and seriality within it; *sovereign*—an individual (or group) who (or that) manipulates series within an institutional group; *alienation*—the condition in which free praxis is taken over and controlled by the Other or by the practico-inert; *transcendence*—the process of going beyond present conditions toward a future that at once negates and incorporates them; *dialectic*—the intelligibility of praxis at every level; *comprehension*—the understanding of praxis in terms of the purposes of its agents.

The underlying theme is that of the possibility of people overcoming their plight of alienation and of domination by the practico-inert and sovereigns through comprehension of their praxis and through transcending their circumstances by way of cooperative action in fused and pledged groups (particularly a revolutionary class).

Assimilation of, and reactions to, the *Critique* were slow in coming, and commentators disagreed as to whether it marked an epistemological break with the earlier *Being and Nothingness.* However, two major contemporaries, Claude Lévi-Strauss and Raymond Aron, subsequently devoted series of seminars or lectures to discussion of the work, and these were published in part in Aron's *History and the Dialectic of Violence* and in Levi-Strauss's case in the chapter of *The Savage Mind* concerned with "History and Dialectic." Lévi-Strauss and Sartre engaged in a celebrated polemical exchange on the meaning of dialectic, which led to numerous articles by other writers who wished to join in the debate. However, the most celebrated account of the relevance and influence of Sartre's ideas in the *Critique* was provided by Epistémon, a professor of psychology at Nanterre, who linked those ideas to the student demonstrations of May 1968. In a book with the title *These Ideas that Have Shaken France* (1969), Epistémon singled out Sartre's ideas on the opposition of series and group, the group in fusion and the idea of the individual escaping his or her solitariness by taking part in a collective action in which all the participants are agents because all of them together, and each separately, spontaneously seek a single, identical object.

A promised second volume of the *Critique* never appeared. Only two chapters were completed: one on boxing, the other concerned with Stalin and the emergence in the USSR of a policy of developing socialism in one country (without reference to world revolution). The purpose of the second volume was to have been to demonstrate the effectiveness of the methods set out in volume 1 by applying them to concrete historical examples. The fundamental question to be answered was How do separate individuals, with their own projects and acts, combine to produce a constituted social world? Some commentators have suggested that Sartre never finished the second volume because he could not answer the question with the methods he had adopted: by starting with the individual and rejecting the sociological concept of a shared social layer internally connecting individuals in groups, he could not explain how boxers *incarnate* violent struggle in their society or how Stalin's praxis incarnated socialism by deviating from it.

A further reason for the failure to complete volume 2 was Sartre's disillusionment with the prospects for a humane socialism in the USSR and for change in the West. In the 1950s he had experienced a certain optimism as he worked furiously on volume 1 of the *Critique*. After its publication, there is a rather bitter and disillusioned tone in his essays on Nizan (1960) and Merleau-Ponty (1961) and a turning away from Europe and its prospects for socialism to a focus on the problems of the Third World, as in his writings on the Cuban revolution (1960) and his preface to Fanon's *Les Damnés de la terre* (1961).

Sartre wrote his self-critical foreword to Nizan's *Aden Arabie* while on a visit to Cuba in February–March. In it, he described the Left in France as a rotting corpse, full of worms, and with nothing to say to young people. Sartre was much impressed with the spontaneity and undogmatic nature of the Cuban revolution, which was in its honeymoon period and resembled his description of such a moment of fusion as set out in the *Critique*. In a discussion with students at the University of Havana, which was subsequently published in various forms, he compared the Cuban revolution favorably with the French and Russian revolutions, stressing its originality and the fact that it forged its ideology in the revolutionary praxis. He gave further views on Cuba in a series of articles in *France-Soir* after his return. On the way back there was a controversial press conference in New York, and then, shortly after their return to Paris, Sartre and Simone de Beauvoir attended a reception for Khrushchev at the Soviet Embassy. In May they visited Yugoslavia and met Tito. Algeria still continued to dominate their political lives, and on 17 June, Sartre was a defense witness at the trial of Georges Arnaud, who had written a report of an illegal meeting about Algeria arranged by Francis Jeanson. Sartre was also among the intellectuals who signed a manifesto expressing their recognition of the right to civil disobedience.

Since their trip to Cuba, Sartre had been toying with the idea of discussing the Cuban experience with other South Americans, and he was convinced by Brazilian friends who said that if he made a visit to Brazil, he could combat the French government propaganda about Algeria and render a service to the Left. During his two-month stay in Brazil, he made numerous speeches on the Algerian situation and on the Cuban revolution. His unpopularity with the French authorities was worsened when he sent back a statement of support for Francis Jeanson, charged with clandestine activities in support of the Algerians; the statement was read in court on 22 September, and it defied the authorities to bring proceedings against Sartre himself, who insisted that he and many other intellectuals were supporters of Jeanson's actions. Feelings against Sartre were running high, particularly among supporters of the military, who condemned Sartre and his fellow signatories of the *Manifesto of the 121*, the "Declaration Concerning the Right of Insubordination in the Algerian War." When Sartre and Simone flew back from Brazil by way of Cuba, arriving in Madrid, they received messages from friends warning them to come back by car rather than plane, so as to avoid a hostile reception at the airport. The French border police had instructions to inform Paris as soon as they crossed the frontier, which they did on 4 November, and they were told to report to the police in Paris. On arrival in Paris they were duly charged; but subsequently the charges were dropped. Sartre countered this by calling a press conference on 1 December, at which he explained his part in the manifesto and gave an exposition of the situation. He called for a rejection of any solution to the Algerian problem that was imposed on the Algerians, and if that was the question to be put by the government in the referendum on 6 January 1961, then he recommended a "no" vote.

1961

Preface to *Les Damnés de la terre (The Wretched of the Earth),* by Frantz Fanon

"Le Peintre sans privilèges" ("The Unprivileged Painter"), preface to the catalog of the exhibition of paintings by Lapoujade at the Pierre Domec Gallery; excerpts were published in *France-Observateur* (9 March); the preface in its entirety appeared in *Médiations,* no. 2 (2nd trimester), pp. 29–44

"Merleau-Ponty vivant" ("Merleau-Ponty Alive"), *Les Temps modernes,* nos. 183–85 (October), pp. 304–76.

This was to be a year of continuing struggle over the war in Algeria, including an attempt to assassinate Sartre, and there were the deaths of two friends with whom Sartre felt great intellectual sympathy—Merleau-Ponty and Frantz Fanon. At the beginning of the year, there were some pleasant interludes. First, there was an interesting dinner at the Soviet Embassy, attended by Mauriac and Aragon. Sartre then went to Milan to receive the Omegna Prize, which had been awarded in recognition of his work and his struggle against the Algerian War. Simone decided they both needed a break from Paris, and so they went to stay in Antibes. It was there that they heard of the death of Merleau-Ponty on 4 May. Back in Paris, they found the pressures as great as ever, and the threats against them increased. Sartre moved his mother out of her apartment and into a hotel, and he moved in with Simone. The precautions were opportune, as, shortly afterward, on 19 July, a bomb was exploded in the entrance to Sartre's apartment, causing great damage but no injuries. It was the work of the OAS (Organisation de l'Armée secrète), which regarded him as an important opponent of its mission to keep Algeria under French control.

Sartre was again burying himself in his work, drugging himself with so much corydrame that he went partly deaf for some time as he wrote the first draft of a lengthy analysis of his whole relationship with Merleau-Ponty, which was to form part of a special issue of *Les Temps modernes* devoted to his old friend and coeditor. Simone de Beauvoir persuaded him that they should have an extended stay in Rome, from the end of July until October, hoping that this would get him away from the work, but he continued working on a revised draft of the article. "Merleau-Ponty Alive" appeared in the special issue of *Les Temps modernes* in October, and it was judged to be one of Sartre's finest articles, although Simone de Beauvoir maintained that Sartre was too hard on himself in it.

In reminiscing about their long friendship, which dated from 1927 and the École Normale Supérieure, Sartre acknowledged that it was Merleau-Ponty who had "converted" him to a genuine appreciation of history as the universal setting of human action. Writing of the turbulent postwar period when they had edited *Les Temps modernes* together, Sartre observed that Merleau-Ponty had shown a much better political sense than he had. Their split had begun when Sartre moved closer to the Communists and published "The Communists and Peace." In his *Adventures of the Dialectic,* Merleau-Ponty had attacked the stand taken by Sartre as ultra-Bolshevik, because it had suggested that the proletariat could only be unified and overcome impotence if there was obedience to party authority. However, an argument can be made that Sartre maintained that there had to be a dialogue between the proletariat and the party and that it was not a question of subservience. Simone de Beauvoir had defended Sartre against Merleau-Ponty's misinterpretations in her article "Merleau-Ponty and Pseudo-Sartrianism" in *Les Temps modernes* (1955). Merleau-Ponty and Sartre had met again, after years of coolness and separation, when they attended a meeting in Venice in 1956, and then again during the summer of 1958 in Italy. Merleau-Ponty had written about their relationship in a preface published in 1960 and had attended a lecture given by Sartre at the École Normale Supérieure in March 1961.

It was while staying in Rome and working on the Merleau-Ponty article that Sartre met with Frantz Fanon, who had asked him to write a preface for his book *Les Damnés de la terre (The Wretched of the Earth)* and had sent him the manuscript via Lanzmann. Born in Martinique, but having completed his medical studies in Lyons, Fanon had been a successful psychiatrist practicing in Algerian hospitals. His exposure to the suffering and oppression in Algeria turned him into a revolutionary and an advocate of violence as the only way in which the oppressed could attain human dignity. This was the theme of *The Wretched of the Earth,* and it corresponded to Sartre's experience of the successful Cuban revolution. The preface was the most violent text Sartre ever wrote, and in it he proclaimed his solidarity with the Algerian terrorists/freedom fighters and with the struggle of all colonial people. Ironically, Fanon's widow had Sartre's preface deleted from the 1968 edition because she disagreed with his stand on the 1967 Arab-Israeli War.

Back in Paris, in November, Sartre took part in a silent demonstration in the Place Maubert to protest against the violent repression of the demonstration by Algerians in Paris on 17 October. He took part in further demonstrations on 18 November and 19 December and attended a large meeting on the Algerian issue in Rome on 13 December. Negotiations about French withdrawal from Algeria were already under way, but the tortures continued, and Sartre took refuge from the constant pressure by burying himself in his study of Flaubert. He took time off to participate in a debate at the Mutualité on the dialectics of nature: the other participants were Garaudy, Hyppolite and Vigier. More than 6,000 people attended the debate, but Simone de Beauvoir thought that the brief time allowed to Sartre meant that he would have been wiser not to have attempted to summarize his thought in such a short time.

1962

Bariona, ou Le Fils du Tonnerre (Bariona, or The Son of Thunder), a
   play written in December 1940 (Paris: Avelier Anjou—copies), lim-
   ited edition.
*Marxisme et existentialisme: Controverse sur la dialectique (Marxism
   and Existentialism: A Controversy About the Dialectic),* with Roger
   Garaudy, Jean Hyppolite, Jean-Pierre Vigier and Jean Orcel (Paris:
   Plon).
"Les Somnambules" ("The Sleepwalkers"), an article; *Les Temps
   modernes,* no. 191 (April), pp. 1397–1401
Reply to a letter by Marcel Péju in *Les Temps modernes,* no. 194 (July),
   pp.182–89
"La Démilitarisation de la culture" ("The Demilitarization of Culture"),
   speech at the World Congress for General Disarmament and Peace,
   Moscow (9–14 July); published in *Literaturnaia Gazeta* and *Mos-
   kovski Komsomoletz* (14 July) and subsequently in *Situations,* vol.
   VII
"La guerra fredda e l'unità della cultura" ("The Cold War and the
   Unity of Culture"), (in Italian); *Rinascita* (Rome), no. 23 (13 October)

The year opened with a second bomb attempt against Sartre's
former address at 42 rue Bonaparte, although Sartre had been
living in an apartment on the boulevard Saint-Germain for a
month. Some of his manuscripts were destroyed. Later in the
year he was to move to a 10th-floor apartment at 222 boulevard
Raspail, where he stayed until 1973. Also in January he gave
evidence for the defense in the trial of the Abbé Robert Davezies,
who was prosecuted for aiding the FLN, the Algerian nationalist organization. His political activities continued to revolve
around antifascist meetings and support for Algerian resistance
movements. With Laurent Schwartz and Jean-Pierre Vigier,
he helped establish an antifascist group of intellectuals, FAC
(Action and Coordination Front), which aimed at uniting Communists and other Leftists in the fight. In a debate published
in *France-Observateur* on 1 February, Sartre took the position
that the FAC should not rule out the need to answer violence
with violence. He attended further meetings of the antifascist
group (FAC) on 11 February and 15 March. On 13 February
he participated in a demonstration protesting the massacre of

demonstrators against the OAS (Secret Algerian Organization) on 8 February, when police had charged the peaceful protesters, who fled down the steps of the Charonne Métro station. These events typified Sartre's troubled relations with the Communists: on the one hand, they were proving difficult partners in the antifascist league, because as individuals they feared being out of step with party orthodoxy; on the other hand, they had his sympathy when they were attacked by the police, as at Charonne.

February 18 saw the declaration of the cease-fire in Algeria. The following day Sartre wrote an article for *Les Temps modernes,* with the title "Les Somnambules" ("The Sleepwalkers"), in which he described the bitter disillusionment of the peace, contrasting it with the Liberation of 1945, when the Parisians felt joy at the deliverance from their sufferings, whereas now they felt relief because they were getting rid of their crimes. He called upon the Left to guard against any attempt by the army to sabotage the agreements, and he repeated his conviction of the need to struggle against the threat of fascism in France.

In June there was a dispute with Marcel Péju, who had been secretary general of *Les Temps modernes* since 1953. Péju had been asked to resign because he was critical of the stance of Sartre and *Les Temps modernes* toward the Algerian National Liberation Front, which he judged too sympathetic. Sartre replied to him in *Les Temps modernes* in a scathing piece, published in July.

June and July were taken up with a trip to Russia and Poland. In Russia Sartre was received by the premier, Khrushchev, and had discussions with the staffs of literary magazines and with other writers. The writers wanted him to take part in a Peace Congress to be held in Moscow, to which they were inviting intellectuals from all over the world. Sartre was amused to remember the names the Communists had called him in the past—"hyena with a fountain pen," "enemy of mankind," "filth peddler," "tool of the bourgeoisie," "gravedigger." Nevertheless, he agreed to take part and lectured on "The Demilitarization of Culture," pointing out how culture had been used to further partisan goals during the Cold War, urging intellectuals to demilitarize it and calling on Marxists to take what was useful from Western culture and not reject it *en bloc.*

The trip was much easier and more official than the one Sartre had made on his own in 1954. He was impressed by the changes in Russia, the greater prosperity and the somewhat easier political and cultural climate. In addition to meeting old friends, such as Konstantin Simonov and Fedin, Sartre and Simone de Beauvoir met some of the younger poets and were amused by the constant debates about the relative merits of Yevtushenko and Vosnesensky. They became firm friends with their translator and guide, Lena Zonina, and when Sartre's autobiographical work *Les Mots (Words)* was being prepared for publication later in the year, it bore the dedication "To Madame Z," who was Lena Zonina.

Much of the rest of the year was spent in Rome, where Sartre worked on finishing *Les Mots* and Simone de Beauvoir wrote *Force of Circumstance*. If *Les Mots* was to be acclaimed as one of his best works, Sartre was less satisfied with some of the other works that came out that year. His contribution to the debate in *Marxisme et existentialisme: Controverse sur la dialectique* was judged by Simone de Beauvoir to be too short to do justice to his complicated thesis, despite the fact that the debate had been followed with rapt attention by an audience of 6,000, as though it were a football match. His position was better explained at length in *The Critique of Dialectical Reason,* where he expressed his fears about the Marxist tendency to postulate the existence of a dialectic of nature by means of an analogy that anthropomorphically projected the dialectical process of historical human development onto the movement of matter. He shared the fear, which Hyppolite expressed during the debate, that the effect might be to naturalize history rather than to historicize nature.

The other unsatisfactory works were the treatment of his script for the movie *Freud,* directed by John Huston and starring Montgomery Clift as Freud and Susannah York as a composite patient character that Sartre had invented. Although he had been highly paid for the script, Sartre disagreed with the changes in it and asked that his name be removed from the credits. Similarly, with Vittorio de Sica's screen version of *The Condemned of Altona,* the result was distasteful to Sartre, despite the list of stars, including Sophia Loren, Maximilian Schell, Frédéric March and Robert Wagner. Although he insisted that the credits should say that the film was "freely in-spired by" his play, he was not able to get his name taken off.

Perhaps the nicest memory of the year, in addition to the peace in Algeria, was the supportive letter Sartre received after the bomb attempt on his apartment. It was from his mother's cousin, the famous Dr. Albert Schweitzer in the leprosy hospital in Gabon, who wrote to say: "Each time I see your name among those fighting against atomic war, I feel how close I am to you."

1963

Les Mots (Words), published in two parts in *Les Temps modernes*, no. 209 (October), pp. 577–649; no.210 (November), pp. 769–823; sub-sequently published as a book by Gallimard in 1964.

"Doigts et non-doigts" ("Fingers and Non-Fingers"), a piece in *Wols: Watercolors, Drawings, Writings;* texts by Werner Haftmann, Henri-Pierre Roché and Jean-Paul Sartre, pp. 10–21.

Preface to *La Pensée politique de Patrice Lumumba (The Political Thought of Patrice Lumumba)*, pp. I–XLVI

"Le Cińema nous donne sa première tragédie: *Les Abysses*" ("The Movies Have Given Us Their First Tragedy: *Les Abysses")*, in support of the film by Nicos Papatakis; *Le Monde* (19 April); reprinted in *Atlas,* vol. 6, no. 2 (August), p. 118.

"Nel sangue di Grimau l'unità della Spagna" ("Spain Is United in the Blood of Grimau"), article in Italian; *Rinascita* (Rome), (27 April); French text in "Grimau," *Libération* (27–28 April)

"Un bilancio, un preludio" ("A Summing Up, a Prelude"), colloquium contribution published in *L'Europa Letteraria*, in Italian, vol. 4, nos. 22–24, pp. 162–68.

28 December–13 January: Sartre and Simone de Beauvoir were back in Moscow, this time with the ostensible purpose of creating an East-West writers' community devoted to encour-aging exchanges of ideas between writers from different ide-ological backgrounds. The organization was to have as its pres-ident the elderly poet Giuseppe Ungaretti, but the optimism about the venture derived from the temporary loosening of cultural controls in Russia, which allowed writers such as Ilya Ehrenburg to publish works that freely discussed Western art and culture. The cultural "thaw" was at its peak during the winter visit, and Sartre attended a Christmas Eve party at a theater where all the guests were dressed in the most elegant clothes and danced to Western jazz music.

By the time of their return visit in July, Khrushchev had clamped down again and had attacked Western influences in the arts. Ehrenburg was personally condemned by Khrushchev for having a bad influence on Sartre and causing him to leave the Communist Party, although Ehrenburg tried without success to point out that Sartre had never been a member of the party. When Khrushchev received a delegation of the writers at his country home in Georgia, he rudely denounced Sartre and his fellow delegates for being henchmen of capitalism. Throughout dinner Khrushchev remained sullen, although he did manage to say that "Still you are against war too, so at least we can eat and drink together." It was only later that Sartre learned that Khrushchev's outburst may have been sparked off by a meeting he had with French Communist Party chief Maurice Thorez, a few hours before their arrival, when he was warned that he was about to meet a bunch of dangerous reactionaries. Soviet writers at the Leningrad conference, 5–8 August, adopted the same line, and the Western writers found their culture accused of corruption and decadence. At a press conference given by participants in the conference on 9 August, Sartre stressed that he took part as a socialist opposed to bourgeois culture, and he affirmed that in his opinion, socialism would win the ideological struggle. However, later in the year, during a visit to Prague from 12 to 24 November, as a guest of the Czechoslovak Writers' Union, Sartre made it clear that his commitment to socialism and his consciousness of decadent elements in capitalist society did not mean that he was prepared to acquiesce in the Leningrad denunciations of important Western authors such as Proust, Freud, Kafka and Joyce as simply decadent. He claimed that it was his reading of Freud, Kafka and Joyce that had helped lead him to Marxism; when people in the East treated these authors as decadent, they outlawed the entire personal culture of Western intellectuals and negated any contribution they might make to dialogue.

The worst signs of decadence in France concerned the decay

brought about by colonialism. Although there was peace at last in Algeria, the aftereffects lingered on, and there was a reluctance to learn the lessons of that war. Sartre took part in a press conference on the fate of AWOLs and deserters on 21 January, and in April he wrote a piece in *Le Monde* commending Nicos Papatakis's film *Les Abysses,* which could be seen to be teaching the same political lessons as the Algerian War. Simone de Beauvoir said Papatakis had the Algerian War in mind when he made this film about two servants who batter their employer's family to death with a flat iron; it was a situation like that described by Fanon, in which the oppressed can break free only by slaughtering the oppressor.

The literary event of the year was the publication in *Les Temps modernes* of Sartre's autobiographical work *Les Mots (Words)*. He had first had the idea of writing an autobiography in 1953 and had written much of it in 1954, before setting it aside and then returning to finish it by early 1963. The original circumstances in which he came to write the book were in the period of the early 1950s when he was reexamining his position in relation to Marxism. He came to realize that he had been living a "real neurosis," similar to that of Flaubert, which was that writing was everything and that the writer's life ought to be understood through his work. In 1953 he came to the realization that this was a bourgeois point of view and that he needed to rethink the value of the written word and just what had made a 9-year-old boy slip into that "neurosis of literature." The method of *Les Mots* was modeled on his prescriptions in *Search for a Method,* and he combined Freudian and Marxian determining factors (e.g., relating to childhood and class) with his existentialist concept of the individual's "projects" to explain how he had developed. The advantage of the autobiographical mode was that it allowed Sartre to explain the meaning or course of a life from the "inside," whereas critics had complained that his works on Baudelaire and Genet had tried to reconstruct meanings from the outside and lacked sympathy.

The book was very well received by the critics, who admired its literary style. Sartre admitted that he had taken the trouble to make this, his farewell to literature, as well written as possible, so that the people who read it would be led to question literature through literature itself. He later said that bourgeois society took the book to be a confession that he had seen the error of his ways and was prepared to give up politics, and so they bestowed on him the Goncourt prize and offered him a Nobel prize, which he was to refuse. Only his mother, the 81-year-old Anne-Marie, saw fit to pronounce a negative judgment on the book, declaring: "Poulou [her nickname for Sartre] hasn't understood anything of his childhood." It is said that she busied herself writing her view of the events of Sartre's childhood, with the intention of putting the record straight, but nothing ever appeared.

1964

Qu'est-ce que la littérature? (What Is Literature?) a book, previously published in *Les Temps modernes* in 1947 (Paris: Gallimard)

Situations, IV: Portraits (Paris: Gallimard), containing 15 pieces published from 1948 to 1963; divided into three sections:

1. "Portrait of a Man Unknown" (on Nathalie Sarraute)
   "The Artist and His Conscience" (on music)
   "Of Rats and Men" (on André Gorz)
2. "The Living Gide"
   "Reply to Albert Camus"
   "Albert Camus"
   "Paul Nizan"
   "Merleau-Ponty Alive"
3. "The Prisoner of Venice" (on Tintoretto)
   "The Paintings of Giacometti"
   "The Unprivileged Painter" (on Lapoujade)
   "Masson"
   "Fingers and Non-Fingers" (on Wols)
   "A Garden of Capucines"
   "Venice from My Window" (these last two pieces are from the abandoned work "Queen Albermarle and the Last Tourist")

Situations, V: Colonialisme et néo-colonialisme (Situations, V: Colonialism and Neocolonialism), (Paris: Gallimard), containing 13 pieces written between 1954 and 1963:

   "From One China to the Other" (preface to a book by Cartier-Bresson)
   "Colonialism Is a System"
   "A Portrait of the Colonized, Preceded by 'A Portrait of the Colonizer,' by Albert Nemmi"

"You Are Really Something"

"We Are All Assassins"

"A Victory" (a response to Henry Alleg)

"The Pretender"

"The Constitution of Contempt"

"The Frogs Who Wanted a King"

"Analysis of the Referendum"

"The Sleepwalkers"

"The Wretched of the Earth" (preface to a book by Frantz Fanon)

"The Political Thought of Patrice Lumumba"

Situations, VI: Problèmes du Marxisme, 1 (Situations, VI: Problems of Marxism, 1), containing five pieces published from 1950 to 1954:

"Portrait of the Adventurer" (Preface to a book by Roger Stephane)

"Which Are False, the Wise Men or the Elephants?" (Preface to a book by Louis Dalmas)

"Are We in a Democracy?"

"The End of Hope" (Preface to a book by Juan Hermanos)

"The Communists and Peace"

Il Filosofo e la politica (The Philosopher and Politics), a selection of political writings published in Italian, two of which had not been published in French; these were:

"The Cold War and the Unity of Culture"

"Peaceful Coexistence and the Confrontation of Ideas"

Foreword to *Reason and Violence: A Decade of Sartre's Philosophy, 1950–1960,* by R. D. Laing and D. G. Cooper

"Sartre parle . . ." ("Sartre Speaks"), an interview by Yves Buin in *Clarté* (monthly of the Union of Communist Students); no. 55 (March–April), pp. 41–47

"Jean-Paul Sartre s'explique sur *Les Mots*" ("Jean-Paul Sartre Explains What He Was Doing in *The Words*"), an interview by Jacqueline Piatier in *Le Monde* (18 April); "A Long, Bitter, Sweet Madness," trans. Anthony Hartley, *Encounter,* vol. 22 (June), pp. 61–63

Paper given on 23 May at the colloquium "Ethics and Society," organized in Rome by the Gramsci Institute; summary in *L'Unità* (24 May); excerpts in *Rinascita,* no. 37 (19 September); subsequently published in collections under the title "Determinism and Freedom"

Statement made at the death of Maurice Thorez, in *L'Humanité* (16 July)

"Il mio amico Togliatti" ("My Friend Togliatti"), in Italian; *L'Unità* (30 August); French text in *Les Temps modernes,* no. 221 (October), pp. 577–87

"L'Ecrivain doit refuser de se laisser transformer en institution" ("The Writer Should Refuse to Let Himself Be Turned into an Institution"), *Le Monde* (24 October); "I Always Refuse Distinctions," *The Times*

(London) (23 October), p. 12; and "Sartre on the Nobel Prize," trans. Richard Howard, *New York Review of Books* (17 December), pp. 5–6

"L'Alibi" ("The Alibi"), an interview; *Le Nouvel Observateur,* no. 1 (19 November), pp. 1–6

The year saw the death of Mme. Morel ("Madame Lemaire" in Simone de Beauvoir's autobiography), at whose house she and Sartre had spent their holidays in earlier years but toward whom they had developed cooler feelings during the years of the Algerian War.

March: Sartre authorized the first performance in 12 years of *Les Mains sales (Dirty Hands),* in Turin. He gave a number of important interviews at this time. Many of the Communist students were interested in his work, and in an interview with Yves Buin—the editor of their monthly journal, *Clarté*—Sartre gave one of his best discussions of the relationship between politics and art. He reaffirmed his commitment to Marxist methodology and gave his views on the task of modern criticism, emphasizing the need to see works of art in terms of their historical conditions and at the same time as surpassing those conditions by virtue of their intentional meanings. In an interview published in *Le Monde* (18 April) on the autobiographical *Words,* speaking of the neurotic drive to produce literature, which had motivated him for 40 years, he declared, "One is no more saved by politics than by literature." Some readers took this to mean that he now despaired of politics, but his point was that salvation was not to be found anywhere. However, he was not at all desperate but rather considered himself an optimist and always happy. This contrasted with his depiction of human beings as "disaster-ridden animals" and his statement that he had discovered that metaphysical evils were secondary compared with man's exploitation of other men: "undernourishment relegated metaphysical evil, which is a luxury, to the background. Hunger is an evil, period." It was in this context that he made the controversial statement, "Weighed against a dying child, *Nausea* doesn't count." His intention was to raise the question of what literature could do in a hungry world, but it was taken by some critics to be a suggestion that a dying child and a work of fiction could be put on the same level and weighed against each other.

23 May: he gave a paper at the colloquium on "Ethics and Society" organized by the Gramsci Institute in Rome. It gained wide notice because of its attack on structuralism and especially "certain Marxists tempted by structuralism (who) are trying to muffle the motor of history, that is, the class struggle."

May–June: Sartre and Simone de Beauvoir went to Kiev to take part in the celebrations honoring the 150th anniversary of the birth of Shevchenko, the great Ukranian poet. In Moscow they found the cultural situation far from encouraging; there was even a temporary doubt as to whether Sartre's *Words* would be published there. Sartre had the impression that ideologically the young were reacting against the "scientific" dogmatism of Stalin and his heirs, not by going back to a purer Marxism but by turning to religion. In Estonia he was impressed by the strong nationalist feelings, which verged on anti-Sovietism.

Two notable Communist leaders died in the summer, and the contrast between Sartre's tributes to the two men served to reflect the different relations he had experienced with the French and Italian Communist parties. In the case of Maurice Thorez, who died on 11 July, Sartre's message to the French Communist Party paid tribute to the man but referred to their "unavoidable differences." For Palmiro Togliatti, who died on 21 August and whose funeral Sartre attended in Rome, there was a much warmer tribute, with the title "My Friend Togliatti," and a reference to the Italian Communist Party as "the most intelligent of parties." Apart from this sad but moving occasion, the summer in Rome was very pleasant. Friends from France would visit them, and Sartre and Simone de Beauvoir spent time in the company of Italian Marxists, including Rosana Rossanda, who was in charge of the Communist Party's cultural policy; they wished the French Communist Party had put cultural matters in such capable hands.

On their return to Paris, they plunged themselves into a fresh initiative to inject new ideas into *Les Temps modernes*. At the beginning of the fall, they held a meeting in Simone de Beauvoir's apartment, to which they invited a number of bright young intellectuals—including Nicos Poulantzas and Régis

Debray, with a view to forming a group that would meet each week to discuss ideas and provide reviews for the journal. The first meeting was rather confused. Many of them were disciples of Althusser and wanted to turn *Les Temps modernes* into a platform for their doctrines. Fewer of them attended the second meeting, and Debray and others never came back. However, the group stayed in existence until 26 June 1966 and for a period met every week: with Sartre and Simone de Beauvoir on alternate weeks; otherwise, by themselves.

The event that came to overshadow everything else that year was the affair of Sartre's refusal of the Nobel prize for literature. It began on 15 October, when Sartre's Italian friend Enzo Paci wrote to ask him if he would send a copy of the speech he would be making on receiving the Nobel prize. Sartre was surprised to learn that such a possibility existed. The next day he wrote to the Swedish Academy informing them that, for strictly personal reasons, he did not wish to figure on the list of possible recipients of the prize. The academy confirmed that it received the letter on 21 October, but it went ahead the following day and awarded him the prize of $53,000. Sartre immediately drew up a statement, which was read in Stockholm on 22 October by a representative of his Swedish editor, with the title "The Writer Should Refuse to Let Himself Be Turned into an Institution." Published in France (in *Le Monde)* and in other countries, the statement set out his reasons for refusing the honor.

He mentioned that he had always refused official honors, such as the Legion of Honor in 1945 and election to the Collège de France. It followed from his conception of the role of the writer, who should persuade and convince solely by the written word and who should remain free of institutions or from the possibility of being turned into an institution. Among the objective reasons for refusing the prize, he mentioned his desire for cultural coexistence of East and West and his fear that, if he accepted awards from either bloc, he would compromise his position. It seemed to him that, at present, the Nobel prize was restricted to Western writers or Eastern rebels; it had not been awarded to Neruda, the great South American poet, nor to Louis Aragon, the Communist. It was regrettable that Pasternak was given the prize before Sholokhov. (This last remark was misunderstood by some of Sartre's Russian friends, who thought he was deserting the "liberal" for the "Stalinist" side.) He said he would have considered accepting the prize if it had been awarded during the Algerian War, when he was signing the *Manifesto of the 121,* because it would have honored not him but the freedom they were fighting for. The academy's citation mentioned freedom, but in the West it is often taken to mean abstract freedom, whereas for him it means a concrete freedom, such as the right to have more than one pair of shoes and to eat when one is hungry. Finally, to accept would be to risk the interpretation of some right-wing circles that, to quote *Figaro Littéraire,* "my controvesial political past would not be held too much against me." Far from wishing to have his controversial political past overlooked, Sartre considered it to be still valid, even though he was ready to admit, among friends, that he had made certain mistakes.

Reactions to this were mixed. They ranged from support from his old schoolmate and now director of Unesco, René Maheu, who declared in *Le Figaro* (26 October) that Sartre could be compared to Socrates, to condemnation by Gabriel Marcel, in *Nouvelles littéraires* (29 October), as an inveterate denigrator and systematic blasphemer who corrupted the young. In an interview in *Le Nouvel Observateur* (19 November), Sartre reaffirmed that his reasons for refusing the prize were that he feared being co-opted, so that some would say, "Finally he's on our side." It was not for the personal reasons that he had seen attributed to him in the newspapers, such as being upset because Camus was given the prize first or being afraid that Simone de Beauvoir would be jealous. What took Sartre aback even more were the letters he received from people who wanted him to take the money and give it to them for such purposes as the protection of animals; the preservation of a certain species of tree; or to buy a business, repair a farm or go on a trip. As Simone de Beauvoir put it, these people accepted the principles of capitalism, so that the fact that Mauriac had used the whole prize to put in a bathroom did not shock them, but Sartre's scorning it filled them with frustration.

The interview in *Le Nouvel Observateur* had the title "The Alibi," which referred to Sartre's comment that talk about young people being depoliticized served as an alibi for people who wished to turn the young away from direct involvement in politics. He rejected the current talk about an end of ideology and the idea that all industrial societies, whether capitalist or socialist, had the same problems—the "convergence" thesis. While deploring the failure of Eastern Marxists to analyze their own societies according to Marxist methods, he made the distinction that a socialist society, such as the USSR, required reforms, not revolution, unlike capitalist societies. In the West the new content of revolutionary struggle should include demands for workers' power in management, and the position taken by those on the Left should be uncompromising, and therefore "scandalous" in the eyes of the established order.

6 December: Sartre sent a message to the reception in homage to Nazim Hikmet, organized by *Les Lettres françaises* at the Salle Pleyel, in which he said of the militant intellectual what Pascal had said of the Christian: "he must never sleep."

9 December: Sartre and Simone de Beauvoir took part in a public debate on the *nouveau roman* (new novel), organized by the journal *Clarté*. Six thousand people were present in the amphitheater of the Mutualité. Sartre had not been one of those originally invited, although Simone had, and it was she who found out that some of the Communists hoped to use the occasion to attack him. He then insisted on taking part, which caused some participants to drop out. German television filmed the proceedings, and the lights caused him to feel weak from the heat, but he and Simone effectively made the case for a committed literature. The debate—under the title "What Can Literature Do?"—was published in 1965.

1965

Situations, VII: Problèmes de Marxisme, 2 (Situations, VII: Problems of Marxism, 2), containing eight pieces published from 1953 to 1962:
  "Reply to Claude Lefort"
  "Operation 'Kanapa' "
  "Reformism and Fetishes" (in reply to Pierre Hervé)
  "Reply to Pierre Naville"
  "The Ghost of Stalin"
  "When the Police Give the Three Raps . . ." (Robert Brasillach)
  "The Demilitarization of Culture"
  "Discussion of the Criticism of *The Childhood of Ivan*"

Les Troyennes (The Trojan Women), an adaptation of Euripides' play; limited edition published by the Théâtre Nationale Populaire. Published by Gallimard the following year.

Que peut la littérature? (What Can Literature Do?), debate with Simone de Beauvoir, Yves Berger, Jean Pierre Faye, Jean Ricardou, Jean-Paul Sartre and Jorge Semprun *Clarté*, no. 59 (January).

"Pourquoi je refuse d'aller aux Etats-Unis: Il n'y a plus de dialogue possible" ("Why I Refuse to Go to the United States: Dialogue Is Not Possible There Anymore"), *Le Nouvel Observateur* (1 April); *The Nation*, with an editorial (19 April), pp. 407–11

"Culture de poche et culture de masse" ("Pocket Culture and Mass Culture"), comments collected by Bernard Pingaud; *Les Temps modernes*, no. 228 (May), pp. 1994–2001

"L'Ecrivain et sa langue" ("The Writer and His Language"), *Revue de'Esthétique*, vol. 18, sections 3–4 (July–December), pp. 306–34

"Avant-garde? De quoi et de qui?" ("Avant-Garde? What and Whose?"), *Le Nouvel Observateur* (26 October), p. 29

Interviews on *The Trojan Women*, in *Bref* (magazine of the Théâtre National Populaire) no. 83 (February), and in *Nin* (Belgrade) 28 March; on why he refused to go to the United States, in *L'Unità* (19 March) and *Le Nouvel Observateur* (1 April); on Simone de Beauvoir, in *Vogue* no. 146 (July) pp. 72–73; on French politics and elections; on Vietnam, in *L'Unità* (18 April) and *The Nation* (31 May) (a message sent to the organizers of a teach-in on Vietnam at Boston University); on the revival of his play *The Condemned of Altona*, in *Les Nouvelles littéraires* (1 July); on the Americanization of culture, in several Greek newspapers

26 January: Sartre put in an application for the adoption of Arlette El Kaim, which was granted on 18 March.

10 March: The première of the Théâtre National Populaire production of *The Trojan Women*, which Sartre had adapted during his stay in Rome the previous summer. In an interview in *Bref* magazine in February, Sartre had explained why and how he had made his adaptation of Euripides' play. He discussed the function of clichés and maintained that the dominant theme of the play was the condemnation of war in general and colonial expeditions in particular. The play had been brought up to date by replacing the contrast between barbarian and Greek with one between Troy (as a symbol of the Third World) and Europe. In an interview with Gisèle Halimi, for the Belgrade journal

Nin, he stressed the political implications of the play and the role of women in it.

March also was marked by controversy concerning Sartre's refusal of an invitation he had earlier accepted to give a series of five lectures at Cornell University on Gustave Flaubert and philosophy. His decision not to go was brought about by the escalation of the war in Vietnam and the American bombing of the North. In a statement published in France and America, he also regretted the powerlessness of the American Left, who found themselves isolated in a country completely conditioned by myths of imperialism and anticommunism. It was his most pessimistic statement about America, and it drew much criticism from intellectuals there, including an editorial in *The Nation,* where the statement appeared. On 8 April, in *Le Nouvel Observateur,* Sartre responded to a letter from a Cornell professor, who had challenged the reasons given for his refusal; he denied that he felt any hatred for America, calling it an absurd suggestion.

In May *Playboy* magazine carried an interview that Sartre had given it the previous year before he was awarded the Nobel prize, although the subtitle described him as the "charismatic fountainhead of existentialism and rejector of the Nobel prize"; in a postscript the interviewer records that Sartre, when contacted again after his refusal of the prize, refused to add anything on this subject, saying that the greatest honor he could have was to be read.

The interview contains many revealing comments, such as that he had been thought of twice as being a traitor—a traitor in the conflict of the generations, and a traitor in the class war. The 1945 generation thought he had betrayed them because they got to know him through *No Exit* and *Nausea,* written at a time when he had not yet worked out the Marxist implications of his ideas.

He said that his duty as an intellectual was to think, and to think without restriction, even at the risk of blundering. He could set no limits within himself, and he must let no limits be set *for* him. As for his relations with the Communist Party, Marxism could work out its full possibilities only if it has "fellow travelers"—that is, friends of the Communists who did not fetter themselves politically and who tried to study Marxism objectively from within.

Literature had to be the work of clear-eyed men who took into account the totality of mankind. Literature had to realize that it existed in a world where children died of hunger. Literature had to realize that it lay within their power, as writers and as human beings, to do something for others. And that others can do something for them.

As a writer, he felt he should deal with what he was best fitted for—what others could not say better than he could. He had often thought that someday he would write about his joys, but then he reminded himself that this side of his life was not really worth holding up as an example.

It was true that he had always tried to surround himself with women who were at least agreeable to look at. Feminine ugliness offended him. He was ashamed of this.

But the main reason he surrounded himself with women was simply that he preferred their company to that of men. As a rule he found men boring. They had specialized sensibilities and they talked shop. But there were qualities in woman that derived from the female predicament, from the fact that she was both a slave and an accomplice. That was why her sensibility ranged so much wider than a man's.

Similarly, what he particularly appreciated in his Jewish friends was a gentleness and subtlety that was certainly an outcome of anti-Semitism. That was why people were always race-conscious, even if they disapproved of racialism.

It seemed to him that people were possessed by the things they possessed—whether it be money or the things it bought. When he liked an object, he always wanted to give it to someone. It was not generosity—it was only because he wanted *others* to be enslaved by objects, not himself.[1]

5 May: Sartre sent a long telegram to the organizers of a teach-in on Vietnam at Boston University, in which he made his most positive statement for some time about America, wishing the American intellectuals more success than the French intellectuals had had during the Algerian War. He said the demonstrations were taking place at a time when "irresponsible men are presenting an odious image of your country to the world,

1. *Playboy* XII, no. 5 (May 1965), pp. 69–76. "Jean-Paul Sartre: A Candid Conversation with the Charismatic Fountainhead of Existentialism and Rejector of the Nobel Prize," interview by Madeleine Gobeil.

and they help us to see that this image is false and that the coming generation is determined to disassociate itself from it completely."

24 June: *Le Nouvel Observateur* published an interview with Sartre in which he attacked one of the socialist leaders, Gaston Deffere, for proposing an alliance between the SFIO (French Branch of the Workers' International) and the MRP (People's Republican Movement). Sartre said the exclusion of the Communists would kill the Left, and he urged support for a single candidate of the Left in the forthcoming presidential election.

1 July: *Les Nouvelles littéraires* published a report of the press conference given by Sartre, Jean Vilar and François Périer on 23 June at the Théâtre de l'Athénée to announce the revival of *The Condemned of Altona*. Sartre confessed he wrote for the theater on impulse, when things were going badly.

July: Sartre and Simone de Beauvoir went to Russia and visited Lithuania. Sartre also went on his own to Helsinki to attend the World Peace Congress (13–14 July). The cultural climate in Moscow seemed better after the fall of Khrushchev, and an appeal by Sartre on behalf of the imprisoned Jewish poet Brodsky may have contributed to securing his subsequent release to a normal life in Leningrad. At the Peace Congress, Sartre made a speech calling for the withdrawal of American troops from Vietnam but managed to upset the Russian delegation, who thought he was taking sides with the Chinese and criticizing the lukewarmness of Russian aid to Vietnam.

September: The new production of *The Condemned of Altona* began playing at the Théâtre de l'Athénée and received good reviews.

6 October: Sartre made a speech in Rome at the congress of COMES (the European Writers' Community) on the theme "The European Avant-Garde, Yesterday and Today." Sartre said that the real avant-garde writer did not simply exploit or play with existing language, as did the false avant-garde, but created a language by writing. It was his opinion that the conditions for a real avant-garde existed only outside Europe.

During the French presidential elections, held in December, Sartre made a statement calling for a vote for Mitterand, as this was the only way to vote against personal rule, as exercised by President de Gaulle, and against the socialist flight to the Right. In a later interview, published in *Le Nouvel Observateur,* before the second round of voting, he said that it was not enough for the Left just to vote for Mitterrand; it also needed to unite around a precise, common program. Sartre's prediction proved correct, and it was not until the Left heeded his advice that its candidate won the presidency in the 1980s.

1966

"Père et fils" ("Father and Son"), excerpt from "Flaubert"; *Biblio,* and its supplement *Livres de France,* vol. 17, no. 1 (January), pp. 19–23

"Entretien avec Jean-Paul Sartre: L'Anthropologie" ("Discussion with Jean-Paul Sartre: Anthropology"), *Cahiers de Philosophie,* nos. 2–3 (February), pp. 3–12

"L'Universel singulier" ("The Singular Universal"), in *Kierkegaard vivant (The Living Kierkegaard),* colloquium organized by Unesco in Paris (21–23 April 1964), pp. 20–63 (Paris: Gallimard)

"La Conscience de classe chez Flaubert" ("Class Consciousness in Flaubert"), *Les Temps modernes,* no. 240 (May), pp. 1921–52; no. 241 (June), pp. 2113–53

"Jean-Paul Sartre répond" ("Jean-Paul Sartre Responds"), interview with Bernard Pingaud; *L'Arc,* special issue "Sartre aujourd 'hui" ("Sartre Today"), no. 30 (October), pp. 87–96

"Saint Georges et le dragon" ("Saint George and the Dragon"), on Tintoretto's painting *St. George Pinning the Dragon; L'Arc,* no. 30 (October), pp. 35–50

"Un Cancer en Afrique . . ." ("A Cancer in Africa"), on apartheid; *Christianisme social,* vol. 74, nos. 11–12, pp. 423–30

Interviews and statements on "The Powers of the Intellectual" on Italian television; on sundry topics during his tour of Japan; for the legalization of the Greek Communist Party on his visit to Greece in August; on behalf of Iranian political prisoners; on the launching of a French National Vietnam Committee; in support of a Swedish publisher expelled by the Swiss government for political reasons

1 January: Sartre's friend the artist Giacometti died in a Swiss nursing home. Their old friendship had grown a little strained in recent years, ever since the artist had taken offense at a remark of his that Sartre had included in *Words*. Giacometti objected to Sartre's interpretation of his remark (after being knocked down by a car) that "At last something is happening to me." Sartre's comment was: "I admire this readiness to welcome everything. If one likes surprises, one should like them to that point."

In February he wrote a preface for the program of Georges Michel's play *La Promenade du dimanche (Sunday Stroll),* which received its première on 26 February. Michel, one of the few writers from a working-class background in France, had received much encouragement and help from Sartre.

The February issue of *Cahiers de Philosophie* published an important interview in which Sartre explained his objections to structuralism. He warned that the concept of structure became misleading if it refers to pure contingency and an external constituent without being related to the historical praxis that constituted the structure. Although the linguistic model of structure had great clarity, it was an abstract model based on an inert synthesis, and it needed to be related to the totalizing praxis of human speech. Sartre insisted on two phases of investigation: the conceptual analysis of static structures (detotalized totalities) and dialectical comprehension, which puts the object of investigation back into the context of human activity, thus integrating the analytic phase as part of the ongoing totalization in practice. He also expressed his agreement with Jacques Lacan's formulation that the unconscious is the discourse of the "other," a discourse that separates through language.

On 27 April, Sartre assisted in a mock trial of the central character of his play *The Condemned of Altona* as part of a course for young lawyers.

2 May–6 June: Sartre and Simone de Beauvoir were in the USSR. Nearly all their conversations with intellectuals revolved around the sentencing of the writers Sinyavsky and Daniel, who had been given seven years and five years, respectively, for allegedly damaging the social and political régime of the USSR. Ehrenburg had courageously sent a petition, signed by 62 writers, calling for the release of the prisoners and offering to be responsible for them. Sartre's friend and translator, Lena, had been one of the signatories. Ehrenburg was surprised that Sartre should make a visit in these circumstances and greeted him with the words, "What are you doing here in the midst of all this?" Sholokov, whom Sartre had said should have received the Nobel prize before Pasternak, had denounced the signatories of the petition and said the men should have been punished even more severely. Solzhenitsyn refused to meet Sartre and reproached him for having cruelly insulted Russian literature by having, in effect, offered the Nobel prize to the "hangman" Sholokov. The next year Sartre and Simone refused to attend the Soviet Writers' Union because it would otherwise look as though they approved of the condemnation of Sinyavsky and Daniel or the silencing of Solzhenitsyn.

July: Sartre agreed to a request from Bertrand Russell that he take part in an international tribunal to consider American war crimes in Vietnam. Sartre was swayed by the advice of his friend Tito Gerassi, who was actively involved in the American antiwar movement.

July and August were spent visiting Greece and Italy. Sartre wrote a short piece on his friend Carlo Levi.

18 September–16 October: Sartre and Simone de Beauvoir undertook a tour of Japan at the invitation of their Japanese publisher and the University of Kyoto. They were greeted at Tokyo airport by swarms of photographers and hundreds of young people, who treated them like film stars. At a banquet arranged by the rector of the university, on the first evening, Sartre ate large quantities of raw fish, after which he was violently sick for the first time in his life and could not eat for two days. They sampled the nightclubs, including a homosexual bar where the main decoration was a poster from a Genet play, which the barman asked Sartre to autograph. During their tour of the countryside and the major cities, Sartre, who had taken a camera with him for the first time in his much-traveled life, "plied it with the ardour of a Japanese," as Simone put it. He gave three lectures on the situation and function of the intellectual, at the universities of Tokyo and Kyoto; he spoke on television and radio and attended a large meeting in protest against American intervention in Vietnam. They visited hospital patients who were victims of the atomic bomb dropped on Hiroshima and then experienced a nearly disastrous accident themselves when their car crashed at Kobe. Fortunately, they were uninjured, although a passenger in the front seat was badly cut. Their stay in Japan was seldom dull!

The October issue of *L'Arc* was devoted to Sartre and contained a rather controversial interview in which he criticized what he saw as a dangerous underlying philosophical trend in the works of Foucault, Lévi-Strauss, Lacan, Althusser and other structuralists. He found in them a common rejection of history and a neo-positivism, which he felt called upon to reject in the name of Marxism. It was not a well-phrased criticism, and it drew bitter counterattacks; Foucault, in a radio interview, expressed his admiration for Sartre but accused him of not having read *The Order of Things*.

9 November: Sartre presided at a conference organized by the Co-ordinating Committee Against Apartheid, held in Paris. Also in November, Sartre helped to launch an appeal announcing the formation of the National Vietnam Committee, which held a large meeting at the Mutualité on 23 November. Meanwhile the Russell Tribunal had begun meeting, holding its first session in London (14–15 November), at which Sartre was elected executive president. After the meeting, Sartre explained its meaning and scope in an interview published in *Le Nouvel Observateur*. He denied that it was "idealist"; the members would be idealists if they sought to set themselves up as a real tribunal and pronounced sentences. But they did have the right to assemble as citizens, to give the concept of "war crime" some force again by showing that every policy may and should be judged objectively in terms of existing juridical criteria.

Another continuing cause that he pursued during the year was on behalf of Iranian political prisoners, acting through the Committee for the Defense of Iranian Political Prisoners, which he had formed in March.

Throughout the year, in five issues, *Les Temps modernes* was publishing extracts from Sartre's forthcoming work on Flaubert, although Sartre was not completely satisfied with them, and they had to be substantially revised before they appeared in their final form in his book, *The Idiot of the Family* (1972).

4 December: Sartre gave a lecture on "Myth and Reality in the Theater" at a conference on the theater held in Bonn. He maintained that, contrary to popular belief, the movies had not dealt a blow to the theater, although they may have hit certain theatrical producers by taking away their audiences. However, these were likely to be producers who staged bourgeois, realist plays, and this sort of realism was much better done in the cinema. The movies had shown the living theater its limitations, and this could be turned into a strength, as all art forms that reflected on their limits had discovered the conditions of what was possible. As for critical theater—which, like all critical art, required from the artist a reflexive attitude toward his or her art—this had begun to emerge since 1950. It involved the rejection of psychological determinism, the rejection of a plot that simply served to distract the audience from what is essential and the rejection of bourgeois realism.

1967

Un Soleil, Un Vietnam (One Sun, One Vietnam), published by the National Vietnam Committee, with lithographs by Matta

"A qui rêve la demoiselle?" ("Who Is the Young Girl Dreaming Of?"), poem for Juliette Gréco, in Jean-Paul Leroux and Michel Chrestien, eds., *Le Livre blanc de l'humour noir (The White Book of Black Humor)*, p. 363

"Myth et réalité du théâtre" ("Myth and Reality in the Theater"), *Le Point* (Brussels), no. 7 (January), pp. 20–25

"L'Universel singulier" ("The Singular Universal"), on Carlo Levi; *Galleria* (Sicily), vol. 17, nos. 3–6 (May–December), pp. 256–258

"Pour la vérité" ("For the Sake of Truth"), preface to the special issue of *Les Temps modernes* devoted to the Arab-Israeli conflict; no. 253a (June), pp. 5–11

"Le Crime" ("The Crime"), on the Russell Tribunal; *Le Nouvel Observateur* (30 November–6 December)

"De Nuremberg à Stockholm" ("From Nuremberg To Stockholm"), on the Russell Tribunal; *Tricontinental,* no. 3 (November–December), pp. 7–19

"Le Génocide" ("Genocide"), on the findings of the Russell Tribunal concerning American war crimes in Vietnam; *Les Temps modernes*, no. 259 (December), pp. 953–71

Interviews and statements on contemporary theater in *Le Point;* on Georges Michel's play *Aggression* in *Bref;* on the Arab-Israeli problem in various publications, particularly during his trip to Egypt and Israel in February-March; a letter to President de Gaulle asking whether the French government was forbidding the Russell Tribunal from holding sessions in France; various speeches at the Russell Tribunal and interviews on its findings; articles and letters on behalf of Régis Debray, imprisoned in Bolivia; a statement on the death of Ilya Ehrenburg; a press conference about the movie *Le Mur (The Wall)* at the Venice Festival

January: Sartre went to London to meet with some of the other members of the Russell Tribunal. They laid down the tribunal's statutes and defined the questions they would try to answer. Other preparatory meetings were held in Paris and at some of these Lanzmann, whom Sartre had named as his deputy, sometimes took his place. The other members of the tribunal, in addition to Sartre and Simone de Beauvoir (although not all of them attended the sessions), included: Bertrand Russell, the honorary chairman, who, at 94, was too old to attend; Dedijer, from Yugoslavia, and Schwartz, from France, who together presided over the sessions; Gunther Anders, a German philosopher; Aybard, a Turkish professor of international law and a member of parliament; Basso, an Italian jurist and a member of parliament; Cardenas, former president of Mexico, who did not attend the meetings in Stockholm; Dellinger, a leader of the American antiwar movement; Hernández, a Philippino poet and former political prisoner; Kasuri, a barrister in the Pakistan supreme court; Morihawa, a Japanese legal expert; Sakata, a Japanese physicist; Abendrath, a German university professor and doctor of law; Isaac Deutscher, the Marxist historian; Laurence Daly, the British miners' union leader; and two famous black Americans, Stokely Carmichael and James Baldwin, neither of whom attended in person. New judges who were subsequently co-opted included Carl Ogleby, the American antiwar activist; Peter Weiss, the playwright; and Melba Hernández, a female comrade of Fidel Castro in the Cuban revolution. There were legal advisers, including Gisèle Halimi, who had been Sartre's lawyer, and Ralph Schoenman, Bertrand Russell's indefatigable and controversial assistant, who acted as organizing secretary to the tribunal. However, full sessions did not begin until later in the year because of difficulties with the British and French governments, which did not want them held on their territories.

During February and March, Sartre took time off from the absorbing business of launching the Russell Tribunal and turned his attention to another international problem—relations between Israel and the Arabs. *Les Temps modernes* was preparing a special issue for May on the Arab-Israeli problem, and Sartre thought a personal visit to Israel and Egypt might help to open up a dialogue between left-wing groups in the two countries. He had been invited to Egypt by President Nasser's close friend and spokesman Heykal, the editor of *Al Ahram,* and he had also received invitations from Israel. He set off for Cairo on 25 February, accompanied by Simone de Beauvoir, Claude Lanzmann and Ali el-Saman, an Egyptian journalist who was working on a thesis in Paris and had helped with documentation for the *Temps modernes* issue.

They were met by Heykal and Lufti el-Kholi, the Marxist editor of a left-wing journal, whom Sartre had met a number of times and whose wife was to act as their guide and interpreter. They were treated as great celebrities, and on some of their trips around the country, they were met by by crowds who chanted in unison, "Long live Sartre! Long live Simone!" President Nasser received them at his residence and talked with them for three hours. Sartre pleaded with him on behalf of 18 young Communists who had been imprisoned without trial, and shortly after the meeting, they were released. He also broached the Palestinian problem and asked whether, if Israel took in all the refugees, Egypt would then recognize the state of Israel. Nasser said that if Israel took in 1.2 million Palestinians, then it would no longer be Israel; it would "burst apart." He gave them the impression that he was not inclined to run the risk of a war. In his talks with the Palestinian leaders, Sartre insisted that a means had to be found of reconciling the rights of the Palestinians and the right of Israel to exist. He said that he would take back a faithful report of the Palestinian leaders' opinions; but they were angered by the fact that he was not prepared to share those opinions. At a press conference before leaving Egypt, he praised Nasser as a prudent, judicious and farsighted leader.

14 March: Sartre and Simone de Beauvoir arrived in Israel via Athens. They were met at Tel Aviv by the president of the parliament and a large group of deputies and intellectuals. During their stay they toured much of the country and met Yigal Allon and Levi Eshkol, along with other Jewish and Arab leaders. In his meetings and in lectures and news conferences, Sartre stressed his neutrality and the need for dialogue. He made clear that he recognized without reservation the two prior conditions for any settlement: Israel's sovereignty and the Palestinian refugees' right to return to Israel. But at the end of the visit, he admitted that these seemed to be insurmountable obstacles for the moment, and he could see no encouraging sign for an Arab-Israeli peace. He reiterated his neutrality in a preface to the special issue of *Les Temps modernes,* under the title "Pour la vérité" ("For the Sake of Truth"). A subsequent appeal that he issued with a few other French intellectuals at the end of May, which called for restraint on both sides and affirmed that they did not think Israel wanted war, aroused strong criticism from many supporters of the Arab cause. A few days later the war began and soon ended in Israeli victory. Sartre's stand was interpreted in some quarters as having constituted approval of Israel's actions, although that was not his intention.

In April the Russell Tribunal was getting ready to meet in Paris, having been denied permission by the British Labor government to meet in London. However, the French government refused a visa to Dedijer, and Sartre wrote to President de Gaulle on 13 April, asking him whether this meant it intended to forbid the tribunal from holding its sessions in France. In his reply announcing that this was the government's decision, despite earlier official assurances, President de Gaulle called Sartre "mon cher Maître" ("Dear Master"). To this Sartre replied that de Gaulle only used this term of address in order to make clear that he was speaking to Sartre the writer, not to the president of a tribunal. For his part, Sartre commented, it was only waiters in cafés who called him "maître," and they knew him as a writer. He added that the Western governments were obviously afraid of the issue of American war crimes; otherwise, why should they forbid a few intellectuals from meeting on their territories?

2–10 May: The tribunal met in Stockholm. The meetings took place in an amphitheater in the House of the People, and there were often 200 people at the public sessions, including two television teams, one Swedish and the other American. There were also private sessions, which were heated at times. Some of the vehemence was generated by Schoenman, who was secretary-general but also claimed to speak on behalf of the absent Lord Russell. Eventually Sartre lost his temper and told him, "Don't carry on like de Gaulle, who says *France* when he means *I*." Russell had asked the American government to send lawyers to plead their cause, and Sartre wrote to the American secretary of state, Dean Rusk, making the same request. Rusk told journalists that he would not "play games with an old Englishman of ninety-four." Sartre publicly read his response to this observation, making a comparison between Rusk and Russell in which he referred to the former as "that commonplace State Department official." Having made the opening speech of the hearings, Sartre also read out its findings at the end of the sessions in Stockholm. It unanimously concluded that the Americans were guilty of aggression in Vietnam and that they had used terrorist bombings to break the people's will to resist.

At a press conference to announce the tribunal's findings, held at the Mutualité on 19 May, Sartre summarized the extent of the evidence that had led them to their decision. He also sent a telegram offering the evidence to the defense in the court-martial of Captain Levy of the U.S. Army, who was being tried for having denounced American war crimes in Vietnam. In September, Sartre and Simone de Beauvoir went to Brussels for a preparatory meeting for the next session of the Russell Tribunal. Dellinger asked for a postponement until 20 November, because in America there was to be a great series of demonstrations against the war starting 21 October. They accepted an invitation to hold the next session in Denmark at a trade union center in Roskilde. At the opening session on 20 November, Sartre listed the questions they still needed to answer, the principal one being whether the Americans had committed genocide in Vietnam, and he again invited the U.S. government to send representatives. In the private sessions Sartre and Simone de Beauvoir expressed doubt that the Americans could be accused of genocide, but eventually they became convinced that the policies of massive bombing of civilian populations, the spraying of vegetation and crops with poisonous substances and the forced removal of villages and the breakup of families constituted genocide. Sartre presented a paper on the subject at the final meeting on 1 December, in which he defined the American actions as genocide on the grounds that, starting from a position in which one society was much more highly developed than the other, the stronger side had then proceeded to wage all-out war against the other, while the weaker side had not reciprocated in kind. Furthermore, the genocidal blackmail was backed up by the blackmail threat of atomic war, and this was slowly degrading all those of the human species who failed to denounce it, because their silence made them accomplices. Years later, after the end of the Vietnam war in 1975, Sartre was to say that the Russell Tribunal had made little impact, especially in America, where it might have counted, but that it had revived the old idea that every man was both his neighbor's judge and his keeper.

There had been little respite from Vietnam and the Arab-Israeli conflict during the year. The visit to Venice for the film festival in September had been an enjoyable occasion, especially as Serge Roullet's direction of *Le Mur* had produced the only film adaptation of any of his works that Sartre felt really happy about. In answer to a question at the press conference, Sartre agreed that it was possible to see parallels between his story of Spanish civil war idealism and that of current Chinese Red Guard ideology—it was idealism in both the best and the worst sense. The Venice trip had also allowed him to have a pleasant reunion with his old École Normale school friend, René Maheu, now director of Unesco.

The year ended with the death on 12 December of Sartre's old love, Simone Jollivet. She had lived as a recluse since the death in 1949 of Dullin, and at the end she had only Sartre and Simone de Beauvoir to offer assistance. Simone visited her in the apartment where she lived in squalor, surrounded by rotting food and vermin, and Sartre paid all her debts. It was left to Simone and the concierge to arrange for her to be taken to a hospital after she was found in a semicoma, lying on the floor, covered with excrement. She died in the hospital of suffocation.

1968

"L'Intellectuel face à la révolution" ("The Intellectual Confronts Revolution"), an interview; *Le Point* (Brussels), no. 13 (January), pp. 18–23

Interview and message on the Havana Cultural Conference, in *Granma* (weekly review, Havana), (21 January)

Text about the paintings of Hélène de Beauvoir (Simone's sister), in the catalog for an exhibition at galleries in The Hague and Tokyo and in *Essais* (Bordeaux), nos. 2–3 (Spring)

Interview by Françoise Gilles on the student rebellion, broadcast on Radio Luxembourg (Sunday, 12 May) and published as a tract by the National Union of French Students

"L'Imagination au pouvoir; Entretien de Jean-Paul Sartre avec Daniel Cohn-Bendit" ("Put Imagination in Power: Jean-Paul Sartre Questions Daniel Cohn-Bendit"), *Le Nouvel Observateur,* special supplement (20 May)

Statement made to the students in the main amphitheater of the occupied Sorbonne (20 May), reported in *Le Monde* (22 May)

"Les Bastilles de Raymond Aron" ("Raymond Aron's Bastilles"), *Le Nouvel Observateur* (19–25 June); reprinted in *Situations,* Vol. VIII

"L'Idée neuve de mai 1968" ("What Was New About May 1968"), *Le Nouvel Observateur* (26 June–2 July); reprinted in *Situations,* Vol. VIII

"Die Revolution kommt wieder nach Deutschland" ("The Revolution Returns to Germany"), interview in *Der Spiegel* (Hamburg), (15 July), pp. 58–64; reprinted as "Communists Are Afraid of Revolution" in *Situations,* Vol. VIII

"Il n'y a pas de bon gaullisme . . ." ("There Is No Good Gaullism"), *Le Nouvel Observateur* (4–10 November); reprinted in *Situations* Vol. VIII

Interviews and statements on the student rebellion in *L'Espresso* (Milan); on the theater, in *L'Avant-Scène Théâtre,* and on the production of his play *In the Mesh,* in *Théâtre de la Ville/Journal;* on the political situation in Czechoslovakia and the Russian invasion, in *Le Monde,* various Czech journals, *Paese Sera* (Rome) and *The Nation,* in which he denounced the Russian aggression as a war crime; on film criticism and the Venice Film Festival, in *Filmcritica* (Rome) and *Paese Sera*

Although he had accepted the Cuban government's invitation to participate in an international conference on culture, to be held in Havana during January, Sartre was unable to travel because of a painful arterial illness. Many Third World intellectuals attending the conference believed that Sartre had not come because he was disillusioned with the direction the Cuban revolution had taken or because he feared meeting the criticisms of Arab participants who were angered by his stand before the Arab-Israeli Six-Day War. Sartre had to content himself with sending a message of support for the conference and giving a telephone interview to a Cuban publication, in which he spoke at length about the Vietnam war and the Russell Tribunal.

A more significant interview appeared in the Belgian journal *Le Point* in January. Its significance lies in the position that Sartre took on the political role of the intellectual and the fact that these very relevant guidelines were laid down well in advance of the student rebellion of May and the Russian intervention in Czechoslovakia. The intellectual must be committed to rationality and universality, which required advocating the cause of the least favored in society. However, radicalism ran the risk of becoming "leftism," which demanded the instantaneous and immediate realization of the universal good. The two safeguards against this were the demand for truth, which requires constant reevaluation of the field of possibilities, and the intellectual's special responsibility to be both disciplined and critical toward the party that stood for the universal interest and good. The main task of Western intellectuals was to carry out critical analysis, not making statements at the level of detailed programmatic objectives but setting forth their principles. In France the objective should be to unite the Left around a common program. A revolutionary situation might result from an electoral victory for the Left, because American imperialism would no longer tolerate radical peaceful reforms.

27 February: Sartre gave evidence as a defense witness at the trial of 18 Guadeloupe nationalists, at which he called upon the French government to enter into a dialogue with the people of Guadeloupe and to see their problems in the wider perspective of Third World problems. He took part in an intellectuals' day of action on Vietnam on 23 March. From the end of March through April, Sartre and Simone de Beauvoir visited Yugoslavia, where they conferred with Vladimir Dedijer about future tasks for the Russell Tribunal. He also spoke to Yugoslavian students and gave an interview in which he reacted to the assassination of Martin Luther King by saying that he believed there were really two Americas. In April he gave a long interview to Czechoslovakian television in which he spoke of his hopes for the development of socialism in the Prague Spring, at a time when it looked as though free debate would give rise to sweeping reforms under the Dubcek régime. The April issue of *Les Temps modernes* carried several articles by Czech progressives. At a meeting in favor of "Black Power," held at the Mutualité on 30 April, Sartre shared the platform with James Forman, Aimé Césaire and Daniel Guérin.

From the beginning of the student rebellion, which started in May, Sartre took the side of the students against the authorities, especially against police repression and brutality. Some commentators looked upon him as the prophet and inspiration of the whole movement. However, Daniel Cohn-Bendit, one of the student leaders, while confessing that they had all read Sartre, nevertheless insisted that there was no single author who had inspired the movement. The disturbances had started as anti-Vietnam war protests, which were followed by arrests of students and then the closing of the university campus at Nanterre by the authorities. Cohn-Bendit and other students from Nanterre then invaded the Sorbonne, at which point they were arrested. On 6 May, the day they were to appear before the disciplinary council of the Sorbonne, there were student demonstrations in the Latin Quarter, which soon turned into battles with the police. Sartre, Simone de Beauvoir and a few friends issued a statement calling upon workers and intellectuals to give moral and material support to the struggle started by the students and professors. This was followed by a statement of solidarity—signed by Sartre, Lacan, Lefebvre and a number of other intellectuals—which appeared in *Le Monde* on 10 May. The night of 10 May was the occasion of epic battles, with barricades in the rue Gay-Lussac, cars burning and the police beating up many students and spectators. Public opinion was outraged. Sartre gave an interview to Radio Luxembourg, broadcast on 12 May, in which he said that these young people did not want the future provided by their fathers, and their challenge could only be violent because violence was being done to them.

In a special supplement of *Le Nouvel Observateur,* which appeared on 20 May, there was a conversation between Sartre and Cohn-Bendit, in which Sartre said that what was interesting about the students' action was that it was putting imagination in power. On the evening of 20 May, Sartre was invited to make a statement and to answer questions in the amphitheater of the Sorbonne, which was packed with several thousand students. At first the reception was rowdy, but after Sartre had uttered a few words, they quieted down. He told them of his hopes for "this wild-flowering democracy that you have created and that upsets all established institutions" (including the trade unions, which could only tag along in their wake). He believed that what was being formed was a new conception of society based on full democracy—a linking of socialism and liberty. On 15 June he also took part in a debate with student militants at the Cité universitaire.

At the beginning of June public opinion began to turn against the students, partly as a result of the violence that accompanied the demonstrations. In an interview published in *Le Nouvel Observateur* (19–25 June), Sartre insisted that the violence was a response to police provocation and that its meaning should not be interpreted as a desire for disorder but as a yearning for a different order. He upheld the students' demand for a new type of teaching and defended them against the criticisms of his old friend Raymond Aron, who he was prepared to bet had never protested in his life and because of that was not worthy to be a professor. Sartre's justification of this judgment rested on his definition of an intellectual as one who was loyal to a political and social order but never stopped contesting it. In a further interview, titled "What Was New About May 1968," which took place after the first round of elections, he said that the movement had only failed for those who thought the revolution was at hand. He answered the Communists' criticisms of the student movement as being anarchistic by asserting that it was not anarchy but a true socialist democracy that they wanted, and such a democracy did not yet exist anywhere in the world. They were making a new demand, that of sovereignty or power over their own fate. The prime mover in revolutions had always been poverty, but in our technocratic society the notion of power had become more important than that of ownership. They saw that, in our dehumanized world, the individual is defined by the object he produces or the function he fulfills.

They rebelled against this state of affairs and claimed the right to decide for themselves what part they should play.

July: Sartre gave an interview to *Der Spiegel* in which he accused the French Communist Party of having betrayed the May movement and therefore of carrying some responsibility for the subsequent strengthening of the Gaullist majority in the recent elections. He believed the Communists had resigned themselves in advance to the Left's losing the elections because they did not want at any price to be in power. This was explained by their fear of having to shoulder responsibility for the economic crisis and by their adherence to the line laid down by Stalin in 1945, according to which they were forbidden to challenge the division of the world arrived at by the Yalta summit meeting.

21 August: While on holiday in Rome, Sartre heard that Soviet tanks had entered Czechoslovakia. He at once gave an interview to the Communist paper *Paese Sera* and accused the Soviets of being "war criminals"; while expressing his deep respect for the history of the Soviet Union and saying that he was anything but an anti-Communist, he condemned the invasion without reservation. He approved of the condemnations by the Italian and French Communist parties but pointed out the contradiction in the attitudes of the latter, which had turned down the demands of millions of French people who had wanted revolution. He concluded by saying that it was clear the Soviet model was no longer valid, as it was suffocating under its bureaucracy, while the model being developed in Czechoslovakia answered the hopes of many people. Further distress was caused by the reaction of Castro; Sartre's Italian Communist friend Rosana Rossanda showed him the text of a speech in which Castro had enthusiastically approved of the invasion.

While in Italy he involved himself in the movement to demand a total reform of the Venice Film Festival and of the film industry. He took part in a round-table discussion, organized by *Paese Sera* and the National Association of Italian Filmmakers, in which he came out in favor of the elimination of competitive world festivals and the substitution of meetings in which film professionals could develop a common policy for producing a culture open to the masses.

11 October: At a meeting called by the Committee for the Fight Against Repression, held at the Mutalité hall, Sartre denounced the repression that had followed the May movement and said the régime was in its very nature an expression of the ruling class the movement was fighting. In a joint letter with Bertrand Russell, Laurent Schwartz and Dedijer, published in *The Times* (London) on 9 October and in *Le Monde* on 17 October, Sartre denounced the complicity between the USSR and the United States in preserving their respective "spheres of influence." At the end of October, he signed another letter with Russell and Marcuse, calling for Russian troop withdrawal from Czechoslovakia.

October: Sartre had had several meetings with his Czech friend, the writer Diehm, who passed on an invitation from the producers to attend the forthcoming production in Prague of *The Flies* and *Crime Passionel*. Sartre accepted but was very doubtful about whether the plays would be allowed and whether he would be granted a visa. In fact Sartre and Simone de Beauvoir landed in Prague on 28 November and went straight to a dress rehearsal of *The Flies*. The theater was packed with students, who proceeded to question Sartre about his position on the Czech situation. He stated that he looked upon the Soviet aggression as a war crime; that he had written *The Flies* to encourage the French to resist; and that he was glad that his play was now being performed in occupied Czechoslovakia. During the subsequent performances of the two plays that they attended, Sartre was given great ovations. He noticed that the audience saw allusions to the situation in Czechoslovakia at many points in the plays and applauded vigorously. In *The Flies,* when Jupiter says to Orestes and Electra, "I have come to help you," laughter broke out all over the theater. And in *Crime Passionel,* when Hoederer says that an army of occupation is never loved—no, not even if it happens to be the Red Army—there was frantic applause. In a television interview, they tried to avoid expressions that might be too compromising, but both Sartre and Simone spoke in veiled but obvious terms about the "misfortune" that had descended upon the Czechoslovak nation and of the nation's "justifiable bitterness." They left Czechoslovakia on 1 December, more hopeful than when they arrived because of the imprssion they had received of the Czechs' will to resist.

28 December: Sartre and the entire cast of *The Devil and the Good Lord* staged a protest at the Palais de Chaillot against the banning of Armand Gatti's play *Passion in Violet, Yellow and Red.*

1969

Les Communistes ont peur de la révolution (Communists Are Afraid of Revolution), a volume in the "Controverses series," consisting of two previously published interviews (Paris: John Didier).

"Le Mur au lycée" ("The Wall in High School"), *Le Monde* (18 January).

"Sartre: Israel, la Gauche et les Arabes" ("Sartre: Israel, the Left and the Arabs"), interview in Italian translation; *Quaderni del Medio Oriente* (Milan), vol. 1, nos. 3–4 (January), pp. 2–11; reprinted in *Situations,* Vol. III

"Un Juif d'Israel a le droit de rester dans sa patrie. En vertu du même principe, un Palestinien a le droit d'y rentrer" ("An Israeli Jew Has the Right to Remain in His Homeland. By the Same Token, a Palestinian Has the Right to Return to His"), an interview; *Le Fait Public,* no. 3 (February), pp. 12–17; reprinted in *Situations* Vol. VIII

"La Jeunesse piégée" ("Trapped Young People"), comments gathered by Serge Lafurie; *Le Nouvel Observateur* (17–23 March); reprinted in *Situations,* Vol. VIII

"L'Homme au magnetophone" ("The Man on Tape"), a psychoanalytic dialogue, with a commentary by Sartre; *Les Temps modernes,* no. 274 (April), pp. 1813–19; reprinted in *Situations,* Vol. VIII

Introduction to a set of documents on Greece, in *Les Temps modernes,* no. 276a (August), pp. 5–6

"La Lune: Una vittoria o una trappola?" ("The Moon: Triumph or Trap?"), interview on the American moon landing; *Paesa Sera* (30 August)

"Masses, spontanéité, parti" ("The Masses, Spontaneity, and the Party"), Italian interview; *Il Manifesto,* no. 4 (September), pp. 46–54; reprinted in *Situations,* vol. VIII

"Itinerary of a Thought," an interview; *New Left Review,* no. 58 (November–December), pp. 43–66

Televised interview on the My Lai massacre; excerpts in *Le Monde* (13 December)

Sartre continued to fight a rearguard action against what he considered to be a government-led backlash against the students in the wake of their rebellion of May 1968. On 18 January he published an article in *Le Monde* protesting against the transfer from the lycée de Vernon of a teacher whose supposed "crime" had been to set the students an essay on Sartre's *Le Mur (The Wall)* and to have asked them to write about topics that appeared in *Le Monde*. Sartre saw this as evidence of a politically orchestrated intimidation of teachers and students, and he demanded to know if the minister of education, Edgar Faure, wished to put the clock back and create a more authoritarian régime than that against which the students had protested. He saw parallels between the short-lived alliance of students and workers in the May events of 1968 in France and the similar alliance he had observed in Czechoslovakia. In an interview on Radio Luxembourg with the French trade union leader Jacques Séguy, on 28 January, he spoke of that alliance in Czechoslovakia and of the recent protest suicide of the Czech student Jan Palach. Sartre said that in his judgment, and in that of some Marxists, such a suicide could have the emotional effect of uniting the masses. On the occasion of Palach's funeral, Sartre called for a protest in Paris to show support for the Czech struggle.

30 January: Sartre's mother died. She had suffered a heart attack on 3 January and had been hospitalized; after a few days it looked as though she might recover, but then she had a stroke, which caused her to decline. Although she was in a comatose state for two weeks before the end and did not seem to recognize her visitors, on two occasions she brought her hand from under the sheets and squeezed Sartre's wrist. She had often said that she did not want a church funeral service, and so they took her straight from the hospital to the graveyard. The next day, Sartre and Simone went to the hotel room in the boulevard Raspail, where she had lived for the last few years, and within an hour had got rid of all her possessions. He gave most of her clothes and the television set to the chambermaids. It seemed an unceremonious end to a life, but he knew that she had been happy in her last years, taking pride in his achievements and seeing him frequently. Only a few weeks earlier, on Christmas Day, they had celebrated by drinking champagne together.

At the beginning of February, *Le Fait Public* (a magazine founded by dismissed journalists of the French television and radio organization) published an interview in which Sartre made the first restatement of his position on the Arab-Israeli problem since the Six-Day War. He advocated a negotiated peace in line with the principles he had always affirmed: return of territory occupied by Israel as a result of the war; recognition of Israeli sovereignty and settlement of the Palestinian refugee problem.

10 February: With Michel Foucault and other intellectuals, he spoke at a meeting called by the National Union of University Professors and the National Union of French Students to protest against the expulsion of 34 students from the University of Paris. He urged the students to resist the educational reforms introduced by Edgar Faure. His criticisms of the reforms were set out in *Le Nouvel Observateur,* under the title "Trapped Young People." He maintained that the so-called reforms were simply a cloak for the "modernization" of the university in the interests of monopoly capital. The only justifiable reform would constitute a revolution, because it would involve inventing a university that had the aim of opening up culture to everyone rather than being a means of selecting an élite.

17 March: Sartre held a press conference on behalf of the Committee for a Strike Against the Vote (set for 27 April), which sought to persuade the French people to boycott the referendum on regionalization measures, proposed by the Gaullist government. Far from promoting participation in government, Sartre said, the exercise would only serve to hide the fact that democracy was a myth, as all the real decisions were made outside the elected assemblies. He had also signed an appeal, published in *Le Monde* on 10 May, in favor of the candidacy of Alain Krivine, of the Communist League, in the presidential election. The appeal suggested that Krivine offered an opportunity for the forces of May 1968 to make themselves heard. However, there is reason to believe that Sartre hoped that Krivine would withdraw before the election.

The April issue of *Les Temps modernes* carried a controversial text of a psychoanalytical dialogue, with a commentary by Sartre, to which were added two replies by Pingaud and Pontalis, who subsequently resigned their *Temps modernes* editorial positions. The next was interesting because, in it, the patient seems to get the better of the psychoanalyst and virtually changes roles. Sartre said he found it fascinating because it spotlights the irruption of the "subject " into the consulting room. The patient with the tape recorder is convinced that the road to independence (facing up to one's fantasies and to other people) cannot pass via a situation of absolute dependence (transference and frustration) but only by a face-to-face encounter in which each accepts his responsibilities in a joint undertaking. Sartre denied his critics' charge that he was a "false friend" of psychoanalysis and preferred the label "critical fellow traveler."

In the June presidential elections, Sartre and Simone de Beauvoir abstained from voting in the second round, when the choice was between Pompidou and Poher.

Summer was spent in Yugoslavia and Italy. In Rome, on 27 August, Sartre took part in a discussion on the theory of the relationship of class and party with staff of the Communist journal *Il Manifesto.* He tried to explain the changes that had occurred in his view of the development of the USSR, especially his appreciation of its imperialist tendencies in light of the interventions in Hungary and Czechoslovakia. He had intended to attempt an explanation of these developments in volume 2 of the *Critique of Dialectical Reason,* but he doubted whether he would ever finish that work. There were also meetings in Rome with some of the leaders of the May 1968 student movement, such as Daniel Cohn-Bendit, who had been spending their summer holidays by the Italian sea. Sartre hoped the different groups might find a forum in *Les Temps modernes* in which to express their views. However, they were all hostile to one another, spoke only of their own parts in the May events and had the air of defeated men. They harshly criticized *Les Temps modernes* and accused it of becoming an institution; so nothing came of the plan of bringing the microgroups together.

The November issue of the *New Left Review,* published in Britain, carried a long interview with Sartre in which he took the opportunity to chart his own intellectual and political progress and suggested some of the directions that his future work might take. On 11 November he signed an appeal with Malraux and Mauriac asking for the release from prison of Régis Debray.

With other intellectuals he signed an appeal denouncing the repression in Czechoslovakia and protested against the expulsion of Solzhenitsyn from the Soviet Writers' Union.

11 December: Sartre took part in his first French television interview since the 1950s. It was on the My Lai massacre in Vietnam, and he rejected attempts to draw a parallel with alleged massacres committed by the National Liberation Front. He presided at a press conference on 19 December, which was also devoted to the Vietnam massacres.

1970

"Le Socialisme qui venait du froid" ("The Socialism that Came in from the Cold"), preface to *Trois générations: Entretiens sur le phénomène culturel tchécoslovaque (Three Generations: Discussions of the Czechoslovak Cultural Phenomenon)*, by Antonin Liehm (Paris: Gallimard).

"Je-Tu-Il" ("I-Thou-He"), preface to *L'Inachevé (The Uncompleted)*, a novel by André Puig (Paris: Gallimard)

Various articles and interviews in *Le Monde, Israel-Palestine, Rouge, La Cause du peuple, Le Nouvel Observateur, Combat, L'Idiot international, Tout!, The Spokesman*

"Coexistences," text of the catalog for a show by Paul Rebeyrolle at the Galerie Maeght

Sartre's thinking, radicalized by the events of May 1968, was leading him to a new assessment of the role of the intellectual. Previously he had thought of the intellectual as the technician of practical knowledge, conscious of the contradiction between the universality of knowledge and the particular interests of the dominant class of which he was the product. The traditional intellectual, enjoying his role, derives a good conscience from his bad conscience and in this way believes himself able to stand alongside the proletariat. The new kind of intellectual, Sartre felt, had to eliminate himself as an intellectual, to go beyond this contradiction by putting himself directly in the service of the masses in order to achieve true universality.

Thus it was that Sartre became heavily involved in the various affairs of *La Cause du peuple,* the newspaper that had run a first series of 21 issues in May–June 1968, under the editorship of Roland Castro. Now, in 1970, edited for the most part by militant workers, it was intended to be a liaison between the factory workers who supported the Gauche prolétarienne (Proletarian Left) and aimed to publicize the various struggles that the worker was engaged in. It likened its followers to resistance partisans, Communist Party members to Nazi collaborators, spoke of the "occupation" of France by the bourgeoisie and the need to liberate the land. It was openly hostile to intellectuals and had even taken Sartre himself to task over his defense of Roland Castro, who had been charged with police assault during a demonstration protesting the death of five immigrant workers asphyxiated in their barracks at Aubervilliers. When, in April, the newspaper having been systematically confiscated by government authorities, its two young editors, Le Dantec and Le Bris, were successively arrested, it was somewhat surprising that other militants in the GP, through the intermediary of Alain Geismar, should ask Sartre to take on the editorship. He accepted without hesitation, thinking that his notoriety might be useful in protecting the Maoists from further repression. After all, it was the first time, with the exception of the German occupation years, that any newspaper editor had gone to jail in France since 1881. During the course of their association with Sartre, the Maoists were obliged to revise their judgment and their tactics with regard to intellectuals.

27 May: Sartre gave evidence at the trial of the former editors of *La Cause du peuple:* they were given a one-year prison sentence on the grounds of having provoked crimes against national security and justifying theft, pillage, arson and murder. This decision was met with a very violent demonstration in the Latin Quarter, and a few days later, when the police surrounded the plant where the newspaper was printed to take its owner, Simon Blumenthal, into "supervisory detention" and to confiscate another press run, the workers surrounded the police vans, forcing the police to leave without Blumenthal, and somehow managed to smuggle out 75,000 copies of the paper to the street corner vendors.

The first number of *La Cause du peuple* to appear under
Sartre's editorship was issued on 1 May 1970, and this date
marked the beginning of a new period of militant action for
him. Apart from taking on the editorship of other papers—no-
tably, *Tout!* and *La Parole au peuple*—and participating in the
foundation of *Secours rouge,* the newspaper of the organization
whose goal was to fight for the political and legal defense of
victims of repression, he went out on the streets to sell *La Cause
du peuple,* thus challenging the authorities to arrest him, which,
of course, they were afraid to do. Sartre said to the many newspaper and television reporters who were in attandance that his
aim was to place the government in a state of self-contradiction,
and judging by the confusion of the police, he had obviously
succeeded. It was also through his association with *La Cause
du peuple* that Sartre met Pierre Victor, alias Benny Levy, an
Althusserian Leninist-Marxist[1] and "Spontex"[2] Maoist, who
was to become his closest friend and collaborator. Sartre's
gradual progression toward the extreme Left had repercussions
among the staff of *Les Temps modernes:* following the publication in April of an article by André Gorz entitled "Destroy
the University," J-B. Pontalis, who had been with the journal
since the beginning, and Bernard Pingaud, who had joined in
1949, decided that they could no longer go along with its orientation and resigned.

Sartre continued to be outspoken on international issues: he
wrote an article in *Le Monde* (13 January) protesting events
in Biafra ("After the assassination of Biafran hopes the reign
of political gangsterism has spread throughout the four corners
of the earth"); he gave a speech at the Mutualité in which he
expressed solidarity with the Brazilian people and stressed the
role of the nationalist bourgeoisie in the establishment of the
dictatorship; in February he gave a filmed interview to the International Committee in Support of the Struggling Mexican
People, saying that the Castroite model was not suitable for
Mexico and that real revolution and real socialism should break

---

1. Victor had been influenced by Louis Althusser's reassertion of the scientific
character of Marxism, stressing its structuralist and historical-materialist
method.

2. So called because the Maoists who believed in sponaneous political action
had chosen the trade name of Spontex scouring sponges to designate their particular brand of "spontaneism."

completely with all previous models and take directives, orders and advice from no one; and in March he became a member of the Israel-Palestine Committee and made clear that his position was the same as the one he had taken before the Six-Day War, which consisted of supporting both the Palestinians' rights to Palestine and the Israelis' rights as a nation. In all these cases he believed that true revolution was the only solution.

Despite his involvement in militant action, Sartre continued to work passionately on his study of Flaubert, much to the disappointment of his Maoist friends, who would have preferred that he write a militant tract or a popular novel. He realized that such a work, written in a complex and "bourgeois" style, would have no appeal for the working class, but nevertheless, since he had been working on Flaubert on and off for 17 years, he was determined to see it through, even though his friends might regard his effort as thoroughly bourgeois. His justification was that, at any historical moment, regardless of the social or political context, it remained essential to understand men, and that his study of Flaubert, with its particular method, would help in achieving this goal.

After spending July traveling in Norway and the Scandinavian countries with Vladimir Dedijer and Arlette El Kaim, and August in Rome with Simone de Beauvoir, he returned to Paris in early September ready to continue the various battles he was involved in. He lived in a small 10th-floor apartment on the boulevard Raspail, opposite the Montparnasse cemetery and very close to Simone de Beauvoirs'. According to her account, he led a fairly routine existence, seeing his old friends regularly—Wanda Kosakiewicz, Michèle Vian—and his adopted daughter, Arlette El Kaim, with whom he would stay two nights a week. Otherwise he would spend his evenings at Simone de Beauvoir's often listening to music—Mozart, Monteverdi, Verdi, Stockhausen, Berg and Webern were among his favorites—and Bost, Lanzmann, Liliane Siegel and Sylvie Le Bon would often drop in and join them.

It was in September that he took over the editorship of *Tout!*, a journal of Maoist-libertarian tendencies, which had been started by the Vive la Révolution (Long Live the Revolution) group, and which involved Sartre in all kinds of legal proceedings, particularly the following year, for its position on homosexuality and drugs. He also apppeared as a witness at the trial of the people who had disseminated *La Cause du peuple*. At a meeting of the "Secours rouge" at the Mutualité, attended by 6,000 people (where, incidentally, he again met Jean Genet, who was now heavily involved with the Black Panthers), he denounced the massacre of the Palestinians in Jordan. In October he refused to appear as a witness at the trial of Alain Geismar, who had been arrested for his part in the demonstration of 27 May, having come to the bitter conclusion that the defense could not get a fair hearing anyway. Instead he decided to go and talk to the workers at the Renault plant in Boulogne-Billancourt, urging unity of action between workers and intellectuals. Although this meeting was attended by several journalists and got worldwide press coverage, very few workers were present to respond to his message. Geismar got 18 months detention.

All of this political activity continued despite the fact that the state of Sartre's health was causing his friends great alarm. He had frequent dizzy spells, which caused him to lurch and stumble. They were eventually diagnosed as circulatory problems. Since he had by now handed over the Flaubert manuscript, he more or less observed the doctor's recommendation to take it easy, and by the end of November he was pronounced cured.

December: Under the aegis of the "Secours rouge," Sartre participated in a "people's trial" at Lens in northern France, an action that he considered most important. In February 16 miners had been killed and several others injured by an explosion of firedamp in the pit at Hénin-Liétard. In reprisal some unidentified young men set fire to the Coal Board offices and were arrested. The trial of the alleged arsonists was to take place on 14 December, but on 12 December the "Secours rouge" organized a people's court in the Town Hall in Lens. On the day of the accident, a fan had been removed, since it was to have been replaced by a more powerful model, but in the meantime the firedamp had accumulated in the shaft. Nevertheless, the miners had been sent down the pit. Sartre argued that the state, as employer, was guilty of premeditated murder, of choosing profit before safety. Such was the publicity surrounding the case that the following Monday the alleged arsonists were acquitted. Although much-criticized for setting himself up as a judge, Sartre felt convinced that by exposing the capitalistic values of the employer, he had helped to radicalize public opinion.

1971

L'Idiot de la famille: Gustave Flaubert de 1821 à 1857 (The Idiot of the Family: Gustave Flaubert from 1821 to 1857), vols. 1 and 2 (Paris: Gallimard)
Preface to *Le Procès de Burgos (The Burgos Trial)*, by Gisèle Halimi (Paris: Gallimard)
Various articles in *J'accuse, L'Idiot international*

Sartre continued to make highly visible, active protests in 1971. In January he spoke at the Mutualité in favor of Russian Jews and their right to emigrate; he actively supported a hunger strike—which had as its headquarters the Saint-Bernard Chapel in the Gare Montparnasse—to demonstrate solidarity with political prisoners, including Alain Geismar, held in la Santé, who were asking for an improvement in their prison conditions; he began to write regularly for a new left-wing newspaper called *J'accuse,* which, in May, merged with *La Cause du peuple.* In February, Sartre and several members from the Gauche prolétarienne attempted to occupy Sacré Coeur in order to focus public opinion on the injuries inflicted on a "Secours rouge" demonstrator by the police. In fact, the CRS (the French riot police) were quickly called in, and although Sartre was spirited away by his friends, the demonstrators were again treated violently by the police. He and Jean-Luc Godard gave a widely publicized press conference on the incident. However, a few days later, Sartre resigned from the "Secours rouge" in the belief that the Maoists were becoming too prominent in the organization and that it suffered from too many defections and internal dissensions. During this period he regularly attended the meetings of *Les Temps modernes'* staff, and according to Simone de Beauvoir's account, he seemed to be in particularly good health. In April he and Simone, along with Arlette and

Sylvie, revisited Saint-Paul-de-Vence and Cagnes, places that they had loved in their youth.

Also in April he signed a letter addressed to Fidel Castro protesting the jail sentence of the Cuban poet Heberto Padilla on charges of homosexuality. This was met by a virulent attack on French intellectuals by Castro, but Sartre had long since become disillusioned about Cuba, feeling that it already demonstrated the "dogmatic obscurantism, the cultural xenophobia, and the repressive system which Stalinism imposed in the socialist countries."[1] He participated in a debate after a showing of the movie *The Sorrow and the Pity,* made by Max Ophuls and André Harris: his main criticism was that it completely eliminated the role that the working class had played in the resistance. In early May a delegation from the "Secours rouge" led by Sartre went to the police station in Ivry-sur-Seine to look into the circumstances in which an Algerian worker, Behar Behala, had been wounded by the police, and a result of this inquiry, a demonstration was organized—an action that again set Sartre at loggerheads with the Communists.

But without a doubt, the major literary event of the year was the publication of the first two volumes of *The Idiot of the Family,* a work that, for its sheer bulk—over 2,000 pages—confounded the critics, who described it as a "verbal Himalaya" and an "anthropological saga." It is an attempt at "totalizing" Flaubert "in the text," using Flaubert's extensive correspondence, and particularly the writings of his youth. Sartre tried to show by his progressive-regressive method, combining psychoanalytic techniques and applied Marxian dialectics, how Flaubert reflected the contradictions of his milieu and class, how he was constituted and became a person—the author of *Madame Bovary.* Sartre's psychological analysis focuses on Flaubert's sexual passivity, caused by the nursing of a cold, rejecting mother and the authoritarian repression of an overbearing father. Both parents clearly favored his older brother, whose abilities were constantly being held up for the young Gustave to emulate, thus further reinforcing his feelings of inferiority—of being the family idiot. The neurosis engendered by his family situation led Flaubert to try to escape into the world of the imaginary, the idea of art for art's sake, to com-

---

1. Sartre quoted in *Le Monde* (22 May 1971).

pensate for his failures in the real world. The Marxist dialectical analysis attempted to situate Flaubert in relation to his time, his class, his relationship to science. In effect, Sartre tried to show through *empathy* how the child interiorizes the social world and its dominant ideologies.

Although Sartre was not very familiar with Lacan's work, his conception of the self as an imaginary construction assumed by the individual after the fact corresponded very closely to Lacan's theory, and, like Lacan, Sartre maintained that by showing the formation and the personalization of the individual, how he moves toward the concrete from the abstract conditioning of the family structures, one can discover all the structures of the self, thus removing the "mystery" in the development of a life. "The fundamental project in my 'Flaubert' is to show that at bottom everything can be communicated . . ., that every human being is perfectly capable of being understood if the appropriate methods are used and the necessary documents are available."[2] In *Madame Bovary* Flaubert inscribes his own defeat—there are numerous passive verbs denoting inner paralysis; but the *triumph* of the book Sartre promised to account for in his totalizing critique, which would constitute his last volume, using structuralist techniques.

May: Sartre suffered a slight stroke: he lost some of the use of his right arm, he experienced difficulty in walking, and his speech became impaired—all signs of circulatory problems in the left side of the brain. However, rest and a course of treatment soon diminished the effects: in the meantime he occupied himself by correcting the proofs of *Situations,* vols. VIII and IX.

Sartre's involvement with *La Cause du peuple* and *Tout!* finally brought him libel suits to answer, but he remained undaunted. He took on another editorship, this time of *Revolution!*, a magazine run by a splinter group of the Communist League. And with Maurice Clavel he founded the "Libération" news service, which, in seeking to provide a forum for journalists "who wish to tell all to people who want to know all," aimed to cut into the monopoly of the "bourgeois" press. Criticisms of Sartre's activities abounded: the weekly magazine *Minute* ran

2. Sartre quoted in *Le Monde* (14 May 1971).

as its cover title "Enough of This Indulgence for Those Who Incite Disorder, Pillage and Hatred: Let's Put Sartre in Jail!" and called him the "red cancer of the nation." A few days later Sartre called for a people's trial of the police in the following words: "A people's tribunal will be held on 27 June. It will examine the role of the police in French daily life since January 1, 1971. This tribunal is absolutely necessary: there is a profound conflict between police activities and the masses." This tribunal, which was to have been held at the Cité universitaire, was banned by police headquarters and was replaced by a meeting—a press conference at the Mutualité—to which Sartre sent a letter and a recorded interview because, due to illness, he was unable to attend. He was suffering from a very sore tongue, which completely dispirited him, causing him to manifest for the first time in his life, and much to the anguish of Simone de Beauvoir, a defeatist attitude toward his fate.

However, after a summer spent on various travels, first with Arlette in Switzerland for three weeks, then for two weeks in Naples with Wanda and finally for several weeks in Rome with Simone, where he finished the third volume of *The Idiot of the Family,* he recovered his good health and his good humor.

On his return to Paris in October, he started the fourth volume of *L'Idiot* and continued to be politically active: he made various appeals on behalf of Iranian political prisoners; along with other intellectuals he called for the granting of emigration rights for Soviet Jews; he worked for the establishment of a Patrice Lumumba African Cultural Center at Nanterre; and in November—along with Michel Foucault, Jean Genet, Claude Mauriac, Michel Leiris and Yves Montand—he participated in a demonstration in the Goutte d'Or section of Montmartre to protest the murder of Djelalli, a young Algerian, who appeared to have been the victim of a racist attack. But Sartre did tire more easily and confided in Simone that he thought he might not be able to finish the work on Flaubert. He bgan to talk about his funeral, which he wanted to be simple, expressing the wish not to be buried in Père Lachaise between his mother and his stepfather but to be cremated. These reflections about his own mortality were, however, interspersed with moments of great optimism, when he thought he might easily last another 10 years.

1972

L'Idiot de la Famille: Gustave Flaubert de 1821 à 1857 (The Idiot of the Family: Gustave Flaubert from 1821 to 1857), vol. 3 (Paris: Gallimard)

Situations, VIII: Autour de 68 (Situations, VIII: Around 1968), (Paris: Gallimard); this volume consists of four parts:

1. Vietnam: The Russell Tribunal

    "Dialogue Is Not Possible There Anymore"

    "An American Writes to Sartre"

    "Sartre Replies" (to David I. Grossvogel)

    "The Crime"

    "Letter to the President of the Republic and Reply" (Charles de Gaulle)

    "Sartre to de Gaulle"

    "Twelve Unangry Men"

    "Russell Tribunal: Opening Speech"

    "From Nuremberg to Stockholm"

    "Genocide"

2. France

    "The Alibi"

    "Let's Refuse to Be Blackmailed"

    "Should the Left Be Killed or Cured?"

    "The Counter Shock"

    "Raymond Aron's Bastilles"

    "What Was New About May 1968"

    "Communists Are Afraid of Revolution"

    "There Is No Good Gaullism . . ."

    "*The Wall* in High School"

    "Trapped Young People"

    "The Masses, Spontaneity and the Party"

    "The Brazilian People in the Bourgeois Crossfire"

    "The Geismar Affair"

    "The Third World Begins in Our Suburbs"

    "The Whole Truth"

    "Words Spoken at the Committee's Press Conference" (Committee for the Liberation of Soldiers in Prison)

    "The First People's Trial at Lens"

3. Israel-The Arab World

    "Interview" (with Claudine Chonez)

    "Israel, the Left and the Arabs"

4. Intellectuals

    "Note" (of introduction)

"A Plea for Intellectuals"
"The People's Friend"
Situations, IX: Mélanges (Situations, IX: Miscellany), (Paris: Gallimard); this volume consists of three parts:
1. On Myself
    "Writers in Person"
    "The Writer and His Language"
    "Anthropology"
    "Sartre on Sartre"
2. Texts
    "Palmiro Togliatti"
    "The Singular Universal" (on Kierkegaard)
    "Mallarmé" (1842–98)
    "Saint George and the Dragon"
    "The Socialism that Came in from the Cold"
    "I-Thou-He" (on *The Uncompleted*, by André Puig)
    "Coexistences" (on Paul Rebeyrolle)
3. "The Man on Tape"
    "Psychoanalytical Dialogue"
    "Reply to Sartre, by J.-B. Pontalis"
    "Reply to Sartre, by Bernard Pingaud"
Foreword to *Les Maos en France (The Maoists in France)*, by Michèle Manceaux (Paris: Gallimard).

Having decided to use his notoriety "for the service of the masses," Sartre continued, in 1972, to be actively militant in various causes, though his health from time to time prevented him from participating as much as he wanted to. In January—along with Michel Foucault, Gilles Deleuze and Claude Mauriac—Sartre tried to hold a press conference inside the Ministry of Justice to protest the penal system as a whole and to indict the minister, Pleven, for not having kept his promise to improve conditions for political prisoners, but the group was unceremoniously dispersed by the CRS (the French riot police). Their press conference was subsequently held at the Libération press agency. The following month, Sartre and Michèle Vian, along with a group of militants, managed to get inside the Renault plant in order to protest the arbitrary firing of Maoist militants, but they were violently expelled by security guards: Sartre accused Renault of fascism. This confrontation with Renault was to have widespread repercussions later.

Meanwhile, Sartre was enjoying having a film made about his life by Alexandre Astruc and Michel Contat, which gave him the opportunity to talk about his past with old friends: Jacques-Laurent Bost, André Gorz, Jean Pouillon and, of course, Simone de Beauvoir. He discussed at length the difference between the classic intellectual—which he himself had been until 1968 and to some extent still was, despite himself—and the new kind of intellectual, who, abandoning his uneasy conscience and his élitist position, follows the masses "without exception." Similarly, he explained how his lifelong search for a morality had finally led him to the conclusion that politics and morality were but one and the same thing—a position he shared with the Maoists. His film was shot during February and March, but because of lack of financial backing, it was not completed until 1976.

Immediately after the filming was over, Sartre went to Brussels to give a lecture on "Justice and the State" to the young bar association of Belgium. He drew the distinction between bureaucratic justice and popular justice, insisting that the role of the intellectual who had decided to work for the latter kind of justice was to do everything in his power to give the people a chance to speak for themselves. He went on to describe the aims of *La Cause du peuple,* and as examples of bourgeois justice he described the cases of Geismar and Roland Castro; he attacked prison conditions and denounced the many and various pressures to which judges were subjected. Unfortunately, the audience was bourgeois in the extreme, failed to be the slightest bit convinced by Sartre's thesis and even took him to task for not dressing properly for the occasion.

On his return to Paris, he learned about the latest incident at the Renault factory in Billancourt. Ever since January there had been demonstrations outside the factory gates against arbitrary dismissals, unemployment and racism. On the night of 25 February, Pierre Overney, who had been sacked the year before, was shot and killed by an armed guard during the course of a demonstration. Sartre himself went along to the factory to look into the facts of the case, proclaiming that he had no confidence in official justice. Although he was not able to walk very far during the demonstration that accompanied Overney's funeral, he was greatly heartened by the massive turnout of 200,000 people, the likes of which had not been seen since 1968, and which seemed to indicate a renewal in left-wing politics. He wrote in his preface to Michèle Manceaux's book *Les Maos en France* that the three immediate characteristics of Maoist revolutionary action were violence, spontaneity and morality. He claimed that the traditional Left parties were still living in the nineteenth century, in the era of competitive capitalism. But the Maoists, with their anti-authoritarian *praxis*, seemed to be the only revolutionary force capable of adapting itself to the new forms of class struggle in the present era of organized capitalism.[1] However, when a group called the New People's Resistance kidnaped Robert Nogrette, the chief of personnel at the Renault factory, in reprisal for the murder of Pierre Overney, Sartre felt unable to condone this action and, according to Simone de Beauvoir,[2] was embarrassed that he might be asked to comment. He was caught in a similar way when *La Cause du peuple* published an article about a murder in Bruay-en-Artois in which the workers appeared to be calling for lynching as the appropriate form of justice for the lawyer who committed the crime. Sartre protested this line of argument but at the same time justified the class hatred that had led the workers to make these suggestions. By this time Sartre was beginning to detach himself from the policies of *La Cause de peuple*. In June he decided to raise his doubts about the direction in which *La Cause du peuple* was moving and published in it an article criticizing its simplistic working-class didacticism; its lack of awareness of other movements of struggle, such as movements of the young, of women, of intellectuals, of small businessmen; and its tendency to become less and less democratic.

Apart from minor attacks of illness, which were often aggravated by his drinking, Sartre's main anxiety was related to his teeth. He would frequently get mouth ulcers, and it appeared increasingly likely that he would have to wear dentures. He felt that this would be the end of his political activities if he could no longer speak in public. He was greatly relieved when, in the fall, an operation was successfully completed, and he suffered no such impediment.

1. Jean-Paul Sartre, preface to Michèle Manceaux, *Les Maos en France* (Paris: Gallimard).

2. Simone de Beauvoir, *La Cérémonie des adieux* (Paris: Gallimard, 1981), p. 48.

June: Volume 3 of *L'Idiot de la famille* appeared. It dealt with the interpretation of Flaubert's neurosis and certain of its consequences from the viewpont of his social environment. The fourth volume, in which he intended to use structuralist methods to analyze *Madame Bovary,* was giving him a lot of trouble, primarily because he had grave reservations about the usefulness of structuralism but also because he was afraid of repeating himself. During the summer—spent in Austria with Arlette, Belgium with Sylvie and Rome with Simone—he worked on it without enthusiasm.

In the fall he gave an interview to a couple of journals, *Esquire* and *Gulliver,* but he derived most pleasure from a series of conversations about politics that he undertook with Benny Lévy and Philippe Gavi, which were to last until March 1974, and which were to form the basis of a book, *On a raison de se révolter (You Are Right to Rebel).* Sartre felt that he could have the type of conversation with them that he had previously only found possible with women, and although they had a considerable rejuvenating effect on him, their drinking habits were altogether too much for Sartre to keep pace with and caused Simone some considerable anxiety.

In the winter of 1972, Sartre became very actively involved in a project to turn the Libération news agency into a popular daily newspaper, *Libération,* which would practice participatory democracy and in which the news and opinions would be furnished by the readers themselves. Sartre willingly undertook to be the editor in chief and put $40,000 of his own money into the venture. For this he finally decided to abandon the final volume of "Flaubert," no doubt with a certain amount of relief.

1973

Un Théâtre de situations, a collection of texts and discussions about the theater, ed. Michel Contat and Michel Rybalka (Paris: Gallimard)

Preface to *Les Paumés (The Mixed-up Ones),* by Olivier Todd

"Sartre parle des Maos" ("Sartre talks about the Maoists"), text of a conversation with Michel-Antoine Burnier; *Actuel* (January).

"Elections, piège à cons" ("Elections, a Trap for Fools"), an article; *Les Temps modernes,* No. 318 (January).

An article in *Le Monde* on prisons; an interview in *Pro Justitia* about bourgeois justice; an interview in *Der Spiegel* about French politics, the "Baader group" and revolution; interview in *Al Hamishmar* about the Arab-Israeli conflict; interview in *Libération* about rape

Much of Sartre's time, energy and money was being devoted to the launching of *Libération,* and on 7 February, despite his deep distrust of the government-run radio and television company, O.R.T.F., he agreed to be interviewed on France-Inter by Jacques Chancel for "Radioscopie" to talk about the project. The interviewer tried to get Sartre to talk about his life and work, as was normally expected in this program, but Sartre refused to talk about anything other than what concerned him—*Libération.* He was able to tell his radio audience that donations were coming in at a rate of about $1,000 a day and that the paper's eventual success would depend on the support given by the people that it was intended for. In response to a question about his presumed abandonment of philosophy for advocacy journalism, he said that he hoped that after six months the paper would be doing well enough for him to be able to take a back seat. A few days later he went to various meetings up and down the country, again to publicize the paper, and was warmly received, particularly by young people.

He was still working on other projects, too: although less actively involved in *Les Temps modernes,* which had a steady circulation of about 11,000, the same as when it first appeared in 1945, he wrote an article in the January issue about the forthcoming legislative elections, entitled "Elections, piège à cons" ("Elections, a Trap for Fools"), in which he argued for abstention, saying that representative democracy deliberately reduced voters to a position of impotence by atomizing and serializing them. During the first round of the elections, he went to the headquarters of *Libération,* and amid all the excitement and confusion, managed to produce an article for its first issue. He was also planning to write a preface to a book on Greece under the colonels. To *Der Spiegel* he gave an interview in which he defended the imprisoned members of the Red Army Faction (the "Baader Gang"), whom he considered as true revolutionaries but whose tactics he disliked.

But in February he had had a touch of bronchitis, which greatly fatigued him, and in March he suffered a stroke, which forced him to cut down on his work just as *Libération* was about to be launched. The hardening of the arteries, which had caused the stroke, was due in large part to tobacco and alcohol, and the doctor insisted that he give up both, a cure that Sartre was not much inclined to follow. During the next few months, he suffered from frequent states of confusion, a condition that gave Simone de Beauvoir and friends cause for great anguish.

By May he had improved somewhat, at least to the point of being able to continue his discussions with Benny Lévy and Philippe Gavi; he wrote a letter, published by *The New York Review of Books,* demanding amnesty for the Americans who had deserted during the Vietnam war; at the staff meeting of *Les Temps modernes* team, he was able to make his usual lucid interventions. In June he granted Francis Jeanson an auto-biographical interview for his book *Sartre dans sa vie.* But just when he looked as if he were on the way to full recovery, he was struck with semiblindness in his one good eye as a result of a triple hemorrhage. For a time Sartre lived in the hope of recovering this lost sight, and during his summer travels in the Midi with Arlette, to Venice with Wanda and Rome with Simone, he accepted his condition with apparent serenity. Simone would read to him—studies on Flaubert, a *Temps modernes* issue on Chile, the latest book by Le Roy Ladurie, two huge volumes on Japan, as well as the French and Italian newspapers—and apart from mealtimes, during which Sartre showed himself to be incapable of eating without making a terrible mess of himself, the holidays passed by, at least for Simone, with a kind of sweet sadness in the face of his obvious fragility.

On his return to Paris in October, Sartre prepared to move from his studio apartment at 222 boulevard Raspail to a larger one on the boulevard Edgar Quinet, which was also on the 10th floor, and which, more important, had two elevators and a spare room, which meant that he would not have to be alone at night.

8 October: Sartre was called before the Paris tribunal to answer charges of defamation made by *Minute* against his articles in *La Cause du peuple* and *Tout!* in 1971. With his lawyer, Gisèle Halimi, Sartre and witnesses prepared a defense—or, more accurately, a counterattack— accusing *Minute* of racism and incitement to murder. In the end Sartre was condemned to paying 1 franc in damages to the plaintiffs and a 400-franc ($50) fine. The pleasure resulting from this moral victory was short-lived , since later the same day the opthalmologist broke the news to Sartre that there was no hope of his recovering his sight, a prognosis that was confirmed by other specialists. The optician encouraged him to try out an instrument that, by making the most of his lateral vision, would allow him to read for perhaps one hour a day; but he found it painfully slow and soon gave it up. This, in addition to diabetes and difficulties in walking, left him in very poor spirits; his medication made him sleepy much of the time, and he was often distant and withdrawn. According to Simone de Beauvoir's assessment, he only had about three hours of reasonable health each day.

Having first abstained from taking a public position on the Yom Kippur War, Sartre nevertheless granted a telephone interview for the Israeli paper *Al Hamishmar* in which he condemned the attitude of the French government and called for the settlement of the Arab-Israeli conflict by direct negotiations. To Lévy he said that he was not for Israel in its present form. But he could not accept the idea of its destruction. They had to fight so that these three million individuals were not blown up or reduced to slavery. One could not be pro-Arab without also being pro-Jewish, and one could not be pro-Jewish without being pro-Arab, as he was . This was a strange position to be in.[1] He subsequently dissociated himself from appeals on Israel's behalf, which Simone de Beauvoir continued to sign.

Toward the end of the year, Sartre took on Benny Lévy as permanent collaborator. Together they were to pursue their thinking about the conditions for a nonauthoritarian socialism, and Lévy would read to Sartre works that he could no longer read for himself. Arlette was furious about the arrangement, fearing that Lévy's will would be imposed on Sartre; Simone, on the other hand, accepted it gladly, realizing that it would give her more free time and that Sartre's morale benefited from time spent in discussion with Lévy.

By December *Libération* was running into serious financial

---

1. Simone de Beauvoir, *La Cérémonie des adieux* (Paris: Gallimard, 1981), p. 81.

difficulty, for which Sartre managed to make several appeals. But his own personal psychological problem, that of coming to terms with his blindness, had for the time being usurped his energies.

1974

On a raison de se révolter, (You Are Right To Rebel), conversations about politics between Sartre, Philippe Gavi and Pierre Victor (Paris: Gallimard)

The beginning of 1974 saw Sartre withdrawing from various commitments, particularly those having to do with extreme left-wing groups and publications, because he was becoming more and more pessimistic about his sight, and his general health continued to be poor; but by the end of the year there was a dramatic improvement, a coming to terms with his semi-blindness, and he again began to throw himself into a variety of activities and projects.

After a recuperative spring spent in the Midi and Venice, he returned to Paris to learn the news of Pompidou's death. Sartre participated in the ensuing political debate, giving an interview to *Libération* on 13 and 14 April in which he expressed the desire for Charles Piaget, who had been the prime mover in the Lip factory workers' occupation, to stand for the presidential elections, adding, privately however, that if he thought Piaget stood a chance of being elected, he wasn't sure whether he would vote for him. He declared himself against Mitterrand's candidacy, which Simone de Beauvoir supported, and for "revolutionary abstention."

At the end of April, Sartre went with Victor and Gavi to Bruay to talk about their book, which was about to be published: *On a raison de se révolter (You Are Right to Rebel).* It appeared in the new collection called "La France sauvage" (Gallimard), which was edited by Sartre and the two former editors of *La Cause du peuple,* Le Dantec and Le Bris. In these published conversations, Sartre had been at pains to defend his notion of socialism and freedom and had tried to convince Victor, the former leader of the Gauche prolétarienne, that the very notion of authority and leadership went against his hope for a society based on complete equality between its members. According to Simone de Beauvoir, this enterprise had greatly refreshed Sartre's thinking, allowing him to "relearn" the theory of freedom and to rediscover the possibility of a political struggle based on freedom.[1] It was shortly after the publication of this book that Sartre invited Herbert Marcuse to his apartment to talk about the position of the intellectual in political life. As a result of this meeting, the German philosopher was to say privately to Michel Contat: "Sartre has always been my super-ego. Although he does not want to be so, he *is* the conscience of the world."

His summer was divided as usual betwen the Midi with Arlette and Rome with Simone. Apart from a few days when he was particularly tired, he and Simone, with a tape recorder between them, spent their time in Rome engaged in a series of "autobiographical conversations," which would complement *Les Mots*. As a constructive form of therapy, this project certainly served its purpose: when Sartre returned to Paris at the end of September, he was again ready for action.

He began by writing a letter to President Giscard d'Estaing asking for Pierre Victor's naturalization as a French citizen to be completed as quickly as possible. The response from the president was prompt and positive, and the required papers quickly came through. He again began attending *Les Temps modernes*' staff meetings regularly; he made various appeals to help save *Libération* from floundering; he continued his discussions with Victor; his diary was constantly full. He even declared himself to be "happy" and took pride in his adaptation to his infirmities.

But the big project was yet to come. Sartre was asked if he would like to produce a series of televised programs on his life and work for Antenne 2. At first he refused, since he regarded the television company as a repressive organ of the state, but after discussion with Victor and Gavi, he came up with another suggestion: a general history of the 20th century as experienced by him. The fact that this idea was approved at the top level—

1. Simone de Beauvoir, *La Cérémonie des adieux* (Paris: Gallimard, 1981), p. 91.

by Marcel Jullian, the head of Antenne 2—seemed to prove that Giscard's new policies of liberalization in television were seriously grounded. Sartre thus began working on this project with Simone de Beauvoir, Victor and Gavi: the four of them, with Sartre in overall charge, constituted the nucleus of a larger team of researchers who were to provide them with material for the scripts. They were to prepare 10 programs of 75 minutes, each of which would be followed by a 15-minute program devoted to present-day problems related to the main theme. By the end of the year, after two months' work, they had managed to produce the outlines of 6 programs, which then needed to be developed by historians.

2 December: Sartre attended a debate, held in La Cour des miracles, with Gavi and Victor on their book *On a raison de se révolter.* According to his friend Georges Michel, who had organized the meeting, Sartre participated little, seemed to have difficulty getting his words out, and pronounced himself very tired.[2] Nevertheless, just two days later, having obtained permission to meet Andreas Baader in prison, Sartre flew to Stuttgart and talked for an hour with the prisoner, who was in his fourth week of a hunger strike. Subsequently, Sartre, with Daniel Cohn-Bendit, gave a widely covered press conference in which he said that, although he disapproved of the activities of the Red Army Faction, he nevertheless hotly denounced the conditions of their imprisonment, which included torture by sensory deprivation. He made an appeal to German intellectuals to support the rights of political prisoners in West Germany. He was harshly criticized in the German press for this visit, and Baader himself was not particularly welcoming, saying that he had expected to see a friend rather than a judge. Sartre himself came to regard it as a failure, especially in its counterproductive effect on German opinion, but in his usual intrepid manner affirmed that if the opportunity presented itself, he would do it all over again.

2. Georges Michel, *Mes années Sartre* (Paris: Hachette, 1981), p. 129.

1975

An interview on Portugal in *Libération* (22–26 April)
An interview on the Russell Tribunal in *Le Monde* (10 May)
An interview on feminism in a special issue of *L'Arc* devoted to Simone de Beauvoir (May)
"Autoportrait à soixante-dix ans" ("Self-Portrait at 70"), an interview with Michel Contat; *Le Nouvel Observateur* (23 June, 30 June, and 7 July)
An interview on Franco's Spain in *Libération* (28 October)

This, his 70th year, saw Sartre absorbed in the various activities relating to his proposed television series: at first there was optimism when it looked as if Jullian would give Sartre and his team a completely free hand; then there was the pleasure for Sartre of working again with young left-wing intellectuals; but as the project progressed, there was the gradual realization that nothing much had changed, that the hassles over financing the series were simply a means of exercising government censorship. The project came to an abrupt end when, on 25 September, Sartre called a press conference at La Cour des miracles during which he recounted in detail the full history of the project and his difficulties with the television authorities, ending with the statement that he would never again have anything to do with television, either in France or elsewhere. He bitterly observed that Michel Droit, a man of the Right, had had no such difficulty in being funded to produce his series chronicling the years 1946 to 1970. Jullian replied accusing Sartre of making exorbitant demands for money and of abandoning much of the work to his assistants. To add further fuel to this bitter press debate, it was rumored that Sartre had retroactively tried to claim the money that accompanied the Nobel prize, which he had rejected in 1964. Sartre issued a vigorous denial.

But prior to all this, Sartre had felt himself well enough to participate in numerous other activities. He decided that he wanted to see at first hand the situation in Portugal, where, the year before, there had been a military coup d'état, which was quickly supported by the population as a whole. So, on 23 March, accompanied by Pierre Victor and Simone de Beauvoir, he set off for Lisbon to talk to members of the MFA (Mouvement

des forces armées), students, workers and writers. On his return, Sartre gave a radio broadcast about Portugal, and *Libération* published (from 22 to 26 April) the transcript of a series
of conversations between Victor, Gavi, Simone de Beauvoir and
Sartre on various aspects of political life in Portugal. Sartre
expressed critical support of the MFA.

May: Sartre sent an open letter in support of the Czech philosopher Karel Kosic, who had denounced the repression suffered by intellectuals in Czechoslovakia. He also signed various
texts condemning repression in the USSR, particularly in the
Ukraine. On 10 May, at the time of the ending of the Vietnam
War, *Le Monde* published a statement by Sartre about the activities of the Russell Tribunal, and on 17 June he made an
appeal (also in *Le Monde*) on behalf of Basque nationalists. In
fact, by the month of June, Sartre was in good health and, having lost some weight, was full of vitality. He was often in the
news, many students were writing theses about his work, and
various books and journals were being devoted to him. He took
pleasure in the feeling of being famous again, having for a few
years prior to this begun to see himself as a "has-been."

On the occasion of his 70th birthday, *Le Nouvel Observateur*
published a series of three interviews between Sartre and
Michel Contat in which he tried to give an account of his life.
He talked with apparent serenity about the loss of his sight
and the consequent destruction of his writing career and said
that he expected to live another 10 years. He stated a very
clear preference for the company of young people, finding his
contemporaries rather set in their ideas. He had particularly
resented the criticism by the press of his visit to Baader when
he had been called an "old dotard," a form of ageism used to
discredit him. Questioned about fame and whether he had been
taken over by his image, he had this somewhat surprising reply,
given the amount of literature devoted to the subject: "No, because I don't have as much of an image (as many famous people).
I know that an image of me exists, but it is the image other
people have of me and not my own. I don't know what my own
is; I don't think about myself as an individual. When I do think
reflexively the ideas I have would apply to everyone."[1] From

1. Jean-Paul Sarte, *Sartre in the Seventies,* trans. Paul Auster and Lydia Davis
(London: André Deutsch), 1978, p. 43.

the enormous mass of writing about him and his works, Sartre claimed that he had never learned anything: "Either I find an accurate presentation of my ideas, at best, or else I cannot see any value in the arguments against me because they are based on a flagrant misunderstanding, in my opinion, of what I was trying to say."[2] In contrast to his statement in 1957—"Marxism is the ultimate philosophy of our time"—Sartre now expressed a certain detachment: "Today I feel, as I try to suggest in *On a raison de se révolter*, that another way of thinking is necessary. We must develop a way of thinking which takes Marxism into account in order to go beyond it, to reject it and take it up again, to absorb it. That is the condition for arriving at a true socialism."[3] Sartre received many warm congratulations for this interview, perhaps not so much for its intellectual content as for the fact that it revealed that the Sartrian spirit was very much alive.

L'Arc published a special issue during the summer on Simone de Beauvoir and feminism, in which she interviewed Sartre on his attitudes toward feminist issues. According to Simone de Beauvoir, Sartre replied to all her questions with a good grace but "rather superficially." He admitted that both in his relationships with women and in his writings there was a distinct element of male chauvinism, which he tried to excuse by the fact that he had always considered himself superior, not only to women but to most men, too! He added that he had always thought of and treated Simone de Beauvoir as his equal. He maintained that he entirely approved of the feminist struggle, arguing that if it kept its ties with the class struggle, it could shake society in such a way as to completely overturn it, creating profound equality between men and women.

For a change Sartre and Simone de Beauvoir went to Greece for the summer, which greatly enchanted both of them, and, for Sartre, the pleasure of being able to see his young Greek friend, Melina, who had by now recovered from a severe mental breakdown—exacerbated, she said, by Sartre's involvement with her—was an extra bonus. However, on their return to Paris, Sartre soon became embroiled in arguments over his television series, which greatly fatigued him and caused blood

2. Ibid., p. 56.
3. Ibid., p. 61.

pressure problems. The medication he had to take caused uri-
nary incontinence, he again had difficulty in walking, and his
balance was far from steady. He could not, however, rest for
long: he began working on his latest book project—*Pouvoir et
liberté (Power and Freedom)*—with Pierre Victor; he made various protests on behalf of 11 militant antifascists who were
condemned to death in Spain; and on 28 October *Libération*
published an interview with Sartre about Spain in which he
made some none too complimentary comments about General
Franco, which were very badly received, since Franco was at
that time on his deathbed.

Through his desire to keep on working just as long as it was
physically possible, Sartre again managed to pull himself out
of a steadily deteriorating condition, and by the end of the year,
he was able to say that he was happy to be alive.

1976

Situations, Vol. X (Paris: Gallimard), which contained the fol-
lowing pieces:
"Self-Portrait at 70"
"Simone de Beauvoir Interviews Sartre" (on feminism)
"On *The Idiot of the Family*"
"The Burgos Trial"
"The Maoists in France"
"Justice and the State"
"Elections: A Trap for Fools"
The Critique of Dialectical Reason, in English trans. Alan Sheridan-
    Smith (London: New Left Books).
Critiques littéraires (Literary Essays) (Situations, Vol. I), in paperback
    (Paris: Gallimard)
L'Etre et le Néant (Being and Nothingness), in paperback (Paris: Gal-
    limard)
Interview about Flaubert (with Michel Sicard), accompanied by un-
    published notes for the fourth volume of *L'Idiot de la famille; Le
    Magazine littéraire,* November.
Articles in *Libération, Le Monde, Corriere della Sera, Le Nouvel Ob-
    servateur*

"Quel beau come-back!" said Simone to Sartre during this year, to which he wryly replied, "Un come-back funéraire." But he was pleased with the amount of attention he was again receiving, and his health was reasonably good. However, according to Simone de Beauvoir,[1] his intellectual form was not what it used to be: he would make big mistakes in recounting past events, but he did not like to be contradicted, which Simone, loyally, almost never did. He was less inventive in discussions and was easily fatigued in the presence of large numbers of people. Simone described him as being at times "burned out" (*éteint*), empty, which was why eating and drinking began to assume a more important place in his life. Nevertheless, his passionate involvement in world affairs continued unabated.

January: Sartre signed a text expressing solidarity with militants from the "Marge" group who had been imprisoned for having occupied one of the Russian embassy buildings in Paris in protest against the system of Soviet oppression. Later in the month he signed an appeal published in *Libération* on behalf of Jean Papinski, a teacher of English, who, having received an unfavorable report from the inspectorate, protested against the decision, claiming that the inspector was unable to pass judgment since he did not speak a word of English. Papinski had demanded reparation and written a pamphlet attacking the inspectorate, which had resulted in his being banned from teaching for life. In protest he had gone on a hunger strike, which, in fact, lasted 90 days. In was during his hunger strike that Sartre made his appeal to the president of the republic.

February: Along with 50 Nobel prize winners, Sartre and Simone signed an appeal, published in *Libération* and *Le Monde*, on behalf of Mikhail Stern, who was imprisoned in the Soviet Union. They subsequently launched a campaign, which eventually brought about his release.

14 March: *Corriere della Sera* published Sartre's reflections on the assassination of the Italian film director Pier Paolo Pasolini,

---

1. Simone de Beauvoir, *La Cérémonie des adieux* (Paris: Gallimard, 1981), p. 120.

whom Sartre had admired, particularly for his evocation of the *sacred* in *Médée*. He had first dictated his article to Simone de Beauvoir, then edited it in his own illegible handwriting and finally recited it back to her by heart. He was happy, not only with the finished article but also with the manner and speed with which he had been able to execute it.

After a brief vacation in Venice with Simone and Sylvie Le Bon, Sartre's return to Paris saw him working with Victor on *Pouvoir et liberté*. And suddenly Sartre's name seemed to be everywhere: *Situations,* Vol. X had appeared at the beginning of the year; *L'Etre et le néant* (Being and Nothingness) was republished in the paperback "Tel" series and *Situations,* Vol. I in the "Idées" collection; *Critique of Dialectical Reason* was published in London; and some interviews that Sartre had given for Australian radio—on Marxism, on Laing, on the role of the intellectual—were published in New York. He gave an interview for the press on the book of the film *Sartre par lui-même (Sartre by Himself),* in which he spoke about his battles with French television. He published a letter in *Libération* about the military use of the plain of Larzac; and for *Le Nouvel Observateur* he wrote a short article about safety precautions in factories. In May he expressed his horror over the death of Ulrike Meinhof in a German prison.

During the summer Sartre traveled a lot: first he spent a month with Arlette in Junas, followed by a visit to Venice with Wanda, then on to Capri with Simone and Sylvie, back to Rome and finally to Athens with Simone, where he had also promised to spend some time with Melina. On his return to Paris in mid-September, his spirits were high, and he quickly took up his work with Victor. And his "come-back" continued: in September *Les Mains sales* was revived at the Théâtre des Mathurins, was well received by the critics, played for 150 performances and then went on tour in the provinces; in October the film *Sartre par lui-même* was finally released, again to a great deal of public enthusiasm; and in November a show entitled *Sartre,* consisting of a montage of texts, created by the actor Gérard Guillaumat, was presented at the Théâtre de la Reprise in Lyon. The *New Left Review* published extracts from the second volume of *Critique de la raison dialectique; Le Magazine littéraire* carried a long conversation between Sartre and Michel Sicard about

Flaubert, accompanied by unpublished notes for the fourth volume of *L'Idiot de la famille. Politique-Hebdo* devoted two issues to him, with articles by Chatelet, Horst and Victor.

9 November: At the Israeli embassy in Paris, Sartre accepted the title of honorary doctor of the University of Jerusalem. In his speech, which he had carefully prepared and learned by heart, he said that he was accepting the degree in order to facilitate the dialogue between Israel and the Palestinians. Although he was a longtime friend of Israel and concerned about Israel's future, he was equally concerned about the Palestinian people, who had suffered greatly.

December: In an interview with *Politique-Hebdo,* Sartre appealed for a public debate on the question of German-American hegemony in Europe and participated in the activities of the Action Committee Against a German-American Europe.

At the end of the year, it was decided by the staff at *Les Temps modernes* that they needed to co-opt some new members, since Bost, who was also deaf, no longer attended meetings, and Lanzmann was too occupied with making his film on the holocaust. Those chosen were Pierre Victor, who acted as an incentive for Sartre to attend more regularly; François Georges, who had often written for the journal; Rigoulet, a young teacher of philosophy; and Pierre Goldman, whom both Sartre and Simone greatly respected. In this way they hoped to revitalize both the *Temps modernes* meetings and the journal itself.

1977

The text of the film by Alexandre Astruc and Michel Contat, *Sartre par lui-même (Sartre by Himself),* (Paris: Gallimard)

"Introduction to Jean-Paul Sartre", 'Socialism in One Country', extracts from the unpublished sequel to *Critique, New Left Review,* no. 100 (November 76–January 77), pp. 138–43.

Various interviews and appeals in *Libération, Le Nouvel Observateur, Le Monde, Lotta Continua*

Despite bouts of severe ill health and a general deterioration in his condition, Sartre continued to give lots of interviews, signed numerous appeals, participated actively in *Les Temps modernes'* staff discussions, traveled a good deal and, to his delight, found himself much in demand by young people, particularly young women. At the beginning of the year, he could hardly walk at all, his legs were very painful, and he would often fall. Simone de Beauvoir anxiously kept a check on his drinking habits, which certain of his young friends failed to do, but it was the smoking that, according to the specialist at the Broussais hospital, would cause him to lose his legs bit by bit; first the toes, then the feet and finally the legs themselves. So impressed was Sartre by the evocation of this piecemeal dismemberment that he finally decided to give up smoking altogether.

6 January: *Libération* published a dialogue between Sartre and Victor about their collaboration, which had started in the fall of 1975 and had kept them occupied for three hours every day, on their project on "Power and Freedom." He tried to explain how this joint work was not merely an expedient because of his infirmities but that he genuinely wished to try to produce a morality and a political position that would express their "we" together but would allow each at the same time to recognize and acknowledge the thought of the other. Later in January the text of the film *Sartre par lui-même (Sartre by Himself)* was published by Gallimard and was a great success; and *Le Nouvel Observateur* published an interview with Catherine Chaine in which Sartre talked about his relationship with Simone de Beauvoir in particular and women in general. He admitted during this interview that he had never felt himself to have been the "contingent love" of someone else but that if he had been, he would not have liked it at all.

February: Sartre flew to Athens with Pierre Victor, having promised Melina that he would give a lecture at the university where she taught. Entitled "What Is Philosophy?" it attracted 1,500 students, who gave him a standing ovation, even though Victor found what he had to say rather "facile." It was shortly after this trip that Sartre's condition deteriorated, and tests indicated that he only had 30 percent circulation in his legs.

The specialist's written summary of his state of health, secretly steamed open by Simone, indicated that if he took special precautions, he might live "a few more years." He was advised not to walk for a while, so his planned trip to Venice, rather than being postponed, started off in a wheelchair. On his return to Paris, he again saw a lot of Melina, whose company he found extremely rejuvenating. But without the possibility of working, he would suffer depressions, and again, much to Simone's distress, he would demand, often angrily, his dose of whisky.

21 June: But on his 72nd birthday, Sartre was able to participate in a meeting with Soviet dissidents, whose cause he had long actively supported. It was the day Brezhnev was received at the Elysée Palace by the president: at the Théâtre Récamier Sartre and other French intellectuals met with a group of dissidents, including Mikhail Stern, whose release Sartre had been instrumental in bringing about the year before.

As usual, he signed numerous appeals, all of which appeared in *Le Monde*: on 9 January an appeal on behalf of *Politique-Hebdo,* which was experiencing financial difficulties; on 23 January an appeal against repression in Morocco; on 26 March a protest against the arrest of a singer in Nigeria; on 27 March an appeal for civil liberties in Argentina; on 29 June a petition addressed to the Belgrade Congress against repression in Italy, which was very badly received by Italian leftists; on 1 July a protest against the worsening political situation in Brazil.

28 July: *Le Monde* published a conversation between Sartre and the musicologist Lucien Malson, in which he talked about his tastes in music—Beethoven, Chopin, Schumann, Berg, Webern, opera and jazz—but deplored the new orientation of France-Musique, which he considered too heavily biased toward modern music and jazz and presented in an incoherent way. Some critics deemed his attitudes toward music "reactionary."

The summer was, as usual, spent in Junas, Venice, Florence and Rome: although unable to walk more than a few yards, Sartre was full of vitality, and Simone read to him books written by Soviet dissidents, which they discussed at length. Toward the end of September, there were demonstrations by the Left in Rome protesting the killing by the police of a student in Bologna, and because of Sartre's condemnation of Italian repression earlier in the summer, he was invited to comment on the present unrest by the *Lotta continua,* an extreme-left journal that had always had good relations with *Les Temps modernes.* In this conversation he took a position against the "new philosophers," declared that he was no longer a Marxist but affirmed his solidarity with the young people protesting the Bologna killing, saying: "Every time the State police shoots a young militant, I am on the side of the young militant." He expressed the wish that there would be no more violence in Bologna.

Sartre decided at the last minute not to go to Athens to see Melina as promised, and when, shortly after his return to Paris, she came over to see him, he told her that he no longer wished to continue the liaison but would honor his promise to pay for her to spend the year in Paris. According to Simone de Beauvoir,[1] he had lots of women in his entourage, which gave him much cause for pleasure.

While continuing to express his opposition to the terrorism as practiced by the Red Army Faction in Germany, he nevertheless signed various protests against the assassination of Baader and his comrades and appealed against the extradition of Klaus Croissant, Baader's lawyer. He was still active within the Committee Against German-American Hegemony in Europe; he was opposed to the use of force against the Polisario Front in Mauritania; and in October he sent a telegram in support of Iranian intellectuals who were opposed to their régime. On 4 December he published in *Le Monde* a short article—"an appeal to his Israeli friends"—encouraging them to respond to the peace initiative made by Egyptian President Sadat.

1. Simone de Beauvoir, *La Cérémonie des adieux* (Paris: Gallimard, 1981), p. 136.

1978

Sartre, images d'une vie (Sartre, Images of a Life), iconography collected
  by Liliane Sendyk-Siegel, with commentaries by Simone de Beauvoir
  (Paris: Gallimard).
An article in *Le Monde* about Daniel Cohn-Bendit and the refusal of
  the French authorities to allow him into France (3 June).
"Moi, Sartre, petit bourgeois," ("I, Sartre, petit bourgeois"), an interview with Jaun Goytisolo; *El País* (11 June).

Sartre's "come-back" continued: Liliane Sendyk-Siegel published her album of photographs, *Sartre, Images d'une vie*,
(Sartre, Images of a Life), with a commentary by Simone de
Beauvoir; Gallimard decided to publish all his novels in the
"Pléiade" series; Michel Sicard was preparing a special number
of *Obliques* on certain unpublished texts; Jeannette Colombel,
among others, came to talk to him about studies of his work;
in March there was a revival of *Nékrassov* at the Théâtre de
l'Est in Paris, directed by Georges Werler; and in May, in Los
Angeles, the first in a series of university colloquia on Sartre
took place. But despite his prominence, he was worried about
money, not for himself but because a number of people were
financially dependent on him, and he hated the thought of let-
ting them down.
  In February he decided that he wanted to go to Jerusalem
to see for himself the response to Sadat's visit to Israel. So,
accompanied by Arlette and Victor, he set off, again having to
use a wheelchair at the airport, on a five-day visit, during which
he talked to Israelis and Palestinians and tried to see as much
of the country as possible. On their return Victor was keen to
write an article for *Le Nouvel Observateur,* which, eventually,
he and Sartre signed. But it was such a weak article that the
editors suggested that they withdraw it; Sartre agreed but ne-
glected to discuss it with Victor, who took it as a huge insult.
Because Simone de Beauvoir had been the intermediary in
these negotiations, relations between her and Victor became
extremely frayed, until finally, at a meeting of the *Temps modernes* staff, at which Sartre was not present, there was a fierce
altercation between Victor, Pouillon and Horst. According to

Simone,[1] Victor insulted them all and left the meeting, never again to return. From then on he and Simone avoided each other. Sartre had expressed the hope that Victor would be the one person to pursue his line of thinking to Sartre's satisfaction, and their relationship appeared to be unaffected by these tensions, but it was a source of considerable sadness for Simone, who had always shared the same friends as Sartre: from then on part of his life was closed to her. For his part, Sartre was deeply attached to their joint project—"Pouvoir et liberté" ("Power and Liberty")—and it was this above all that absorbed his interest.

April: Sartre participated in the making of a film about Simone de Beauvoir by Josée Dayan and Malka Rybowska, which was released the following year. In June he made an appeal in *Le Monde* on behalf of Daniel Cohn-Bendit, who, since his part in the activities of May 1968, had been refused entry into France. Later in the same month he gave his name to a protest about Heide Kempe Böltcher, a young German woman who had been severely burned during a police interrogation in Paris in May.

October: Sartre met with a delegation of farmers from Larzac. He was particularly interested in their struggle to prevent military encroachment on their land and especially their active nonviolent resistance, which was proving to be a real problem for the establishment. Several of them were going on a hunger strike, and Sartre was invited to attend their press conference, but since he was too tired to come in person, he sent a statement, supporting their cause. Their farmers' cause and their methods fascinated Sartre, and he wanted to be more involved in their struggle, but his failing health would not allow it.

1. Simone de Beauvoir, *La Cérémonie des adieux* (Paris: Gallimard, 1981), p. 140.

1979

A special issue of *Obliques* devoted to Sartre, edited by Michel Sicard
An interview about the theater with Bernard Dort; *Travail théâtral*
(January).
An interview about music with Jean-Yves Bosseur and Michel Sicard;
Magazine littéraire (June).
An interview with Catherine Clément; *Le Matin* (about politics and
feminism (10 November).

Two major political activities concerned Sartre during this year.
Under the aegis of *Les Temps modernes,* Victor, with Sartre's
support but without the participation of any of the other members of the *Temps modernes* staff, organized an Israeli-Pales-
tinian colloquium in Paris in March. Held in the home of Michel
Foucault, the meetings were opened by a short statement by
Sartre but, according to Simone de Beauvoir, produced nothing
new. Although Sartre shared Victor's enthusiasm and optimism
about the outcome of these discussions, he in fact contributed
very little, and when the text of the conference appeared in the
October issue of *Les Temps modernes* under the title "Peace
now?" he was disappointed by its very lukewarm reception.

His second major polticial activity of the year saw him side
by side with Raymond Aron, his student friend from the École
Normale days, but with whom he had since rarely seen eye to
eye, pleading their cause for more aid to be given to the boat
people fleeing from Vietnam. So far their committee "A Boat
for Vietnam" had successfully arranged for the boat *Ile-de-Lu-
mière,* anchored off Poulo-Bidong, to provide help and safety
for thousands of refugees, but now they wished to intensify the
rescue operations by providing air transport between the camps
in Malaysia and Thailand and the transit camps in the West.
To this end Sartre and the rest of the committee presented their
demand to Giscard at the Elysée Palace in June, and at a press
conference, Sartre stressed the point that they were concerned
with saving people's lives, regardless of their political affilia-
tions. The press made much of Sartre's "reconciliation" with
Aron, seeing it as an indication of a move to the Right—which
Sartre himself strongly denied.

Shortly after the Easter holidays, which had been spent in Aix-en-Provence, Sartre was physically attacked at the door of his apartment by a Belgian poet, Gérard de Clèves, who, in between stays in psychiatric hospitals, would pester Sartre for money. On this occasion, when both money and entry were refused, he drew a knife on Sartre and managed to slash his thumb through the half-open door.

The summer holidays, spent in Aix and Rome, ended on a sad note: Pierre Goldman, member of the managing committee of *Les Temps modernes,* and for whom Sartre and Simone felt a great deal of affection, was brutally murdered. Despite his considerable fatigue, Sartre insisted on being present at his funeral on 27 September.

His work on "Pouvoir et liberté" continued, but, since he and Victor did not always agree, it was still far from being finished. In November he gave an interview to Catherine Clément for *Le Matin,* in which he recognized the diminishing influence of the intellectual and the disarray of the Left. In December, in an interview with Bernard Dort for *Travail théâtral,* he talked about his favorite playwrights—Pirandello, Brecht and Beckett—and his own plays. According to those close to him during his public appearances he created a terrible impression, looking, as he was, close to death, whereas in private he would astonish by his indomitable vitality.

1980

"L'Espoir maintenant" ("Hope Now"), a dialogue between Sartre and
    Benny Lévy; *Le Nouvel Observateur* (10, 17 and 24 March).
An interview in *Le Gai Pied* (April).
An interview on Flaubert with Catherine Clément and Bernard Pin-
    gaud; *L'Arc* (May).

Sartre began this, his final year, in typical fashion—in protest: first, in January, against the house arrest of Andrei Sakharov and then in support of the boycott of the Olympic Games in Moscow to protest Russian intervention in Afghanistan. He gave interviews for *Le Gai Pied,* the monthly homosexual magazine, and on Flaubert for the May issue of *L'Arc.* He continued his discussions with Victor for their proposed book, "Pouvoir et liberté" ("Power and Liberty"), which they intended to publish at the end of the year. In the meantime they decided to talk about their work together and how it had changed Sartre's thinking. These dialogues were published in three successive issues of *Le Nouvel Observateur* in March (Benny Lévy on this occasion abandoning his pseudonym of Pierre Victor) and produced considerable consternation among Sartre's friends, since, instead of the "plural thinking" that Sartre was hoping to arrive at, there appeared nothing more than a vague, woolly philosophy that seemed to owe much to Benny Lévy but was attributed to Sartre. When Sartre was apprised of the unfavorable reaction to these dialogues, he nevertheless went ahead and had them published but, according to Simone de Beauvoir, suffered a good deal of anxiety about the criticism, which, on at least one occasion, led him to drink to dangerous excess.

20 March: Sartre was urgently hospitalized for a pulmonary edema. His condition did not at first give cause for serious alarm, and when his fever and the accompanying state of delirium had passed, he and Simone talked about their proposed trip to Belle-Ile. Arlette and Simone took turns sitting by his bedside, but his condition deteriorated: his kidneys ceased to function, and because of his poor circulation, gangrene set in. On 13 April he went into a semicoma, and Sartre died, unconscious, on 15 April at 9 p.m. The news was broadcast on radio and television at 11 p.m. and made major headlines in all the Parisian newspapers the next day.

The reaction was very strong, both at home and abroad. After the first 48 hours of unanimous homage, there followed various and diverse appreciations, which followed old political cleavages. Giscard d'Estaing said that he knew Sartre would not have wanted a state burial but did offer to pay for the ceremony, which was refused. Instead Giscard went personally to the Broussais hospital to pay homage to Sartre. *Pravda,* on 16 April, announced Sartre's death in three lines, as did *Hanoi Moi,* and made no further comment. French press coverage surpassed that given to de Gaulle.

19 April: A crowd of about 500,000 people, without pomp or organization—comprising intellectuals, students, actors, political figures, ordinary people—accompanied Sartre's body to the Montparnasse cemetery. According to his wishes, he was cremated, three days later, at Père-Lachaise during a private ceremony and his ashes were placed in a tomb at the Montparnasse cemetery, not far from the apartment at 31 boulevard Edgar-Quinet where he had spent his last years. The tomb bears the simple inscription: "Jean-Paul Sartre, 1905–1980."

Bibliography

Major Works by Sartre

Baudelaire. Paris; Point du Jour, 1946; Paris: Gallimard, 1947. Trans. as *Baudelaire* by Martin Turnell. London: Horizon Press, 1949; New York: New Directions, 1950.

Cahiers pour une morale. Paris: Gallimard, 1983.

Carnets de la drôle de guerre. Paris: Gallimard, 1983.

Critique de la raison dialectique. Paris: Gallimard, 1960. Trans. as *Critique of Dialectical Reason* by Alan Sheridan-Smith. London: New Left Books, 1976.

Entretiens sur la politique, with David Rousset and Gérard Rosenthal. Paris: Gallimard, 1949.

Esquisse d'une théorie des émotions. Paris: Hermann, 1939. Trans. as *The Emotions: Outline of a Theory* by Bernard Frechtman. New York: Philosophical Library, 1948.

Huis clos. First published in *L'Arbalète,* 1944, then Paris: Gallimard, 1945. Trans. as *No Exit* by Stuart Gilbert in volume with *The Flies.* New York: Knopf, 1947. English edition titled *In Camera,* London: Hamish Hamilton, 1946.

Kean. Paris: Gallimard, 1954. Trans. as *Kean* by Kitty Black. London: Hamish Hamilton, 1954.

L'Age de raison. Paris: Gallimard, 1945. Vol. 1 of *Les Chemins de la liberté.* Trans. as *The Age of Reason* by Eric Sutton. New York: Knopf, 1947. Revised trans. London: Penguin Books, 1961. Vol. 1 of *The Roads to Freedom.*

La Mort dans l'âme. Paris: Gallimard, 1949. Vol. 3 of *Les Chemins de la liberté.* Trans. as *Iron in the Soul* by Gerard Hopkins. London: Hamish Hamilton, 1950; and as *Troubled Sleep,* New York: Knopf, 1951. Vol. 3 of *The Roads to Freedom.*

La Nausée. Paris: Gallimard, 1938. Trans. as *Nausea* by Lloyd Alexander. New York: New Directions, 1949; trans. as *Nausea* by Robert Baldick, London: Penguin Books, 1965.

La Putain respectueuse. Paris: Nagel, 1946. Trans. as *The Respectful Prostitute* by Lionel Abel. In *Three Plays,* New York: Knopf, 1949.

La Transcendance de l'ego. Published in *Recherches Philosophiques,* vol.VI, 1936–37, pp. 85–123; and as a book, edited by Sylvie le Bon, Paris: Vrin, 1965. Trans. as *The Transendence of the Ego* by Forrest Williams and Robert Kirkpatrick. New York: Noonday Press, 1957.

Le Diable et le bon Dieu. Paris: Gallimard, 1951. Trans. as *Lucifer and the Good Lord* by Kitty Black. London: Hamish Hamilton, 1953; and trans. as *The Devil and the Good Lord* by S. and G. Leeson, New York: Knopf, 1960.

Le Mur. Paris: Gallimard, 1939. Trans. as *The Wall and Other Stories* by Lloyd Alexander. New York: New Directions. 1948.

L'Engrenage. Paris: Nagel, 1948. Trans. as *In the Mesh* by Mervyn Savill. London: Andrew Dakers, 1954.

Les Jeux sont faits. Paris: Nagel, 1947. Trans. as *The Chips Are Down* by Louise Varese. New York: Lear, 1948.

Les Mains sales. Paris: Gallimard, 1948. Trans. as *Dirty Hands* by Lionel Abel. In *Three Plays,* New York: Knopf, 1949. Trans. as *Crime passionnel* by Kitty Black. In *Three Plays,* London: Hamish Hamilton, 1949.

Les Mots. Paris: Gallimard. Trans. as *Words* by Irene Clephane. London: Hamish Hamilton, 1964, and Penguin Books, 1967. Trans. as *The Words* by B. Frechtman. New York: G. Braziller, 1964.

Les Mouches. Paris: Gallimard, 1943. Trans. as *The Flies* by Stuart Gilbert. New York: Knopf, 1947.

Les Séquestrés d'Altona. Paris: Gallimard, 1960. Trans. as *Loser Wins* by Sylvia and George Leeson. London: Hamish Hamilton, 1960. Trans. as *The Condemned of Altona* by Sylvia and George Leeson. New York: Knopf, 1961.

Le Sursis. Paris: Gallimard, 1945. Vol. 2 of *Les Chemins de la liberté.* Trans. as *The Reprieve* by Eric Sutton. New York: Knopf, 1947. Revised trans., London: Penguin Books, 1963. Vol.2 of *The Roads to Freedom.*

L'Etre et le Néant: Essai d'ontologie phénoménologique. Paris: Gallimard, 1943. Trans. as *Being and Nothingness* by Hazel Barnes. New York: Philosophical Library, 1956.

Les Troyennes. Paris: Gallimard, 1966. Trans. as *The Trojan Women* by Ronald Duncan. New York: Knopf, 1967.

Lettres au Castor et à quelques autres. Edited by Simone de Beauvoir. 2 vols., Paris: Gallimard, 1983.

L'Existentialisme est un humanisme. Paris: Nagel, 1946. Trans. as *Existentialism* by Bernard Frechtman. New York: Philosophical Library, 1947. Trans. as *Existentialism and Humanism* by Philip Mairet. London: Methuen, 1948.

L'Idiot de la famille, vols. 1 and 2. Paris: Gallimard, 1971; vol. 3, Paris: Gallimard, 1972. Vol. 1 trans. as *The Family Idiot* by C. Cosman. Chicago: University of Chicago Press, 1982.

L'Imaginaire: Psychologie phénoménologique de l'imagination. Paris: Gallimard, 1940. Trans. as *Psychology of the Imagination* by Bernard Frechtman. New York: Philosophical Library, 1948.

L'Imagination. Paris: Librairie Félix Alcan, 1936. Trans. As *Imagination: A Psychological Critique* by Forrest Williams. Ann Arbor: University of Michigan Press, 1962.

Morts sans sépulture. Lausanne: Marguerat, 1946. Trans. as *The Victors* by Lionel Abel. In *Three Plays.* New York: Knopf, 1949. Trans. as *Men Without Shadows* by Kitty Black. In *Three Plays,* London: Hamish Hamilton, 1949.

On a raison de se révolter, with Philippe Gavi and Pierre Victor. Paris: Gallimard, 1974.

Orphée noir, introduction to *L'Anthologie de la nouvelle poésie nègre et malgache* by Léopold Sedar Senghor. Paris: Presses Universitaires, 1948. Trans. as *Black Orpheus* by Arthur Gilette. New York: University Place Book Shop, 1963.

Question de méthode. First published in *Les Temps modernes,* no. 139 (September 1957), pp. 338–417, and no.140 (October 1957), pp. 658–98; then in *Critique de la raison dialectique.* Separate volume, Paris: Gallimard, 1967, Trans. as *Search for a Method* by Hazel Barnes. New York: Knopf, 1963; and with the title *The Problem of Method,* London: Methuen, 1964.

Réflexions sur la question juive. Paris: Morihein, 1946, and Gallimard, 1954. Trans. as *Anti-Semite and Jew* by George J. Becker. New York: Schocken, 1948. Trans. as *Portrait of the Anti-Semite* by Eric de Mauny, London: Secker and Warburg, 1948.

Saint Genet, comédien et martyr. Paris: Gallimard, 1952. Trans. as *Saint Genet, Actor and Martyr* by Bernard Frechtman. New York: G. Braziller, 1963.

Sartre on Cuba. New York: Ballantine Books, 1961.

Situations, I. Paris: Gallimard, 1947. Trans. (in part) as *Literary and Philosophical Essays* by Annette Michelson. New York: Criterion Books, 1955.

Situations, II. Paris: Gallimard, 1948. Trans. (in part) as *What is Literature?* by Bernard Frechtman. New York: Philosophical Library, 1949.

Situations, III. Paris: Gallimard, 1949. Trans. (in part) as *Literary and Philosophical Essays.* New York: Criterion Books, 1955.

Situations, IV. Paris: 1964. Trans. as *Situations* by Benita Eisler and Maria Jolas. New York: G. Braziller, 1965.

Situations, V. Paris: Gallimard, 1964.

Situations, VI. Paris: Gallimard, 1964. Trans. of part as *The Communists and Peace* by Martha E. Fletcher. New York: G. Braziller, 1968. Trans. as *The Communists and Peace* by Irene Clephane. London: Hamish Hamilton, 1969.

Situations, VII. Paris: Gallimard, 1965. Trans. of part as "A Reply to Claude Lefort" by Philip Berk in *The Communists and Peace*. New York: G. Braziller, 1968. Trans. of part as *The Ghost of Stalin* by Martha E. Fletcher. New York: G. Braziller, 1968.

Situations, VIII and Situations, IX. Paris: Gallimard, 1972. Trans. of parts of both volumes as *Between Existentialism and Marxism* by John Matthews. London: New Left Books. 1974.

Situations, X. Paris: Gallimard, 1976. Trans. as *Life/Situations* by Paul Auster and Lydia Davies. New York: Pantheon Books, 1977; and published as *Sartre in the Seventies,* London: Andre Deutsch, 1978.

Un Théâtre de situations. Paris: Gallimard, 1973. Trans. as *Sartre on Theater* by Frank Jellinek and compiled by Michel Contat and Michel Rybalka. New York: Pantheon Books. 1976.

Secondary Works Referred to in the Text

Beauvoir, Simone de. *La Cérémonie des adieux*. Paris: Gallimard, 1981.
———. *La Force de l'âge*. Paris: Gallimard, 1960. Trans. as *The Prime of Life* by Peter Green. New York: Harper Colophon, 1976; London: Penguin Books, 1965.
———. *La Force des Choses*. Paris: Gallimard, 1963. Trans. as *Force of Circumstance* by Richard Howard, New York: G.P.Putnam, 1964. London: Penguin Books, 1968.
———. Memoirs d'une jeune fille rangée. Paris: Gallimard, 1958. Trans. as *Memoirs of a Dutiful Daughter* by James Kirkup. London: Penguin Books, 1963,
———. *Toute compte fait*. Paris: Gallimard, 1972. Trans. as *All Said and Done* by Patrick O'Brian. London: Penguin Books, 1977.
Contat, Michel, and Rybalka, Michel. "Chronologie", in Jean-Paul Sartre. *Oeuvres romanesques*. Paris: Gallimard, 1981, pp. XXXV–CIV.
———. *Les Ecrits de Sartre*. Paris: Gallimard, 1970. Trans. as *The Writings of Jean-Paul Sartre* by Richard C. McCleary. 2 vols. Evanston, Ill.: Northwestern University Press, 1974.
Jeanson, Francis. *Sartre dans sa vie*. Paris: Editions du Seuil, 1974.
Laing, R. D., and Cooper, D. G. *Reason and Violence: A Decade of Sartre's Philosophy, 1950–1960*. Foreword by Jean-Paul Sartre. London: Tavistock, 1964. Revised edition. New York: Vintage Books, 1971.
Lapointe, Francis H., *Jean-Paul Sartre and His Critics: An International Bibliography (1938–1980)*. Bowling Green, Ohio: Bowling Green State University Philosophy Documentation Center, revised edition, 1981.
Madsen, Axel. *Hearts and Minds: The Common Journey of Simone de Beauvoir and Jean-Paul Sartre*. New York: William Morrow, 1977.
Manceaux, Michèle. *Les Maos en France*. Foreword by Jean-Paul Sartre. Paris: Gallimard, 1972.
Michel, Georges. *Mes Années Sartre*. Paris: Hachette, 1981.
O'Brien, Conor Cruise. *Albert Camus*. New York: Viking Press, 1970.

Sartre. Text of a film made by Alexandre Astruc and Michel Contat. Paris: Gallimard, 1977. Trans. as *Sartre by Himself* by Richard Seaver. New York: Urizen Books, 1978.

Sartre: Images d'une vie. Photographs compiled by Liliane Sendyk-Siegel, with commentary by Simone de Beauvoir. Paris: Gallimard, 1978.

Todd, Olivier. *Un fils rebelle.* Paris: Grasset, 1981.

Tynan, Kenneth. *Tynan Right and Left.* New York: Atheneum Publishers, 1967.

Index of Names

Index of Places

Index of Works